The Ultimate Guide to

G.I. JOE

1982-1994

Identification & Price Guide

Mark Bellomo

©2005 Mark Bellomo
Published by

An Imprint of F+W Publications

700 East State Street • Iola, WI 54990-0001
715-445-2214 • 888-457-2873

Our toll-free number to place an order or obtain
a free catalog is (800) 258-0929.

G.I. Joe, all associated character, vehicle, and group names, and their
respective likenesses, are trademarks of Hasbro, Inc.

Library of Congress Catalog Number: 2004098436

ISBN 13-digit: 978-0-87341-669-6
ISBN 10-digit: 0-87341-669-4

Designed by Brian Brogaard
Edited by Karen O'Brien

Printed in United States of America

CONTENTS

FOREWORD

by Larry Hama

This Mark Bellomo guy can be a real pain in the butt. He's always e-mailing or calling to ask all sorts of questions about G.I. Joe. He's trying to nail down the details. You know what details are, don't you? That's where God lives, according to Mies van der Rohe.

Yes, Bellomo is a pain, but it's his job to be a pain. And he asks the right questions. He gets it. He understands the subtext and was able to suss out the importance of meter in the writing of the file cards. He doesn't ask, "Who's stronger, Snake-Eyes or Storm Shadow?" He asks, "Why did you choose the *I Ching* hexagram #63 *After Completion* to be the sigil of the Arashikage ninja clan?"

How am I supposed to remember something like that twenty years after the fact? Luckily I still had my copy of the *I Ching* that I used back then (the Richard Wilhelm translation with the forward by C.G. Jung [from *I Ching: Book of Changes*]) and my margin notes and yellow hi-lighting were intact. Synapses were triggered, memories were dredged—Aha! I chose that hexagram because the pattern of the lines was easy to remember, and if the line reading was appropriate, well, there you have it— synchronicity, *nicht wahr*?

The questions weren't easy. I got the feeling that Mark bugged everybody else as persistently because *he wanted to get it right.* Hey, if the questions were easy, would I want to read the book? Flippancy and glibness may stand you in good stead at a cocktail party when the folks you are talking to are working on their fifth Cosmopolitan of the evening, but they make for reading material that can be knocked over by the merest zephyr.

I have found myself waxing logorrheic whilst being interviewed by others, settling into a veritable fugue state of flippancy and glibness from which, disembodied, I observed myself babbling like a panel of writers at a comic book convention. Horrors! The question that runs through my mind during most interviews is, "Why are they asking me such dumb questions?" The question that ran through my mind whenever Mark bugged me was, "How did he ever figure that out?"

You may have thought that in the fog of dotage I have wandered from the point, but in fact I have arrived by the side door. What you are holding in your hands is not your usual compendium of facts and figures, not the same old rehashing of readily available file cards and company hype, but a well tempered tome, thoughtfully written by a guy who really loves the material and has a goodly understanding of the original sources of that material.

When I sat down to write this Foreword, I cast the three copper coins to consult the *I Ching*, and I came up with #45, Ts'ui, *Gathering Together*. The judgment reads, (among other things) "success… it furthers one to undertake something." Nothing like the *I Ching* to haul you out of the sludge of indolence and put your fingers to tapping at the keyboard.

Larry Hama
Oct. 31, 2004

INTRODUCTION

Walking down the crowded aisle of a Kay-Bee toy store in early summer of 1982, I was picking through the latest selection of *Star Wars: The Empire Strikes Back* characters, and was about to abscond with an ESB Zuckuss when a selection of figures from a new toy line caught my attention. On the end cap of the action figure aisle were a mustering of 3-3/4″ military action figures. They looked pretty alluring to an eleven-year old. Their packages were bold and fully painted. Their articulation was incredible. Their accessories were astonishing. They even came with biographies on the back of the packaging known as "Combat Command File Cards." WOW! I focused back on the *Star Wars* figure I thought I had committed to, held out the package in my hand, and regarded the ESB Zuckuss with a sense of disappointment; of unfulfillment and disdain. Zuckuss came with a big awkward gun, a little bit of poseability, and looked, well, *boring* in comparison.

That day I bought two G.I. Joe items: a Mortar Soldier code-named "Short-Fuze" and a jeep known as the "VAMP" with its driver, "Clutch." I went home, unwrapped the packages, slapped on the figures' accessories and the jeep's labels and played outside for hours until the streetlights came on. Short-Fuze included a mortar, its stand, a helmet, a visor, a backpack, and a bio/file card. The jeep was free-wheeling and came replete with blueprints, two gas cans, a mounted gun that with the press of a lever would simulate automatic firing, and (of course) its tough-looking driver, Clutch with his file card. All of this product for under $15.00…

Later that week, I did a few odd jobs around the neighborhood and managed to score some cash in order to accrue a nice G.I. Joe collection consisting of counter intelligence agents and commandos, rangers and laser rifle troopers, missile systems, and jet packs. The toys were sturdy enough to be played with in the out of doors, and the "snap-on, stay-on" accessories allowed characters to fall from (ahem) great heights without losing their rifles, backpacks, or helmets. And the poses. The wonderful poses you could make a G.I. Joe figure hold. Remarkable. But what about a back story?

The frontispiece of Hasbro's initial 1982 G.I. Joe product catalog reads, "The forces of evil are on the rise. The enemy army of COBRA Command (An international paramilitary terrorist force) want to conquer the world! Only one group of heroic, dedicated, fighting soldiers can stop them. Code name… G.I. Joe! This crack mobile strike force will go anywhere and do any thing to fight COBRA. Each member of the squad is an expert in the use of ultra-modern small arms, vehicles and weapons systems. They are specialists, trained in the latest fighting techniques. Read their Combat Command File

Cards and select the best team members for each perilous mission. 'Duty, Honor, Courage' is the motto of G.I. Joe… a Real American Hero."

Now I knew where the Joes stood. I knew their mission. And complementing the toy line was an accessible cartoon produced by Marvel/Sunbow animation, and a fantastic and realistic comic written by the uber-talented Larry Hama, who also drafted the biographies (hereafter referred to as "file cards") for nearly all of the characters from 1982-1994. Mr. Hama would get a production sketch or painting of a character from Hasbro with the action figure's MOS attached (Military Occupational Specialty), and then render their personality in proper and distinct fashion.

Oddly enough, the 1982 Joe Team was not Marvel Comics' original intention. In 1981, Mr. Hama had pitched Marvel a comic entitled "Fury Force"—a book revolving around the exploits of Nick Fury's son and his team of young soldiers, "An elite unit of seven Army Special Forces Green Berets whose primary mission is the neutralization of terrorists, insurgents, and espionage agents." Mr. Hama wrote further that, "The FURY FORCE has access to the very latest in military high-tech hardware. From hand-held heat-seeking ground to air missiles to laser lock gunsites and passive night vision devices. They can be inserted into target areas by HALO (high altitude low opening) parachutes, low vector 'radar invisible' helicopters, conventional and nuclear submarines, VTOL aircraft (Harrier, etc.), or they can just walk in through customs wearing civilian clothes and carrying cleverly designed luggage."

Kirk Bozigian suggested that the 3-3/4″ G.I. Joe line was supposed to be an *action vehicle* line initially, focusing on super-detailed laser cannons, 4WD vehicles, and aircraft. But it was the figures that really sold the line from 1982-1994. And we'll more than likely never see another bunch of meticulously crafted figures and accessories like that again—as a kid, assembling a Joe vehicle was akin to putting together a super-detailed model kit.

Regardless of how the beginning of the 3-3/4″ Joe era happened—and people have cited the 1980 Olympic Games, Fury Force, the Reagan Era, the deregulation of children's television programming by the FCC—G.I. Joe: A Real American Hero succeeded and *endured*. In recent years, the G.I. Joe Collector's Club and its devoted following have become some of the most dedicated and loyal fans in the entire world.

It is for these fans (and casual collectors alike) that I have carefully constructed the text of this book. In my descriptions and whenever possible I have tried to reference Mr. Hama's original prototype Psychological Profiles along with Hasbro's Combat Command File Card biographies—with tidbits thrown in from the Marvel comics of the '80s and '90s, the current Devil's Due comics, and the Sunbow and DIC cartoon shows. I hope that by providing this information to you, that it will enhance your book-reading experience, for how often do action figure guides come without any new information for the die-hard reader?

It should be noted that the G.I. Joe figures came alive in their biographies and in the Marvel comic where Larry Hama adopted a Hemingway-esque "Iceberg Theory" approach to the Joe universe: as a good deal of the subtext was "underwater for every part that shows." In the realm of G.I. Joe—if you read carefully enough—there is always something important lurking under the surface. Mr. Hama was deliberate in his rendering of fictional Joe and Cobra characters, taking into consideration proper military nomenclature in allusions, and evinced his devotion to cadence and meter when writing biographies and dossiers. These bios should, as he put it, "roll off the tongue in your mind," for if children were going to read these file cards then Mr. Hama knew that the rhythmic flow and particular arrangement of words should be memorable. Yes, kids could read up on their favorite Joes, but at the same time adults could gape at the realism injected into the product—some of that realism is mentioned in the bios contained herein.

You see, certain levels of the G.I. Joe: A Real American Hero universe are *not* for kids, but Mr. Hama spectacularly suspended a child's disbelief and at the same time impressed the adult collector.

I suppose that the final topic I should broach is why does the 3-3/4″ G.I. Joe line endure? What made these characters last for nearly thirty years? Was it their military prowess? Their uncanny ability to avoid danger? Their discipline and honor and sense of duty? Maybe not. Maybe it was something else altogether. Maybe it was because Hasbro and Larry Hama and Buzz Dixon made them three-dimensional dynamic human beings. When commenting on his writing the initial prototype file cards, Mr. Hama suggested, "I was just trying to nail very distinctive characters and give them a few human foibles. Foibles and eccentricities were usually the first things to get edited out." And I think that's what drew us to the characters on the Joe team, Tripwire's case of the dropsies, Deep-Six's coldness, Beach Head's overly aggressive nature, and Clutch's misogynistic attitude. The Joes were admirable men and women who often had a small flaw, an eccentric quirk of personality that brought them closer to us as children, and now as adult collectors. Blowtorch hates fire. Cover Girl drives a tank. Short-Fuze loses his temper. But ultimately, they all became much, much more than just static characters on a cartoon or in the four-color pages of "the funny books."

—*MWB*

ACKNOWLEDGMENTS

This book would not be possible without constant encouragement on *www.yojoe.com* message boards, at local and distant collectible shops, and during hour-long telephone conversations with die-hard Joe fans—you know who you are. This book is for YOU.

I'd also like to thank my mom and dad, Larry Hama, Kirk Bozigian, Derryl DePriest, Paula Sacchi-Walsh, all the moderators at YoJoe, Dave Dorman (www.davedorman.com) for the original prototype pencil sketch images, Adam "The Kid" Romano, the Stonebacks ("Get that book *done!*"), Ernest "My Man" Hemingway, and my stupid cat Boo-Boo Kitty who bites me all the time and gets his own snail mail (it's true).

Super duper extra special thanks with whipped cream on top to Karen O'Brien who put this together (1300+ images and 60,000+ words she had to get through)—you are a saint and scholar, to Brian Brogaard who I never met but is hands-down one of THE best designers in the industry (as you can tell), Sir Thomas Bartsch for giving me a chance at *Toy Shop*—which is all I could ever ask for, and most importantly to my gorgeous and patient fiancée Jessica Lynn Rivers for putting up with endless nights of tak-a-tak writing, my poring through too many musty old boxes, 10,000 times hearing me curse at the top of my lungs at an inanimate piece of hardened plastic, noting my conspicuous absence for days on end during photo shoots, and basically not setting my collection on fire while I slept.

Thank you all for your continuous support of my "glorious obsession."

—*MWB*

HOW TO USE THIS BOOK

This book is an identification and price guide to the 3-3/4" G.I. Joe figures, vehicles, and accessories produced from 1982 through 1994. As a guide, the prices are suggested values reflecting the current market trends in the hobby. Although derived from the author's expertise and experience with the hobby, the prices contained herein are only a guide.

The book is organized chronologically by year. Within a given year, G.I. Joe figures are listed first, followed by Cobra figures, then the Vehicles/Playsets. Each section is in alphabetical order.

1982 GRAND SLAM

1) → GRAND SLAM
2) → Laser Artillery Soldier (straight-arm)
3) → (Includes: Helmet, Visor)
   Included with the HAL.
4) →

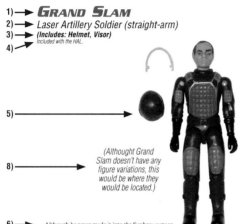

5) →

8) → (Although Grand Slam doesn't have any figure variations, this would be where they would be located.)

6) → Although he never made it into the Sunbow cartoon show, and his appearances in the Marvel comic were few and far between, Grand Slam was always one of my favorites of the 1982 figures due to the introspection that Mr. Hama's prototype file card provides: "...outwardly soft-spoken and calm. Intelligent enough to have doubts about his own sanity. Was a late bloomer and still exhibits discomfort in social situations. Indulges in escapist fantasy (reads science fiction)." As an introvert, Grand Slam's character spoke to me directly, despite making sporadic (but nonetheless important) appearances in the Joe canon. It has been suggested that Grand Slam is currently training new Joe members in some capacity.

7) → **NOTE:** Be careful to note that the color of Grand Slam's fatigues and helmet are of a dark green, as opposed to the regular olive drab of Breaker, Clutch, and Flash, or the light green of Steeler and Zap. The easiest way to tell the difference is to hold Grand Slam or his helmet up to another figure.

9) → MLC: **$12**

1) "Code Name" as it appears on the figure package or file card.

2) MOS ("Military Specialty" or "Military Occupational Specialty") as it appears on the figure package or file card.

3) "Includes" line contains the figure's accessories as they appear on the original card front, near the bubble.

4) States what vehicle or playset the figure was packaged with.

5) Photo of figure with equipment.

6) A brief biography from the action figure's "Combat Command File Card" (the official Hasbro name for the dossier printed either on the back of the package, or placed inside a boxed accessory). These bios were enhanced using tidbits of information from the Sunbow G.I. Joe cartoon, the Marvel and Devil's Due comic books, and some rare prototype dossiers written by Larry Hama before they were sent to Hasbro. Also contained here are notes on existing variations, along with any miscellaneous notes describing minor unusual features.

7) Important variations or notations (optional depending on the action figure).

8) Photo of the unusual variation (optional depending on the action figure).

9) Values. The goal here was to provide a **conservative** estimate of what you'd expect to receive as a value for the figure, but remember that prices adjust based on supply and demand between individual buyers and sellers.

1982 MOBAT

1) → MOBAT
2) → (Motorized Battle Tank/Super Duty Battle Tank/ Multi-Ordnance Battle Tank)
   Modern Army Action Tank—The G.I. Joe Mobile Strike Force Tank
3) → (Includes: Steeler figure)

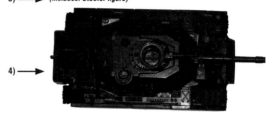

4) →

5) → Growing up in the 1980s, almost every kid I knew had a MOBAT. The MOBAT wa the main battle tank for the Joes in 1982, and the tank served them well. Although non of the sculpted hatch covers on the MOBAT flip up, the vehicle had plenty of actio for kids. With an extendable 130mm main cannon, and a .50 caliber machine gun fo Steeler to man while sitting in the command turret, this tank had it all!

Easily lost/removable pieces: The .50 caliber machine gun tip is difficult to find attached to the command turret of the tank. Check to see if the battery cover is on the bottom of the MOBAT.

6) → **NOTE:** There are two different tread variations for the MOBAT—solid tank treads or notched tank treads. Neither of these variants is more rare or more valuable than the other.

Collector's note: remember to always remove batteries from Joe figures and vehicles when not using them, or they might corrode and ruin the toy.

7) →

MISB: **$200**, MIB: **$150**,
8) → MLC: **$15-20**

The MOBAT's easily lost pieces.

1) "Code Name" or acronym (abbreviation) as it appears on the package or blueprints.

2) Military function as it appears on the package or blue print.

3) If the vehicle or accessory includes a figure in its package, the figure is listed here.

4) Photo of vehicle or accessory.

5) A brief notation of the vehicle/accessory specs from the official Hasbro packaged blue prints included inside a boxed vehicle or accessory. These specs have been enhanced by using tidbits of information from the Sunbow G.I. Joe cartoon, the Marvel and Devil's Due comic books, or some rare prototype dossier info as written by Larry Hama before they were sent to Hasbro. Also contained here is a list of the most common and most frequently (easily) lost or removable pieces of the vehicle/accessory, and variations if they exist, along with any miscellaneous notes describing minor unusual features.

6) Important variations or notations (optional depending on the vehicle or accessory).

7) Photo of the unusual notation (optional depending on the vehicle or accessory).

8) Values. The goal here was to provide a **conservative** estimate of what you'd expect to receive as a value for the vehicle/accessory, but remember that prices adjust based on supply and demand between individual buyers and sellers.

ABBREVIATIONS

MISB (Mint in Sealed Box): This is the most rare condition in which to find a vehicle or accessory—mint condition box, unopened and sealed with factory tape (when applicable), and all contents sealed in their factory baggies. MISB toys are pretty rare finds. Toys with sealed boxes in less than mint condition cannot be considered MISB, and prices should be adjusted accordingly.

MISP (Mint in Sealed Package): See MISB.

MIB (Mint in Box, Mint and Loose in Box): This is the price for a mint-condition vehicle or accessory in a mint-condition box that is not factory sealed (box is open and baggies may be opened) but **all** of the toy's respective accessories and pieces are present and in mint condition.

MOC (Mint on Card) or MOSC (Mint on Sealed Card): This is the price for a figure still sealed on its mint-condition card. (If a card has never been placed on a retail peg, it is considered "unpunched," as its pegboard tab hasn't been punched off the card. These are pretty rare finds, and command premium prices above the MOC value.) If a card is in less than a mint condition (bent, water damaged, dents in the bubble, etc.), it cannot be considered MOC, and prices should be adjusted accordingly.

MLC (Mint Loose and Complete): The figure, vehicle, or accessory is in mint condition with no packaging or box and complete with all pieces and equipment. Buyers and sellers must realize that a mint toy is **not** in MLC condition if it does not come with every one of its respective pieces. Incomplete toys in mint condition and complete toys not in mint condition cannot be considered MLC, and prices should be adjusted accordingly.

MISBaggie or Mint in Sealed Baggie: Some mail away exclusives were not packaged on cards or in boxes, but arrived from Hasbro in plastic baggies. See, The Fridge (1986) as an example of a mail away with this designation.

NOTE: As this guide does not deal with file cards, blueprints, and other paper work, keep in mind that these items hold some value as well. The more rare the vehicle or accessory is, usually the more rare the blueprint will be. For example, a U.S.S. FLAGG blueprint set is quite valuable (somewhere in the realm of $10-20 depending on the condition), but an LCV Recon Sled blueprint is worth much less (think $.75 to $1.00).

1982 G.I. JOE FIGURES

BREAKER
Communications Officer (straight-arm)
(Includes: TV-Radio Back Pack, Helmet, Radio Headset)

Breaker was the fun loving RTO (Radio Tele-communications Operator) of the original Joe team. In early issues of the Marvel comic, Breaker could be found toting an M-16 rifle and blowing a seemingly endless supply of bubble gum during high-stress situations. Sadly, the jovial and upbeat linguist (spoke seven languages) from Gatlinburg, Tennessee died on a mission in Trucial Abysmia. He was killed by a Cobra S.A.W. Viper *(Marvel Comics, G.I. Joe, issue #109)*. It is curious to note that Breaker was the only Joe figure in 1982 to come equipped without a weapon.

NOTE: *Some collectors require a truly "straight" cord attached to his radio headset, or the figure is not "mint."*

MOC: **$100**, MLC: **$15**

CLUTCH
VAMP Driver (straight-arm)
(Includes: Helmet)
Included with the VAMP.

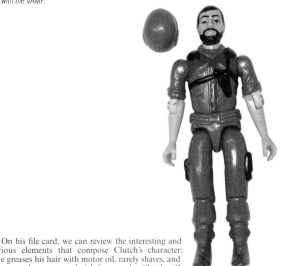

On his file card, we can review the interesting and curious elements that compose Clutch's character: "He greases his hair with motor oil, rarely shaves, and chews on the same toothpick for months. Clutch still calls women 'chicks.'" In early Marvel comic book lore, he became one of the more popular Joes, but in the Sunbow cartoon was relegated to a few select appearances. After the initial Joe team disbanded in 1994, he joined the Indy Racing Circuit. Since then, he has come back into the fold for a few selected missions, and is still a member of the current Joe team.

MLC: **$10**

FLASH
Laser Rifle Trooper (straight-arm)
(Includes: XMLR-1A [Shoulder-Fired Laser Rifle], Power Pack, Helmet, Visor)

Flash, perhaps because of his orange pads and slew of accessories, was one of the most popular Joe characters throughout the original team's long tenure from 1982-1994, and strangely enough there was only one action figure ever made based on this character. Flash was the electronics and CBR (Chemical, Biological, and Radiological) expert of the original team, and tragically, he was killed in action while on a mission to blow up a radar station (Devil's Due Comics, *G.I. Joe issue #25*).

NOTE: *Some collectors require a truly "straight" Flash cord attached to his shoulder-fired laser-rifle, or the figure is not "mint."*

MOC: **$125**, MLC: **$15**

GRAND SLAM
Laser Artillery Soldier (straight-arm)
(Includes: Helmet, Visor)
Included with the HAL.

Although he never made it into the Sunbow cartoon show, and his appearances in the Marvel comic were few and far between, Grand Slam was always one of my favorites of the 1982 figures due to the introspection that Mr. Hama's prototype file card provides: "...outwardly soft-spoken and calm. Intelligent enough to have doubts about his own sanity. Was a late bloomer and still exhibits discomfort in social situations. Indulges in escapist fantasy (reads science fiction)." As an introvert, Grand Slam's character spoke to me directly, despite making sporadic (but nonetheless important) appearances in the Joe canon. It has been suggested that Grand Slam is currently training new Joe members in some capacity.

NOTE: *Be careful to note that the color of Grand Slam's fatigues and helmet are of a dark green, as opposed to the regular olive drab of Breaker, Clutch, and Flash, or the light green of Steeler and Zap. The easiest way to tell the difference is to hold Grand Slam or his helmet up to another figure.*

MLC: **$12**

GRUNT
Infantry Trooper (straight-arm)
(Includes: M-16 Rifle, Combat Pack, Helmet)

Grunt was the infantry-man of the original Joe team, and his name reflects his job: "grunt" by military definition is an infantryman or foot solider. Grunt is pictured on the front of the 1982 product catalog, charging into battle with his rifle. Grunt has since retired from the Joe team, and has received a degree in engineering from Georgia Tech. He now works in the private sector, and sometimes joins with the Joe team on special missions. In Mr. Hama's original file card prototype, Grunt was an "...apprentice gunsmith in his home town prior to enlistment." Hama claimed in his Psychological Profile that Grunt "Does not enjoy his work (this is a favorable assessment) but believes it is in the best interest of his country."

MOC: **$100**, MLC: **$12**

HAWK
Missile Commander (straight-arm)
(Includes: Helmet, Visor)
Included with the MMS.

Although he did not show up in the Sunbow cartoon until the beginning of the second season, Hawk, the G.I. Joe Commander (here known as "Missile Commander"), was the first character introduced in Marvel Comics' run and is a recurring character in the current Devil's Due comic. Hawk was appointed field commander of the Joe team during its inception and has recruited many of the original members of the team (i.e. Snake Eyes, Stalker). In 1982, Hawk is ranked as a Colonel (O-6), and briefs (and frequently) leads the early Joe teams' missions. His file card states that Hawk graduated from West Point at the top of his class, and comes from a very wealthy family, but in spite of his lavish upbringing, "He is keenly intelligent and perceptive and is capable of totally selfless acts in support of his teammates. An excellent leader!"

MLC: **$15**

ROCK 'N ROLL
Machine Gunner (straight-arm)
(Includes: Heavy Machine Gun with Bipod, Helmet)

Rock 'N Roll was a surfer and bass player in a band prior to enlistment, and even sported a bit of long hair in the first comic run. Even though long hair and beards are not army regulation, in special ops teams dress code was never very important—and this allowed many Joe characters to change their outfits with impunity according to their military specialty or personal preference. During his initial Marvel comic book appearances, Rock 'N Roll is portrayed as his file card states: "a man of contradictions." From Hama's prototype: "...obstinate but pliable; forceful but shy; proud but self-deprecating..." With his dedication to the cause, Rock 'N Roll has risen in the Joe ranks, and is now one of the Joe team's field commanders. The weapon shown is reminiscent of a 7.62 mm, M-60 Series (Medium Machine Gun)—the army's "general purpose" machine gun since the late 1950s.

NOTE: *The color of Rock 'N Roll's fatigues and helmet are of a dark green, as opposed to the regular olive drab of Breaker, Clutch, and Flash, or the light green of Steeler and Zap. The easiest way to tell the difference is to hold Rock 'N Roll or his helmet up to another figure.*

MOC: **$150**, MLC: **$15**

SCARLETT
Counter Intelligence (straight-arm)
(Includes: XK-1 Power Crossbow)

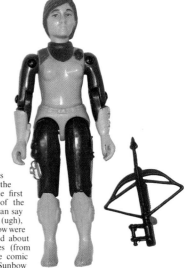

Scarlett's popularity has endured and grown over the past 20+ years. She was the first (and only) female member of the Joe team, and whatever you can say about her terrible face sculpt (ugh), her body sculpting and crossbow were fantastic. A lot has been said about her affairs with Snake Eyes (from the Marvel and Devils' Due comic books) and Duke (from the Sunbow cartoon), but Larry Hama's file card intended her to be a serious and lethal warrior. Her 1982 file card states: "...it's remarkable that a person so deadly can still retain a sense of humor." Scarlett is a qualified expert with throwing stars, Ka-Bar knives (military/tactical edged weapons), and a garotte (an instrument *of execution for* execution by strangulation). Apparently she is much deadlier than we initially thought. From her prototype file card, her MOS is listed simply as "Girl." Her military training on the proto dossier reads as long as an arm, and her Peer Personality Assessment by teammate Grunt affirms her uncanny prowess as a fighter.

NOTE: *Scarlett's feet have no "holes" in the bottom of them, so she can not be posed on battle stands or Joe vehicles with pegs.*

MOC: **$250**, MLC: **$18-20**

SHORT-FUZE
Mortar Soldier (straight-arm)
(Includes: M-1 [81mm Medium Mortar] with Stand, Ammo Pack, Helmet, Visor)

Short-Fuze's nickname is appropriate, as he was the "hothead" of the original Joe team. On occasion, he would lose his temper, which was forgivable because he was such an expert with explosives and mortar rounds. Short-Fuze was from a career military family, and could "plot artillery azimuths (the lateral deviation of a projectile or bomb) and triangulations in his head." It should be noted that in the comic, Short-Fuze wore glasses. In the prototype file card, Hama states that Short-Fuze is a "fastidious dresser who maintains an unusually high level of personal discipline." Hama goes on with a very sophisticated assessment of Short-Fuze in his Psychological Profile: "Has a tendency to explode into verbal abuse involving very imaginative vitriolic content… however, vituperative outbursts are merely a smokescreen masking a vulnerable ego."

NOTE: *Short-Fuze came equipped with one of three different types of mortars: type 1 (closed, thin handle), type 2 (open, thin-handle), or type three (open, thick handle). Types 1 and 2 were available with the straight-arm version of Short-Fuze, while type 3 came with the swivel arm version.*

MOC: **$125** *(depending on mortar variation)*, MLC: **$15**

SNAKE EYES
Commando (straight-arm)
(Includes: Uzi Gun, Explosives Pack)

Snake Eyes' original prototype was dubbed "Spook" and he donned a hood in the drafts of Marvel's nascent post-G.I. Joe project entitled "Fury Force." With the introduction of Snake Eyes, whether Commando (1982) or Ninja (later years), the mute character with no file name has become the most popular figure in the entire G. I. Joe canon. Valiant, honorable, silent, and deadly, the commando known only by the slang expression "Snake Eyes" has become one of the most identifiable characters in the line. When we look at his 1982 figure, it does seem a bit bland, but rumor has it that Hasbro created an all-black plastic molded character to save on production costs. Little did they know that with excellent characterization by Larry Hama, and some renderings by talented artists, Snake Eyes would end up as an enduring pop-culture icon.

As a soldier, a commando's job is to make quick destructive raids against enemy held areas, and that's what Snake Eyes showcased as early as issue #1 of the Marvel comic. His file card that states the following regarding his military training: "Has received extensive training in mountaineering, underwater demolitions, jungle, desert and arctic survival, and some form of holistic medicine." After consulting Mr. Hama about this, he claimed that most of Snake Eyes' military training was acquired in the Army during the Vietnam conflict *prior* to his experience with Storm Shadow and his infamous Arashikage ninja clan. Snake Eyes was in a LRRP (Long Range Reconnaissance Patrol) in the war. In reference to the phrase "holistic medicine," however, Mr. Hama claimed he wasn't sure how he has come to terms with that in relationship to Snake Eyes. Hama stated further that "holistic medicine" refers to esoteric and herbal forms of healing practiced by ninjas (mercenary agent martial artists) and yamabushi ("those who sleep in the mountain") mountain warrior monks.

MOC: **$350**, MLC: **$35**

STALKER
Ranger (straight-arm)
(Includes: M-32 "Pulverizer" Sub-Machine Gun)

Stalker was the only African-American member of the 1982 G.I. Joe team, and his file card states that he was the "warlord of a large urban street gang" in Detroit, Michigan, prior to his enlistment in the Army. According to the Marvel comic, part of his army experience was to serve on the same LRRP (Long Range Reconnaissance Patrol) as Snake Eyes and Storm Shadow. After his experiences in Southeast Asia, Stalker came back to the States and became the first member of Hawk's G.I. Joe team. Stalker led many of the Joe's earliest adventures, has been involved in some very harrowing missions, and is still active with the Joe team.

Even though Stalker has a lower rank than some of the men and women under his command, Mr. Hama explains that, frequently, "Special op units do not go by a strict time-in-grade and 'shoulder rank' chain of command. Chain of command may depend on who has the most experience in the specific area of operations or mission." This explains a lot in regards to rank in the G.I. Joe Universe, where we often observe a soldier of lower rank taking control of a mission. Special Ops teams simply rely on the trooper who has the most experience in a chosen field to take charge.

MOC: **$150**, MLC: **$15**

Stalker's camouflage variations.

STEELER
Tank Commander (straight-arm)
(Includes: Helmet, Headset, Uzi Gun)
Included with the MOBAT.

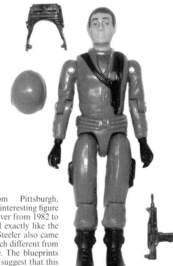

Ironically hailing from Pittsburgh, Pennsylvania, Steeler was an interesting figure as he was the only vehicle driver from 1982 to have a weapon, an uzi pistol exactly like the one carried by Snake Eyes. Steeler also came with a unique black visor much different from that of Flash or Short-Fuze. The blueprints from Steeler's MOBAT tank suggest that this visor/headset has an infra-red lens, a zoom-control knob, a shutter release button, and a motor drive. Steeler's rank is O-1 (2nd Lieutenant) on his finished mass-produced file card, but on the prototype, his rank is E-5. Described as "Tank Commander," it is implied that he is of a high rank, and his file card states: "Young, reckless, often clashes with authority (superior officers), but he's one tough soldier." From his prototype Psychological Profile: "…he is either the most normal, well-adjusted man in the world or the best disguised psychotic. There's something seething beneath the surface… He lies to me all the time fabricating the most outlandish…" In the Sunbow cartoon show, Steeler remained on the Cobra controlled earth in the "World Without End" episode.

NOTE: *The color of Steeler's fatigues and helmet are of a light green, as opposed to the regular olive drab of Breaker, Clutch, and Flash, or the dark green of Grand Slam and Rock 'N Roll. The easiest way to tell the difference is to hold Steeler or his helmet up to another figure.*

MLC: **$20**

ZAP

Bazooka Soldier (straight-arm w/both v.1 and v.2 single-handled)
(Includes: Bazooka, Ammo Pack, Helmet)

Zap was the bazooka-man of the G.I. Joe team in an age when the term "bazooka" has been rendered obsolete (since about WWII). Regardless, the character of Zap was Hispanic in origin (Raphael J. Melendez), and this showed that both Mr. Hama and Hasbro were willing to push the envelope when it came to recruitment. Zap is usually pictured with a thin black moustache, but it wasn't until 1991 that his figure acquired one. His prototype dossier states that he is a "gregarious, fun-loving type. Tendencies towards extreme self-criticism but not overly paranoid. Extremely pragmatic outlook on life characteristic of explosive ordnance personnel."

NOTE: *The color of Zap's backpack, fatigues, and helmet are of a light green, as opposed to the regular olive drab of Breaker, Clutch, and Flash, or the dark green of Grand Slam and Rock 'N Roll. The easiest way to tell the difference is to hold Zap (or his accessories) up to another figure.*

HELMET NOTE: *Even though all of the 1982 helmets (hereafter referred to as "regular issue" helmets) had holes drilled into their sides, not every Joe came with a visor to attach to their helmet. Only Flash, Grand Slam, Hawk, and Short-Fuze came with clear visors that attached to their helmets. Steeler came with a black visor/helmet headset. The other helmet-wearing Joes (Breaker, Grunt, Rock 'N Roll, and Zap) did not come with visors. Perhaps Zap should have come with a clear visor to protect his eyes from the missile-firing blasts of his "bazooka"?*

NOTE: *Zap came equipped with one of three different types of bazookas: type 1 (two-handled bazooka), type 2 (single-handled, thin), or type 3, the most common (single handled, thick). Types 1 and 2 were available with the straight-arm version of Zap, while type 3 came with the swivel-arm version. Type 1 is the most rare, and Hasbro stopped its production because it broke the fingers off of many straight-arm Zaps.*

NOTE: *G.I. Joe helmets came in three different color variations to reflect the color of the Joe uniforms. Thus, since Grand Slam and Rock 'N Roll have dark olive drab colored uniforms, they wear dark olive drab colored helmets. Since Zap and Steeler have light olive drab uniforms, they don't have light olive drab helmets. Remaining team members (Breaker, Clutch, Flash, Grunt, Hawk, and Short-Fuze) wear medium olive drab colored helmets. Look at the picture to note the difference.*

MOC: **$175** (depending on bazooka variation),
MLC: **$12-18** (depending on bazooka variation, as I have seen his rare bazooka sell for $10 itself!)

1982 COBRA FIGURES

ENEMY LEADER

Cobra Commander,
(Includes: "Venom" Laser Pistol)
Mail Away Exclusive

Although this figure's code name is "Enemy Leader," most G.I. Joe fans refer to the character as "Cobra Commander." Regarding Cobra Commander's origin, there are two conflicting versions. The Sunbow cartoon states that Cobra Commander was once a genius biochemist who, a few thousand years ago, was sent out by Golobulus (see Golobulus, 1987) to rule the world for the strange empire of Cobra-La. In contrast, the Marvel comic book suggests that Cobra Commander was a used car salesman who, when faced with insurmountable failures in life, decided to create his own empire and this (eventually) became Cobra Command. The figure shown here is Cobra Commander wearing his silver-masked battle helmet. Cobra Commander's pistol fits securely into his back.

Cobra Commander was a mail-away figure in 1982, and was not offered on a card until 1983. The only way to receive this figure in '82 was to send five "Flag Points" (proof-of-purchase seals from G.I. Joe packages) and 50 cents for shipping and handling to Pawtucket, Rhode Island, the headquarters of Hasbro Industries. Collectors of the line soon learned that any time a package postmarked from Pawtucket arrived via the USPS, there was a real treat inside.

NOTE: *There were two versions of the "straight-arm" Enemy Leader/Cobra Commander figure. The earliest straight-arm version had what collectors refer to as the "Mickey Mouse" Cobra logo. This Cobra sigil is much less sophisticated in design than the more common release. The later straight-arm version of Enemy Leader/Cobra Commander had the corrected, highly detailed Cobra logo.*

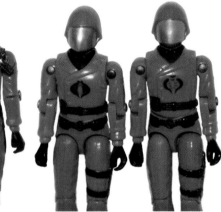

Cobra Commander with "Venom" laser pistol in his back.

Cobra Commander logo variants, "corrected" on left, Mickey Mouse on right

Mint in Mailer box: **$50-$150**, MLC: **$25-30**, MLC: ("Mickey Mouse" version of logo) **$50-60**

Cobra Commander with mailer box, mailer file card, 1982 catalog, and club membership form.

Cobra Commander and Major Bludd mail-away coupons.

MAJOR BLUDD
Mercenary
(Includes: Rocket Launcher, Missile Backpack)
Mail Away Exclusive

NOTE: *Even though Major Bludd is usually included with the figures from the 1983 series, the good (or bad) Major was indeed an unadvertised late mail away from 1982 (with strict rules for redemption, including dated cash register receipts, etc.). Apparently, the only way to mail away for him in '82 was to be sent a coupon in the mail only after having sent away for your Cobra Commander mail away. Hasbro reportedly put you on a mailing list, and then sent the coupon to members of the list.*

Major Bludd's right arm is covered in armor to protect him from the blast of his rocket launcher, and has articulation only at the shoulder. His left arm, however, is closer to the 1983 Joe figures, as it possesses swivel-arm type of articulation. According to his file card, Major Sebastian Bludd is a reprehensible evil-doer with no redeeming qualities whatsoever. He lends his talents to the highest bidder, and according to his prototype dossier he served in the Australian Special Air Service in Southeast Asia, the French Foreign Legion in Algeria, worked as a military advisor in Africa and Central America, and is wanted for "various unnamed crimes in Rhodesia and Libya." He was originally called "Major Chill" (Sebastian Chill) but Hasbro changed the name to its current and more appropriate moniker. He is a terrible poet, and his file card comes with two different versions of his awful, belligerent, (but oddly catchy) poetry.

Mint in Mailer Box: *(quite rare)* **$50-$150,**
MLC: **$10-12** *(common figure)*

Major Bludd with mailer box, mailer file card, 1982 catalog, and club membership form.

THE ENEMY
Cobra (straight-arm)
(Includes: Dragunov [SVD] Sniper's Rifle)

From his file card: "One of the nameless, faceless legions of COBRA Command." Even though his code name on the file card states "The Enemy," casual enthusiasts and aficionados alike refer to this figure as "Cobra" or "Cobra Soldier." This character represents the grunts of the Cobra legions—the offal Cobra uses used to "conquer the world for their own evil purposes." It should be noted that both the Cobra and the Cobra Officer figures came with either red or black painted eyebrows. It has been suggested that earlier versions of the 1982 figures came with red eyes and eyebrows, while later versions were painted in black. Neither version is more difficult to find. This figure is the very first "army builder" of the Joe line. Most kids and collectors bought a lot of these characters to create a Cobra army.

NOTE: *The logo on his chest is red in color, not silver like 1983's The Enemy: Viper Pilot. If you find a figure without a logo on his chest, it is most likely a Viper Pilot figure with the silver logo rubbed off, as the paint application was weak.*

MOC: **$225**, MLC: **$18-28**

THE ENEMY
Cobra Officer (straight-arm)
(Includes: AK-47 Assault Rifle)

Cobra Officers were the leaders of various Cobra divisions, possessing a rank of O-4 (major) or equivalent. Although his code name on the file card states "The Enemy," collectors refer to this figure as "Cobra Officer." According to the file card, Cobra Officers are "front line fighters who lead COBRA attack units into battle." In 1982, this figure was renowned for having one of the most sought-after accessories from the line—an AK-47 assault rifle. Collectors should treat the figure's silver Cobra sigil with care, as it rubs off easily. It is rumored that an editor at Marvel Comics casually suggested that the Joes needed an adversary, unlike the original 12″ Joe line. The name "Cobra" was suggested and it has stuck ever since.

MOC: **$225**, MLC: **$18-28**

Headband and Wristband set mail-away.

MISP: **$15-30**, MLC: **$5-15**

1982 Catalog.

★★★ To the Rescue ★★★

The two G.I. Joe mail-away posters, "Stars and Stripes Forever" and "To The Rescue."

MISP: **$30-50**, MLC: **$30-40**

1982 VEHICLES/PLAYSETS

FLAK
(Attack Cannon/Field Light Attack Cannon)
Modern Army Action Weapon—The G.I. Joe Mobile Strike Force Attack Cannon

Based on the U.S. Army's top-secret weapons systems, the FLAK is usually manned by an artillery soldier such as Grand Slam or Zap, but Stalker is pictured in the cannon's blueprints. This weapon is used primarily as an anti-aircraft cannon, and shoots 105mm shells, High Explosive rounds, smoke tracers, and the barrel can fire 20,000 rounds without being replaced.

Easily lost/removable pieces include 3 hydraulic support legs and the seat. Take care not to force the seat back into its tabs, as the tabs may break easily.

MIB: **$25-35**, MLC: **$8-15**

The FLAK's easily lost pieces.

Series One

(COBRA) MISSILE COMMAND HEADQUARTERS

Sears Exclusive

(Includes: Three straight-arm or swivel-armed figures, Cobra, Cobra Commander, and Cobra Officer—majority came w/straight-arm figures, and only a few came w/swivel-arm figures)

The Sears Exclusive Missile Command Headquarters could be considered one of the three "Holy Grails" of the domestic vintage 3-3/4" line (including the 1987 Defiant and the 1985 U.S.S. FLAGG). Offered through the 1982 Sears Christmas catalog and made of brittle chipboard, it is nearly impossible to find in good condition. The play set features a Cruise Missile (so described on the instructions/blueprints) that pivots up and down.

Cruise Missiles constructed during the Cold War period were inexpensive to build and designed to overwhelm defenses by sheer numbers. They could be small, with low-thrust engines that can penetrate radar and infrared-detection networks. This machinery seems to fit perfectly with Cobra Command, as the technology to construct these weapons is simple and available to any country that builds even rudimentary aircraft.

The easily lost/removable pieces for the CMCH include three chipboard seats, a bag of plastic parts, movable chipboard Cruise Missile, and a movable chipboard elevator. All the tabs are fragile, as is the entire play set.

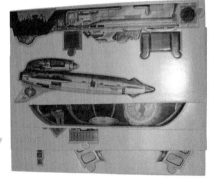

The four cardboard inserts, unassembled.

MISB: **$500-750**, MLC: **$150-300**

The three sealed figures in box.

The plastic attachments for the CMCH.

The file card holder assembled.

The file card holder unassembled.

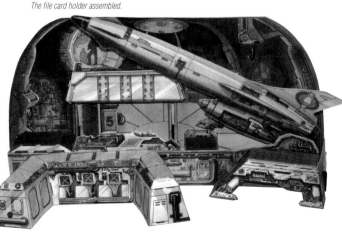

Assembled Cobra Missile Command H.Q.

The packaged figures included with the CMCH.

HAL
(Heavy Artillery Laser)
Modern Army Action Weapon—The G.I. Joe Mobile Strike Force Laser Cannon

(Includes: Grand Slam figure)

The HAL weapon is a laser cannon with barrels that have to be replaced after every thirty hours of use. It is a large weapon that is somewhat unwieldy to transport, but operates wonderfully when stationary. The HAL also comes with two tow hooks on the end of both hydraulic trail legs in order for it to be towed by the VAMP jeep (1982). With a removable CRT sighting and locating computer, the HAL is one of the first lines of defense for the Joes.

The easily lost/removable pieces for the HAL are the hydraulic stabilizer and CRT sighting computer.

MISB: **$150**, MIB: **$60-80**, MLC: **$15-25**

Some of the HAL's easily lost pieces.

MMS
(Mobile Missile System)
Modern Army Action Weapon—The G.I. Joe Mobile Strike Force Mobile Missile System

(Includes: Hawk figure)

Hawk's MMS fires three Patriot missiles approximately thirty miles at an approximate speed of Mach 3 (three times the speed of sound). The MMS is a fabulous toy, and can be towed by the VAMP or MOBAT (1982) from its towhook. Like the HAL, FLAK, and JUMP of the same year, the MMS has the capability to be a stationary unit. Simply pull down its hydraulic support legs and its hydraulic stabilizer legs, and the MMS is operational. Place Hawk by the portable remote control firing box, and simulate launching the missiles.

Easily lost/removable pieces include three patriot missiles, remote control firing box (usually attached to system), and a stand for the firing box.

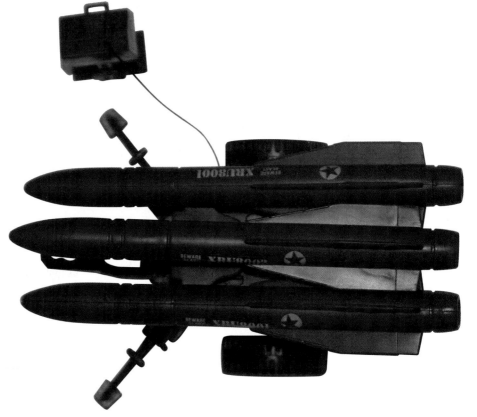

MISB: **$175**, MIB: **$100-125**, MLC: **$15-25**

The MMS's easily lost pieces.

JUMP
(Jet Mobile Propulsion Unit/Jet Pack/Jet Propulsion Unit)
Modern Army Action Weapon—The G.I. Joe Mobile Strike Force Jet Pack

The JUMP Jet Pack was used by frequently Stalker in the comic, and proved useful to the Joes in the Sunbow cartoon as well. Indeed, having a portable jet pack would be the envy of any Special Ops team. The jet pack's titanium launch pad was designed for portability and field durability, as all four hydraulic support legs are movable. With a two-hour fuel supply, and an average speed of 150 mph, the JUMP is a leap in technology not yet arrived at in the real world. Its laser blaster has a range of 100 yards. The easily lost/removable pieces for the JUMP are the power cord, jet pack, laser blaster, jet pack mount, base, and four support legs.

MISB: **$75**, MIB: **$30-40**, MLC: **$10-20**

The JUMP's easily removable pieces.

MOBAT
(Motorized Battle Tank/Super Duty Battle Tank/ Multi-Ordnance Battle Tank)
Modern Army Action Tank—The G.I. Joe Mobile Strike Force Tank

(Includes: Steeler figure)

Growing up in the 1980s, almost every kid I knew had a MOBAT. The MOBAT was the main battle tank for the Joes in 1982, and the tank served them well. Although none of the sculpted hatch covers on the MOBAT flip up, the vehicle had plenty of action for kids. With an extendable 130mm main cannon, and a .50 caliber machine gun for Steeler to man while sitting in the command turret, this tank had it all!

Easily lost/removable pieces: The .50 caliber machine gun tip is difficult to find attached to the command turret of the tank. Check to see if the battery cover is on the bottom of the MOBAT.

NOTE: *There are two different tread variations for the MOBAT—solid tank treads or notched tank treads. Neither of these variants is more rare or more valuable than the other.*

Collector's note: *remember to always remove batteries from Joe figures and vehicles when not using them, or they might corrode and ruin the toy.*

MISB: **$200**, MIB: **$150**, MLC: **$15-20**

The MOBAT's easily lost pieces.

RAM
(Rapid Fire Motorcycle)
Modern Army Action Vehicle—The G.I. Joe Mobile Strike Force Motorcycle

The RAM's easily lost pieces.

Every kid wanted ten RAMs so there would be at least one for every member of the Joe team. The motorcycles with sidecars were useful and portable, and Joe figures, especially Rock 'N Roll (1982), looked great driving them. With a fuel-injected twin cam engine, heavy rear shock absorbers, dual strut front suspension, and a 20mm electronic Gatling cannon mounted on its sidecar, the RAM was built for durability. The RAM also came with a support stand that you could flip down to stand up the motorcycle when the sidecar was disengaged.

Easily lost/removable pieces include two saddle packs (labeled #1 and #2), and the sidecar.

MISB: **$60-75**, MIB: **$30-40**, MLC: **$10-15**

VAMP
(Multi-Purpose Attack Vehicle)
Modern Army Action Vehicle—The G.I. Joe Mobile Strike Force Jeep

(Includes: Clutch figure)

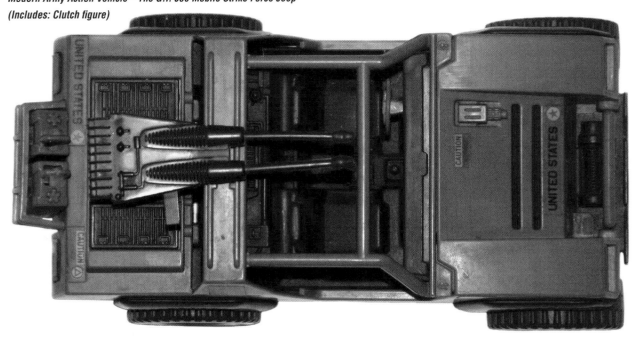

The most durable toy ever. I literally threw my VAMP off of a cliff and it bounced and rolled over onto its wheels. This free-wheeling, standard-use jeep of the Joe team is featured prominently in the Sunbow cartoon as well as the Marvel comic. With a range of 550 miles and a maximum speed of 150 mph, the VAMP was a fantastic utility vehicle for the Joe team. Its 7.62mm computer synchronized machine gun and roll bar gave the Joes an edge when completing perilous missions.

Easily lost/removable pieces are the machine gun, steering wheel, and two gas cans (labeled #1 and #2).

MISB: **$180**, MIB: **$140**, MLC: **$20-30**

The VAMP's easily lost pieces.

(SERIES II, 1983)

The figures released in 1983 were fantastic, and a few from 1982 were re-released with the new "swivel-arm battle grip" feature. All figures released in 1983 and thereafter contained a new swivel joint in the figure's bicep. This "swivel-arm battle grip" made it easier for figures to hold their rifles and accessories. Listed first are the 1983 re-released figures with "swivel arm battle grip." There was a new waist piece manufactured for these re-released figures as well—one that was not as bulky as the 1982 waist.

NOTE: *The swivel arm battle grip re-released 1982 figures are notoriously difficult to find, so with a few possible exceptions (Snake Eyes and Scarlett) these should command higher values than their 1982 versions.*

1983 inserts and promotionals.

Larry Hama's dossiers.

The 1983 catalog.

1982-83 SWIVEL-ARM FIGURES

BREAKER
Communications Officer (swivel-arm)
(Includes: TV-Radio Backpack, Helmet, Radio Headset)

For a full bio of this character see Breaker (1982).

CLUTCH
VAMP Driver (swivel-arm)
(Includes: Helmet)
Included with the VAMP (1982).

For a full bio of this character see Clutch (1982).

ENEMY LEADER
Cobra Commander (swivel-arm)
(Includes: "Venom" Laser Pistol)

NOTE: *This is the first time Cobra Commander would appear carded on store shelves, and so he commands premium prices ($600+up) for mint on card specimens. All carded specimens of Cobra Commander were swivel-arm versions of the figure.*

For a full bio of this character see Enemy Leader (1982).

FLASH
Laser Rifle Trooper (swivel-arm)
(Includes: XMLR-1A [Shoulder-Fired Laser Rifle], Power Pack, Helmet, Visor)

For a full bio of this character see Flash (1982).

GRAND SLAM
Laser Artillery Soldier (swivel-arm)
(Includes: Helmet, Visor)
Included with the HAL (1982).

For a full bio of this character see Grand Slam (1982).

GRUNT
Infantry Trooper (swivel-arm)
(Includes: M-16 Rifle, Combat Pack, Helmet)

For a full bio of this character see Grunt (1982).

HAWK
Missile Commander (swivel-arm)
(Includes: Helmet, Visor)

Included with the MMS (1982).

For a full bio of this character see Hawk (1982).

ROCK 'N ROLL
Machine Gunner (swivel-arm)
(Includes: Heavy Machine Gun with Bipod, Helmet)

For a full bio of this character see Rock 'N Roll (1982).

SCARLETT
Counter Intelligence (swivel-arm)
(Includes: XK-1 Power Crossbow)

For a full bio of this character see Scarlett (1982).

SHORT-FUZE
Mortar Soldier (swivel-arm)
(Includes: M-1 [81mm Medium Mortar] with Stand, Ammo Pack, Helmet, Visor)

For a full bio of this character see Short-Fuze (1982).

SNAKE EYES
Commando (swivel-arm)
(Includes: Uzi Gun, Explosives Pack)

For a full bio of this character see Snake Eyes (1982).

STALKER
Ranger (swivel-arm)
(Includes: M-32 "Pulverizer" Sub-Machine Gun)

For a full bio of this character see Stalker (1982).

STEELER
Tank Commander (swivel-arm)
(Includes: Helmet, Binocular Headset, Uzi Gun)

Included with the MOBAT (1982).

For a full bio of this character see Steeler (1982).

THE ENEMY
Cobra (Soldier) (swivel-arm)
(Includes: Dragunov [SVD] Sniper's Rifle)

For a full bio of this character see The Enemy: Cobra (Soldier) (1982).

THE ENEMY
Cobra Officer (swivel-arm)
(Includes: AK-47 Assault Rifle)

For a full bio of this character see The Enemy: Cobra Officer (1982).

ZAP
Bazooka Soldier (swivel-arm)
(Includes: Ammo Pack, Helmet)

For a full bio of this character see Zap (1982).

Note: *Only came w/the pictured Type 3 Bazooka.*

1983 G.I. JOE FIGURES

ACE
Fighter Pilot
(Includes: Helmet)
Included with the Skystriker Combat Jet.

Ace was the original fighter jock for the Joe team, and on his prototype file card we learn he was a senior instructor at USAF Fighter pilot combat training school, code-named "Top Gun" (Hasbro edited that last part out, and listed his previous duty as, "senior instructor USAF Fighter Weapons Squadron 'The Aggressors.'"). Ace was the best of the best fighter pilots. His prototype file card comments that he became interested in poker (his favorite game because he never loses) when "he grew bored with the quality of his chess opponents." Ace is currently a member of the Joe team.

Ace is a very common Joe figure to obtain, as many children bought Skystrikers.

MLC: **$10**

AIRBORNE
Helicopter Assault Trooper
(Includes: Helmet, Assault Pack, XM-16 Attack Rifle)

On the Sunbow cartoon, Airborne had a psychic bond with his brother, perhaps displaying, as his file card states, his spooky and prescient "far-seeing look." His prototype file card states that his parents were "oil rich Navahos who indulged their eldest son with skydiving lessons in the mistaken belief that the panache associated with the daring sport would be an asset to his political career once he finished law school." He passed the Arizona State Bars and never looked back. He loved jumping out of airplanes too much. Airborne is a current member of the Joe team.

NOTE: *This version of Airborne is not the same character as the 1990 Sky Patrol version.*

MOC: **$150**, MLC: **$15-20**

Airborne's parachute variations. The parachute on the left has no cross on the inside, while the one on the right does. The one on the right seems more difficult to obtain.

COVER GIRL
Wolverine Driver
Included with the Wolverine.

Cover Girl's original code name was Hurricane Helga, and she was noted as "Tank Driver," until Mr. Hama drafted her file card and the name of the "Wolverine" tank as we now know it. Her prototype file card states that she is "...A prime example of denial. She finds herself to be so beautiful that she must work against it. She is compelled to learn and master decidedly un-feminine disciplines, but in the end—the self assurance this provides only makes her more alluring and compliments her already stunning good looks with a maddening charismatic attraction that reduces most men to stuttering fools." The package artwork on the box of the Wolverine is striking and accurate in her depiction. She is currently an active member of the Joe team.

MLC: **$18**

DOC
Medic
(Includes: Helmet, Stretcher, Rescue Flare Launcher)

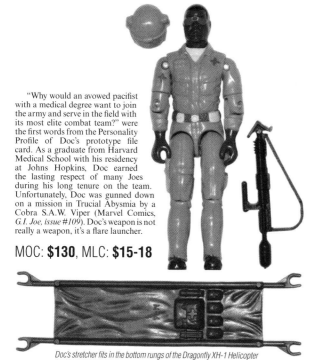

"Why would an avowed pacifist with a medical degree want to join the army and serve in the field with its most elite combat team?" were the first words from the Personality Profile of Doc's prototype file card. As a graduate from Harvard Medical School with his residency at Johns Hopkins, Doc earned the lasting respect of many Joes during his long tenure on the team. Unfortunately, Doc was gunned down on a mission in Trucial Abysmia by a Cobra S.A.W. Viper (Marvel Comics, *G.I. Joe*, issue #109). Doc's weapon is not really a weapon, it's a flare launcher.

MOC: **$130**, MLC: **$15-18**

Doc's stretcher fits in the bottom rungs of the Dragonfly XH-1 Helicopter for Medevac purposes.

GRAND SLAM
Laser Jet Pack Soldier
(Includes: Helmet, Visor)
Included with the JUMP Jet Pack only in 1983.

Since this version of Grand Slam was included with the JUMP during the 1983-84 year, this short span and the fact that the paint wears off of the figure *very* easily may suggest why the "Silver Pads" Grand Slam is a very difficult find. A mint "Silver Pads" Grand Slam is a truly rare find and is highly prized. For a full bio of this figure, see Grand Slam (1982).

MLC: **$25-40**

DUKE
First Sergeant
(Includes: Binoculars, Helmet, Assault Pack, Sticker, M-32 Submachine Gun)
Mail Away Exclusive

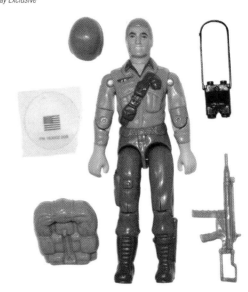

Duke became one of the most enduring and iconic characters in the line, and Mr. Hama commented that he gladly accepted Duke as the team's field leader because, up until 1983, "the top sergeant… [is] the one slot that's glaringly missing from the roster." After Hama and Hasbro debated between giving the Joes a new officer, or a high-ranking enlisted man, they decided that Carl (later changed to Conrad) Hauser, Duke, would be a Master Sergeant.

Duke's prototype file card is influenced by the Vietnam conflict. After enlisting in the army in 1960, he graduated Special Language School focusing on languages that would help him on his tour of duty. Duke "went Special Forces in 1963 and did his first tour in the Republic of South Vietnam… in the boonies working with Montagnard tribesmen." This suggests that Duke, trained indigenous Montagnard tribesmen to fight against the Viet Cong. As a First Shirt, Duke was "…the old vet [He] did three tours 'In Country' and ran four different Special Forces schools… Has a tendency to become 'one of the boys' and commands by winning respect." Duke is still the field commander of the current Joe team.

The figure itself was a mail-away exclusive and is a common find, but the flag sticker that was issued with the mail-away version (only) is quite rare, although the figure is considered complete without it. This is why many mail-away Dukes have a sticky part on their left or right shoulder—the flag sticker was there, but is now missing.

Mint in Sealed Mailer Box with flag sticker: **$50-75**, MLC: *(with flag sticker)* **$30**, MLC: *(no flag)* **$20**

Duke mail away. Pictured is his helmet with "no holes," the impossible-to-find flag sticker, full head-shot file card, and brown mailer box.

GRUNT
Falcon Pilot
(Includes: Helmet)
Included with the Falcon Glider.

Collectors know this figure as "Tan Grunt." This sculpt, the second version of the figure, suggests a desert theme, not unlike the "tan" Clutch figure offered with the VAMP Mark II 1984). Hasbro smartly repainted and reused the molds of old figures to save on the cost of producing new molds. This practice has saved them quite a bit of money over the last thirty years. For a full bio of this figure, see Grunt (1982).

The only difference in the character from 1982-83, is that his file card now reads, "Graduated: Falcon Glider School." Keep in mind that this version of Grunt only came with a helmet. There is a tendency for collectors to give him a tan backpack from the Battle Gear Accessory Pack #1 (1983), but this is incorrect.

MLC: **$10-15** *(beware of inflated prices, as this figure is common)*

GUNG-HO
Marine
(Includes: Jungle Pack, XM-76 Grenade Launcher)

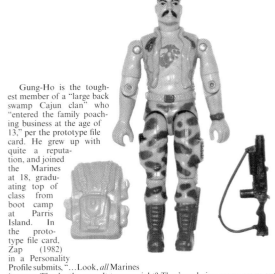

Gung-Ho is the toughest member of a "large back swamp Cajun clan" who "entered the family poaching business at the age of 13," per the prototype file card. He grew up with quite a reputation, and joined the Marines at 18, graduating top of class from boot camp at Parris Island. In the prototype file card, Zap (1982) in a Personality Profile submits, "…Look, *all* Marines is crazy. They're the assault troops, right? They're a hairy, scary, crazy outfit!…" And Gung-Ho is the craziest of them all, "the hairiest, scariest craziest jar-head that ever scratched, kicked and bit his way out of that hole in the swamp they call Parris Island!" In the comic, Gung-Ho had a turn-on turn-off Cajun accent, mixing French and Creole English. In the cartoon, Gung-Ho became a fan favorite, and appeared in many episodes. Gung-Ho is currently active on the Joe team.

MOC: **$200**, MLC: **$15**

SNOW JOB
Arctic Trooper
(Includes: Skis, Poles, XMLR-3A Laser Rifle, Polar Pack)

Snow Job was a "major Olympic Biathlon contender" prior to enlistment because he could shoot well and ski well at the same time. He rearranged priorities "to the consternation of Army PR flacks" and was accepted onto the Joe team. According to Rock 'N Roll (prototype file card), he's called Snow Job because, "He's always got some sort of deal cooking and whenever you think you've got him pegged—he pulls the double whammy on you!" Snow Job made sporadic appearances on both the Sunbow cartoon and the Marvel comic book, and has participated in a few missions with the new team. It is unsure whether he is still active.

NOTE: *Snow Job's XMLR-3A Laser Rifle was the most commonly used weapon in the heyday of Sunbow's animated smash-hit G.I. Joe: A Real American Hero. The rifle is apparently an upgrade of Flash's (1982-83) XMLR-1A laser rifle, as it does not need a power source (backpack) to function. The "XM" designation in the Army means "experimental model."*

MOC: **$160**, MLC: **$12-18**

TORPEDO
SEAL (Sea, Air, and Land)
(Includes: Scuba Tanks, Swim Fins, Harpoon Rifle)

Torpedo has made sporadic appearances on the Sunbow cartoon and in the Marvel comic, where he seemed more gregarious than his file card indicated. He's a SCUBA instructor, holds black belts in three martial arts, and "Has absolutely no sense of humor. Period. Spends off duty hours perfecting his fighting skills and marksmanship. Competes in combat pistol matches and various swim meets. Strict vegetarian. Regarded by his team-mates has a highly competent professional albeit a Psycho-Chicken to the MAX" (prototype file card). Torpedo is an active member of the Joe team.

MOC: **$150**, MLC: **$12-16**

TRIPWIRE
Mine Detector
(Includes: Minesweeper, 3 Land Mines, Mine Detector Backpack)

Tripwire dropped out of high school and "spent two years in a Zen monastery pondering the meaning of life until he was expelled for breaking too many dishes and spilling every conceivable liquid. Joined the Army at age 19 and received spiritual awakening on the grenade range." It appears that explosives are the only thing that can calm him down. Tripwire is an active member of the Joe team.

MOC: **$140**, MLC: **$12**

WILD BILL
Helicopter Pilot
Included with the Assault Copter Dragonfly.

Wild Bill has become one of the most popular Joes, perhaps because he was, according to Mr. Hama, "based on a real man who served in the 1st Air Cavalry as a helicopter pilot." His prototype file card states that he "served as a combat infantryman and participated in LRRP (Long Range Reconnaissance Patrol) operations during [the] South East Asian debacle." He thinks of himself as a country western singer, and is "totally honest in personal dealings, [but] he is not beyond spinning a tall tale for the amusement of comrades…" With his Colt revolvers and a western drawl, Wild Bill functions as a pilot on the current Joe team.

MLC: **$10-15** *(depending on condition of his easily rubbed off belt buckle)*

1983 COBRA FIGURES
DESTRO
Enemy Weapons Supplier
(Includes: High Density Laser Gun, Armed Attaché Case)

On his prototype file card, the masked man known as Destro was called "Warmaster," and, like his acceptable name, is "the faceless power behind one of the largest multi-national corporations in the world, M.A.R.S. (Military Armaments Research System), [the] largest manufacturer of state-of-the-art weapons." Hama was so prescient when he wrote Destro's file card in 1983, that he commented, "He is one of the very few holders of the American Express Platinum card…"

The prototype file card delves deeply into Destro/Warmaster's past and claims that he believes in two things, "War and family tradition." Hama explains, "…his sliver battle mask [is]… a family tradition, from the time an early ancestor was sealed in such a mask as punishment for breaking the peace to strike at an enemy. The same ancestor defiantly wore the mask when he returned from exile to crush those who punished him."

Destro supplies weapons for Cobra Command, or "against them, if it is better for business." Destro "admires the G.I. Joe team for their combat skills and expertise, but abhors them for wasting such skills to maintain peace. Respecting them, he considers them all the more dangerous and is totally dedicated to seeing them… destroyed." Destro is currently an adversary of the Joe team, and joins with Cobra if it suits his purposes. He was a prominent character on the Sunbow cartoon, the Marvel comic, and currently the Devil's Due comic.

MOC: **$300**, MLC: **$12-15** *Destro's opened armed attaché case. If only you could assemble that rifle…*

MAJOR BLUDD
Mercenary
(Includes: Rocket Launcher, Missile Backpack)

Major Bludd was no longer a mail-away in 1983, he was available on the card. For a full bio of this figure, see Major Bludd (1982).

MOC: **$275**, MLC: **$10-12**

THE ENEMY
Cobra H.I.S.S. Driver
Included with the Cobra H.I.S.S.

This version of the generic trooper code-name "The Enemy" applies to the strange Cobra H.I.S.S. Driver figure. The H.I.S.S. Driver is a bright red departure from the standard black and blue colored Cobra Troopers. They are selected from "the best and most evil of Cobra Command's thousands of yearly recruits. Each is chosen for his physical strength and total dedication to evil!"

MLC: **$10-20** *(depending on the condition of his easily rubbed off Cobra sigil)*

THE ENEMY
Viper Pilot
Included with the Viper Glider.

The Enemy: Viper Pilot is one of the most difficult Joe figures to find in *good* condition. The silver Cobra sigil on his chest is frequently scratched, nearly gone, or is totally absent, as the paint application of the logo was weak. If you find a The Enemy: Cobra (1982) figure that is missing a Cobra logo, then it is most likely a Viper Pilot. I have only seen a handful of copies of this figure with a mint Cobra symbol. The Enemy: Viper Pilot did not come with any accessories.

MLC: **$15-75** *(depending on the condition of his Cobra sigil)*

1983 VEHICLES/PLAYSETS

APC
(Amphibious Personnel Carrier)

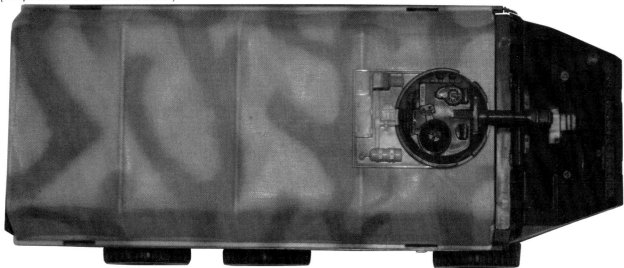

The APC became the first troop transporter for the Joe team. It is a very common vehicle to find. The APC's front and top are removable, and the vehicle can hold up to 28 G.I. Joe figures. The seat belts hold the figures in place, and the 50mm auto-control cannon also snaps off the top. The rear bumper of the vehicle can function as a carrying handle, and the APC is rumored to float on water, but I have not found that to be true with the four that I own. The mail-order version of the APC had a dark green non-camouflaged top, and is a bit more rare that the original version.

Easily lost/removable pieces include the steering wheel, two seat belts, and top cannon.

MISB: **$130**, MIB: **$75**, MLC: **$15-20**

The APC's easily lost pieces.

ASSAULT COPTER: DRAGONFLY (XH-1)

(Includes: Wild Bill figure)

Wild Bill's Dragonfly Copter is a trademark vehicle in the G.I. Joe line. With its four Sidewinder air-to-ground missiles, and two Sidewinder H.E. (high explosive) missiles, the XH-1 provides strong air support for the ground troops. The copter is replete with a dual M-34 grenade launcher/ 2mm Vulcan Gatling cannon mounted on its nose, a winch with rescue hook, and a side-mounted 160mm cannon pod. Pushing a button turns the rotor blades, and the cockpit holds two figures.

Easily lost/removable pieces include six missiles, two red blade tips, side cannon, side cannon power cords, and the grenade launcher/Gatling cannon.

NOTE: *There are two variations of the nose cannon—one cannon has stationary grenade launcher/Gatling cannons, while the grenade launcher/Gatling cannon are separately movable on the other version.*

MISB: **$200**, MIB: **$125**, MLC: **$25-35**

Variations of the grenade launcher/Gatling cannon.

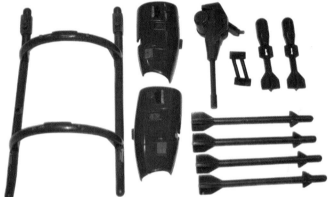

The Dragonfly's easily lost pieces.

BATTLE GEAR ACCESSORY PACK #1

Includes:

4 brown Helmets

4 clear Visors

1 gray Binocular Headset (Steeler)

1 gray Communications Headset (Breaker)

1 tan Ammo Backpack (Short-Fuze/Zap)

1 tan Communications Backpack (Breaker)

1 tan Laser Backpack (Flash)

1 tan Combat Backpack (Grunt)

1 gray XK-1 Power Crossbow (Scarlett)

1 gray M-16 Rifle (Grunt)

1 gray XMLR-1A Laser Rifle (Flash)

1 gray M-11 Submachine Gun (Stalker)

NOTE: *The original name for this gun was "M-32 'Pulverizer' Submachine Gun"*

2 gray Uzi Guns (Snake Eyes/Steeler)

1 gray M-60 Heavy Machine Gun and Bipod (Rock 'N Roll)

1 gray Explosives Pack (Snake Eyes)

2 tan Battle Stands

NOTE: *These weapons are not the same colors as the regular Joe equipment, so if you find a weapon or accessory for a Joe figure that doesn't match the colors designated in this book, then it's from the current Joe line (1997 to present), or from a Battle Gear Accessory Pack. For example, the weapons included in the 1983 Battle Gear Accessory Pack were gray in color, not the dark deep gray or black used for the weapons of the original carded figures.*

MMC: **$20**, MOC: **$12-15**, MLC: **$10-12**

Cobra F.A.N.G.
(Fully Armed Negator Gyrocopter)

The Cobra F.A.N.G. was the popular light-attack helicopter designed for quick Cobra raids. The F.A.N.G. weighs 2,200 lbs, can max out at speeds up to 197 mph, and has a range of 550 miles. The F.A.N.G. comes equipped with four heat-seeking air-to-air rockets and a joystick control.

Easily lost/removable pieces include four missiles, a bomb, and the rollbar. These copters were seen on the Sunbow cartoon as well as in the Marvel comic.

The F.A.N.G.'s easily lost pieces.

MISB: **$100**,
MIB: **$50-60**,
MLC: **$18-25**

Cobra H.I.S.S.
(Includes: The Enemy figure)

The High Speed Sentry, known as the Cobra H.I.S.S., came with, "Double 'Diablo' [90mm twin] cannons you can swivel and elevate," and perhaps this is why many H.I.S.S. tanks today have broken tabs that elevate these guns. The H.I.S.S. was Cobra's main battle tank, and was used prolifically in all aspects of the G.I. Joe canon. There's a tow hook on the H.I.S.S., which leads me to believe that Hasbro was planning on the success of the line, as there weren't any tow-able Cobra weapons until next year when the Cobra Assault System Pod 1984) was released. With some imagination, it could tow captured Joe weapons.

NOTE: *The Cobra H.I.S.S. came with three different sticker variations of the '788' stickers on the front sides of the H.I.S.S.: clear numbers (early retail versions), red numbers (later retail versions), and white numbers (mail-in versions). There were no loose parts to the H.I.S.S.*

MISB: **$200**, MIB: **$100**, MLC: **$20-25**

The three H.I.S.S. sticker variations.

Collector's Carry Case
(MIP, with unapplied stickers)

The case's easily lost pieces.

The G.I. Joe Collector's Carry Case was a fascinating way to carry and display figures, as there were two holes on the back that could be used to wall mount the case. It held twelve figures, their weapons (barely), and their file cards (mostly). The case came with labels appropriate to the 1982-83 line, and a small instruction sheet with flag points. Most of these cases have holes punched out in order to make them wall-mountable.

Easily removable pieces include three straps to hold figures and the accessory holder cover.

NOTE: *The earliest late 1982 versions of the case came with stickers appropriate to the figures released in late 1982 (see Breaker-Enemy Leader, 1982), while later versions of the case, those released in early-late 1983, came with labels for those figures (see Airborne-Major Bludd, 1983). This case therefore can be placed in the 1982 section as well, but it was first displayed in Hasbro's 1983 catalog.*

MISB: *(tough to find)* **$30**, MLC: **$10-18**

The case with unapplied stickers.

COMBAT JET: SKYSTRIKER (XP-14F)
(Includes: Ace figure)

Unwrapped Skystriker parachute.

The Skystriker was another impressive 1983 vehicle. With six removable missiles (two Site-5 Sidewinder, two Site-3 Sparrow, and two Site-3Z Phoenix), two working parachutes with ejection seats, variable wings that swept back and forth with the movement of a lever, and two Vulcan Cannons (one front-mounted, and one on the plane's underbelly), the Skystriker was the crown jewel of many a collection. It is still highly sought after in good condition, but be wary—finding this popular vehicle isn't difficult, but finding one in mint loose complete condition, or (even less frequently) MIB or MISB is a challenge.

Easily lost pieces include six missiles, two ejector seats, and two parachutes w/seats.

NOTE: *There are two variants of the Vulcan Cannon on the nose of the plane, one has a grid behind it, while one does not. Neither is more difficult to find.*

MISB: **$250**, MIB: **$125**, MLC: **$35-60**

Skystriker w/wings folded.

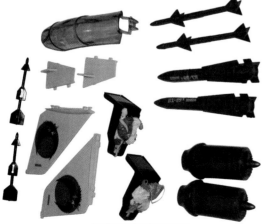

The Skystriker's easily lost pieces.

FALCON GLIDER
(G.I. Joe Attack Glider, Flying Armed Light Reconnaissance)
(Includes: Grunt figure)

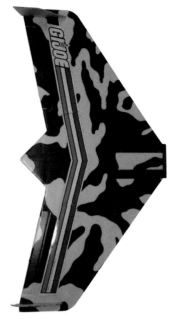

The Falcon Glider is one of the most fragile of all G.I. Joe toys. Its body, ailerons, and vertical stabilizers are made of graphic foam and are easily broken. Over time, the labels for the glider can lose their adhesive and come off. According to the blueprints (which come in two different color variations, green [rare] and blue [common]), a real Falcon Glider would have a wingspan of 30.4', and has two .30 caliber mini-machine guns that are mounted on the hard plastic weapon system reinforcement. In the sealed box, the glider also came with a small black rubber band that helps to attach Grunt to the bottom of the hard plastic reinforcement. The glider is still considered complete if this rubber band is missing. The Falcon Glider is rarely found in any condition other than poor fine, and is difficult to find in high grade, especially MIB.

Easily lost pieces include the black rubber band, weapon system reinforcement, and two vertical stabilizers.

MISB: **$300**, MIB: **$150**, MLC: **$50**

The Falcon's easily lost pieces.

Falcon Glider box.

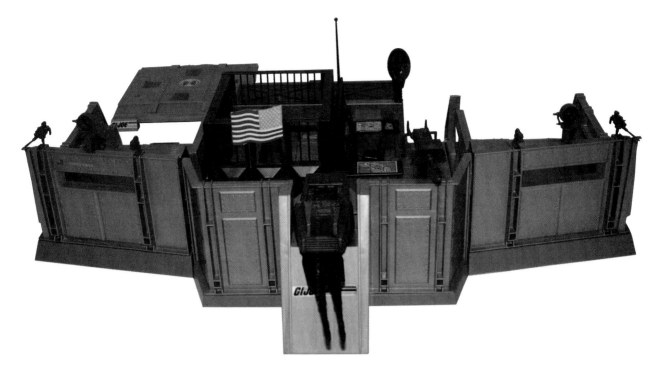

HEADQUARTERS COMMAND CENTER

The G.I. Joe Headquarters Command Center is one of the most popular of all Joe toys. It was portrayed in the Marvel comic as a "prefabricated" fortress in issue #24, "The Commander Escapes." Die-hard comic fans recognize that this version of G.I. Joe's Headquarters is not "The Pit"—the actual G.I. Joe Command Center below the Fort Wadsworth motor pool portrayed in the Marvel comic. Cartoon fans, however, recognize the HQ, and all loyal Joe fans appreciate the care and time it took to craft this amazing base.

The HQ has a bevy of action features including a helipad for Wild Bill's Dragonfly, a mechanic's lift for Clutch's VAMP, two secret storage facilities (one for weapons, one for file cards), a stockade with opening door for captured Cobra prisoners, a computer console replete with maps and diagrams, two search lights, a radar dish, a laser cannon, two infrared surveillance cameras, two 20mm machine guns, a big "double devastation" cannon, and an American flag with Joe logo on the back.

The HQ could be split into four parts: a helipad; a heavy equipment supply depot; a motor pool; and the command center. It was easily disassembled, and very durable. It is common to find HQ's at garage sales in heaps of parts thrown into a large cardboard box. Be careful to inspect your two searchlights, two machine guns, and two infrared cameras, as the tabs to attach these to the walls of the HQ are frequently missing. Inspect the jail door carefully—this super-fragile piece is almost always broken.

Easily lost pieces include two search lights, two machine guns, two cameras, flag, radar dish, laser cannon, generator cover, weapons hatch, and file card hatch.

MISB: $150-180, MIB: $70-80, MLC: $60

The computer console.

The stockade.

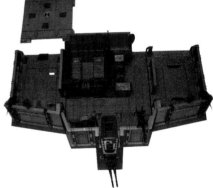

Top view.

The HQ's easily lost pieces.

The hidden weapon storage.

The lift.

The hidden file card compartment.

The helicopter landing pad.

A mint-in-sealed-box (MISB) Headquarters.

JUMP
(Jet Mobile Propulsion Unit/Jet Pack/Jet Propulsion Unit)
(Includes: Grand Slam figure)

This version of the JUMP jet pack included Grand Slam, "Silver Pads" and is quite desirable MIB or MISB, as it was only on store shelves for about a year and most Joe fans had already purchased a JUMP. Compound Grand Slam's popularity with the rarity of finding a mint condition Grand Slam with Silver Pads (his silver paint wore off easily), and this toy is an investment quality item. For a full description of the JUMP, please see JUMP (1982).

MISB: **$225**, MIB: **$100**, MLC: *(with Grand Slam)* **$50**, *(without Grand Slam)* **$10-15**

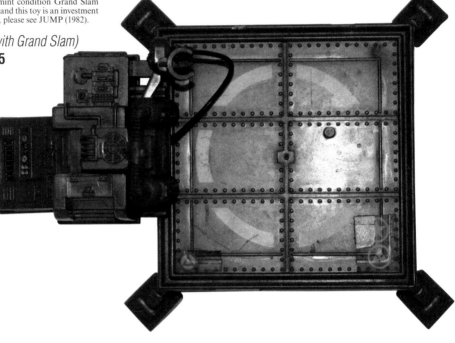

PAC/RAT
(Programmed Assault Computer/Rapid All Terrain)
Flamethrower

With four twin-stage boosted missiles, the remote control PAC/RAT Flamethrower adds extra firepower to the G.I. Joe arsenal without putting troops in harm's way. The Flamethrower's tiny remote control is rarely, if ever, found with the vehicle. Most collectors consider the vehicle complete without the remote control activator.

MISB: **$30-35**, MIB: **$20-25**, MLC: **$5-10**

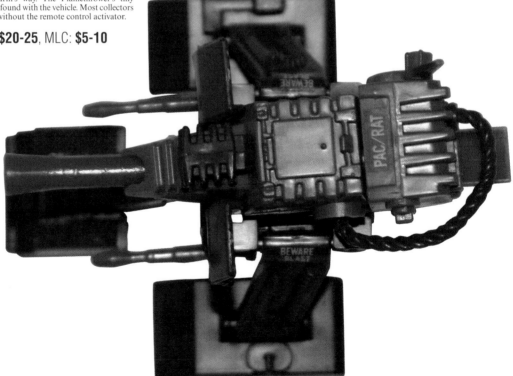

PAC/RAT
(Programmed Assault Computer/Rapid All Terrain)
Machine Gun

With four gun barrels, the remote control PAC/RAT Machine Gun adds extra firepower to the G.I. Joe arsenal. The Machine Gun's tiny remote control is rarely, if ever, found with the vehicle. Most collectors consider the vehicle complete without the remote control activator.

MISB: **$30-35**,
MIB: **$20-25**,
MLC: **$5-10**

PAC/RAT
(Programmed Assault Computer/Rapid All Terrain)
Missile Launcher

With four twin-stage boosted missiles, the remote control PAC/RAT Missile Launcher adds extra firepower to the G.I. Joe arsenal. Take care not to lose the Missile Launcher's remote control, which is rarely, if ever, found with the vehicle. Most collectors consider the vehicle complete without the remote control activator.

Easily lost pieces are the remote control and four two-stage missiles.

MISB: **$30-35**, MIB: **$20-25**,
MLC: **$5-10**

The Missile Launcher's easily lost parts.

POLAR BATTLE BEAR
(Skimobile)

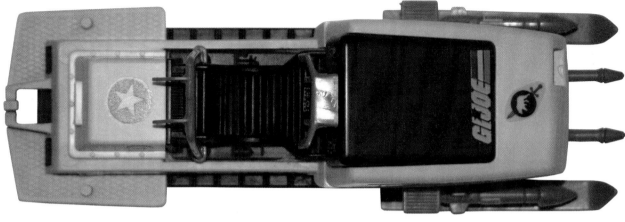

The Polar Battle Bear (usually driven by Snow Job [1983]) is a fascinating bit of Joe machinery and was very popular with kids. It was durable, and could hold the driver as well as two other Joes on its rear battle deck. With synchronized twin 55mm cannons, two heat seeking missiles, a roll bar, a 160hp V-6 engine, and a tow hook to carry the Whirlwind (1983) or the MMS or HAL (1982), the Skimobile had it all. Be careful that the two front cannons (attached within the hull of the vehicle) are not drooping, as the guns can become disengaged from the gun-slide inside the vehicle. The Skimobile is prone to discoloration of its white exterior.

Easily lost pieces include two missiles, rollbar, and the engine cover.

MISB: **$100**, MIB: **$50**, MLC: **$12-20**

The Polar Battle Bear's easily lost pieces.

POCKET PATROL PACK

The Pocket Patrol Pack was used to transport three Joes and their weapons from place-to-place. The pack attached to a child's belt and slid off easily. Not the greatest accessory, but very common to find. There are two logo variations for the Pocket Patrol Pack, and these changed when the carded Joe logo changed in late 1985/early 1986. The Pocket Patrol Pack was also available in black as a mail-away with the Rapid Deployment Force in 1993.

MISP: **$20**,
MLC: **$2-5**

COBRA S.N.A.K.E. BATTLE ARMOR
(System: Neutralizer–Armed Kloaking Equipment)

The S.N.A.K.E. armor is an intricate accessory for Cobra Command, as it has several pieces, and required assembly before each use. It came with a two-part chest piece (external maintenance module), two two-part legs, two arms, a rubber stand to store the armor (in lieu of a figure), two arm brushings (to hold the arms in the chest piece), and four arm attachments: remote claw, flamethrower arm, machine gun arm, and rocket. This makes a truly complete loose S.N.A.K.E. a hard find. The armor is not an expensive piece, as many were produced from 1983-84. In 1985, the S.N.A.K.E. was released in a dark blue color, and was very difficult to find at retail. A figure could fit inside the armor (without their accessories), and used the suit as battle armor. In the Marvel comic, a brainwave device could be implanted inside the armor in order to utilize captured Joes against their teammates. As the armor was molded in white, it is common to find it in a yellowed condition.

Easily lost pieces include—actually, the whole S.N.A.K.E. Armor is composed of easily lost pieces.

MISB: **$90**, MIB: **$40**, MLC: **$10-18**

TWIN BATTLE GUN
(Whirlwind)

The Whirlwind is an easy find, and this is good because it's a fantastic piece. With its twin 20mm armor piercing main gun systems that rotate when you spin a thumb wheel, its 360 degree rotation, two collapsible tow wheels/isolation pads, and a universal tow arm that can attach it to any Joe vehicle with a tow hook (Wolverine [1983], MOBAT [1982]), the Whirlwind is an all-purpose weapon. Be careful that the two foldable wheels are not broken, and that the two ammunition emergency access panels are intact. The box front indicates that Rock 'N Roll is the Joe who usually sits in the command seat.

Easily lost pieces include two machine gun covers, computer/hand attachment, and two wheels.

MISB: **$60-70**, MIB: **$40**, MLC: **$8-12**

The Whirlwind's easily lost pieces.

COBRA VIPER GLIDER
(Cobra Command Attack Glider)
(Includes: The Enemy: Cobra Viper Pilot figure)

The Viper Glider's easily lost pieces.

The Viper Glider, like its cousin the Falcon Glider, is a very fragile G.I. Joe toy. Its body, ailerons, and vertical stabilizers are made of graphic foam and are easily broken. Over time, the labels for the glider can lose their adhesive and come off. According to the blueprints, a real Viper Glider would have a wingspan of 30.4', and has two .30 caliber mini-machine guns that are mounted on the hard plastic weapon system reinforcement. In the sealed box, the glider also came with a small black rubber band that attaches The Enemy: Cobra Viper Pilot to the bottom of the hard plastic reinforcement. The glider is still considered complete if this rubber band is missing. The Viper Glider is rarely found in any condition other than poor-fine, and is difficult to find in high grade, especially MIB – even more so than the Falcon Glider.

Easily lost pieces include the black rubber band, weapon system reinforcement, and two vertical stabilizers.

MISB: **$300**, MIB: **$150**, MLC: **$50**

WOLVERINE
(Armored/Armed Missile Vehicle)
(Includes: Cover Girl)

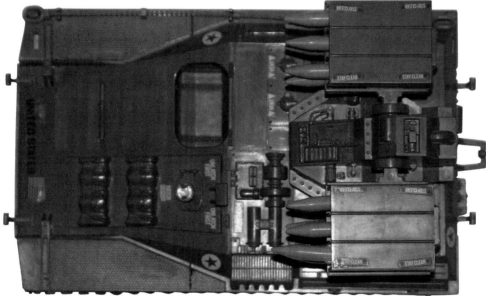

Wolverine sticker sheet outlining all the missile stickers.

Cover Girl's armor plated Wolverine tank was a very popular vehicle in 1983, as it came with twelve individually labeled Stinger ground-to-ground missiles that were numbered 1-12, a tow hook in the rear in order to attach the Whirlwind (1983), a removable engine cover, and a rescue cable. Although the tank itself is common to find, the Wolverine's rescue cable is a tough part to locate. It is one of the most commonly lost or broken Joe vehicle parts. If yours includes the cable, be very careful not to force it onto the vehicle, as it might actually be a bit shorter than where it shows to be attached.

Easily lost pieces are those twelve missiles and the rescue cable.

MISB: **$175-200**, MIB: **$100**, MLC: **$25-35**

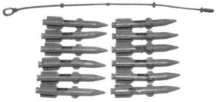

The Wolverine's easily lost pieces.

(SERIES III, 1984)

This series of G.I. Joe figures and vehicles featured prominently in the Sunbow cartoon and jump-started the line's stride towards icon status. With the addition of Zartan, Hasbro pushed toward a more supernatural element in G.I. Joe. This establishes a fundamental difference between G.I. Joe and Cobra characters. The stalwart Joe characters are the more military-type honorable soldiers. Cobra characters, especially as portrayed in the cartoons, emerged as over-the top and more akin to super-villains with Destro, Cobra Commander, and Zartan in their ranks.

The 1984 catalog.

Carded 1984 Figures.

Duke/MANTA Mail-Away promotional.

1984 G.I. JOE FIGURES

BLOWTORCH
Flamethrower
(Includes: M-7 Manpack, Flamethrower, Helmet, Oxygen Mask)

Blowtorch's other operative code names were Pyro and Hot-Foot (from the prototype file card), and he has "made a study out of fire… [and] knows [its] effect on known construction materials, vegetation, protective shields and explosives." As the Joe's original flame-thrower (and there have been a few), the ulti-mate irony in his character is that he is paranoid about fire, and his file card states that he "…can't sleep un-less he's near a smoke detector," an action based on "intimate knowledge."

Blowtorch's figure has three variants worth noting, neither worth more than the other. His face can have either dark or light eyebrows. His flamethrower can either be made be of a stiff, hard green plastic (earlier versions of the figure), or softer, more durable plastic (a later version)—made when Hasbro realized that the harder cord to the flamethrower broke frequently. His helmet is available with or without holes in the side (neither is more rare), and strangely enough—it is quite difficult to attach a 1982 clear visor to the helmet. These holes are assumed to be a product run that was stopped.

Blowtorch helmet variations.

MOC: **$120**, MLC: **$15**

CLUTCH
VAMP Mark II Driver
(Includes: Helmet)
Included with the VAMP Mark II.

This version of the character is frequently referred to as "Tan Uniform" Clutch because this casting is exactly like the 1983 version of Clutch, but it features a desert paint scheme. For a full bio on the character, see Clutch (1982).

MLC: **$12-15**

S
E
R
I
E
S

T
H
R
E
E

CUTTER
Hovercraft Pilot
Included with the Killer W.H.A.L.E. Hovercraft.

This figure is the most hopeful Joe character ever. I say this because both he and I are fans of the same ball club—he proudly wears a Boston Red Sox hat on his head (NOTE: Since then, yes, the Sox have won the World Series!). There are Cutter figures out there that have many different shades of color for his facial hair, ranging from dark brown to a red-brown. Cutter's real name is "Skip A. Stone," and on the Sunbow cartoon he spoke with a Massachusetts accent. Cutter has a strange sense of humor, and is the first member of the Joe team from the Coast Guard. He is on their current roster.

MLC: **$12-15**

DEEP SIX
S.H.A.R.C. Diver
(Includes: Bellows)
Included with the S.H.A.R.C.

Deep Six's bellows.

Deep Six is considered to be complete with or without the bellows system that accompanies the S.H.A.R.C. The bellows is a pump that allows a child to (according to the S.H.A.R.C.'s box text) "make 'Deep Six' submerge or surface." The figure is odd in that his helmet is non-removable, and his only poseable feature are his arms which move at the shoulder—a frustrating aspect of his figure to me as a child. It is suggested that his head mold is the same as Ace (1983), but after destroying a sub-par Deep Six figure, I have concluded that the sculpts are indeed different. As a character, Deep Six has a reputation for being introverted, soft-spoken, even solitary—he became a diver "So I can be alone" (from his file card). Deep Six enjoys bottlecap collecting, New York Times crossword puzzles, and solitaire.

MLC: **$10-12**

DUKE
First Sergeant
(Helmet variation without holes and 1/2-body file card)
(Includes: Binoculars, Helmet, Assault Pack, M-32 Submachine Gun)

This is the first time that Duke was available carded, as all previous versions of the character were mail-aways. His carded version never included the flag sticker of the 1983 Duke, and the figure is considered complete without that minuscule patriotic label. On the Sunbow cartoon, Duke is second in command of the Joe team. For a full bio on this character, see Duke (1983).

NOTE: *Some Duke figures have cuffed sleeves like some of the early Joes (see Stalker, 1982). Dukes with these cuffed sleeves are a more difficult to find variant of the figure.*

MOC: **$200-250**, MLC: **$18-20** *Duke helmet variants with and without holes.*

MUTT
Dog Handler (K-9)
(Includes: "Junkyard," Ingram MAC-11 with Silencer, Night Stick, Leash, Face Mask, Helmet)

Mutt and Junkyard (now Junkyard II, as the original Junkyard has since retired) have a fond place in the hearts of many Joe fans. Their operative code names according to their prototype dossiers were Dog-Face and George (or even "Dawg"), and the file card states that Mutt is considered, "A natural with animals. He gets along better with dogs than people." His figure is impressively colored, and it comes with many appropriate accessories including a muzzle, leash, and night stick. Mutt's helmet, like Blowtorch and Rip Cord's from 1984, is available with or without holes in the side (neither is more rare). It is fairly difficult to attach a 1982 clear visor to the helmet, and these holes are assumed to be a product run that was halted.

MOC: **$150**, MLC: **$15**

RECONDO
Jungle Trooper
(Includes: Cross Country Backpack, M-1 4E2X Rifle)

Recondo's two different camouflage patterns—neither one is more rare.

Recondo is the Joe's resident jungle specialist, and his original name was "Boonie-Rat" (a term for 'combat infantryman' from the Vietnam War). Recondo loves the jungle and hates the cold, as "There's nothing he likes better than to be hauling a rucksack through the brush and sweating through his cammies. When he's in the jungle, he owns it." Recondo has been on many perilous missions for the Joe team, slogging through jungles throughout the world. Recondo's figure is well-camouflaged, and his rifle is a fantastic sculpt as it looks like he's wrapped the barrel in camo cloth. His backpack has a handle and can be carried by the figure. Recondo is currently a reserve member of the Joe team.

NOTE: Recondo comes with two different variations of camouflage patterns.

MOC: **$125**, MLC: **$15**

RIP CORD
HALO Jumper (High Altitude Low Opening)
(Includes: Parachute Pack, Helmet, Oxygen Mask, SLR-W1L1 Rifle with sight)

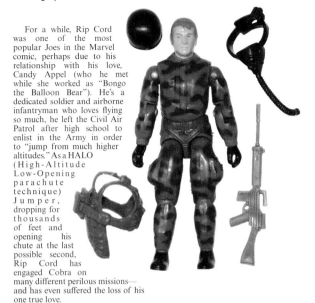

For a while, Rip Cord was one of the most popular Joes in the Marvel comic, perhaps due to his relationship with his love, Candy Appel (who he met while she worked as "Bongo the Balloon Bear"). He's a dedicated soldier and airborne infantryman who loves flying so much, he left the Civil Air Patrol after high school to enlist in the Army in order to "jump from much higher altitudes." As a HALO (High-Altitude Low-Opening parachute technique) Jumper, dropping for thousands of feet and opening his chute at the last possible second, Rip Cord has engaged Cobra on many different perilous missions—and has even suffered the loss of his one true love.

Rip Cord's helmet, like Mutt and Blowtorch's from 1984, is available with or without holes in the side (neither is more rare). It is fairly difficult to attach a 1982 clear visor to the helmet, and these holes are assumed to be a product run that was stopped.

MOC: **$160**, MLC: **$15**

ROADBLOCK
Heavy Machine Gunner
(Includes: Backpack, M-2X Machine Gun with Tripod, Ammo Box, Helmet)

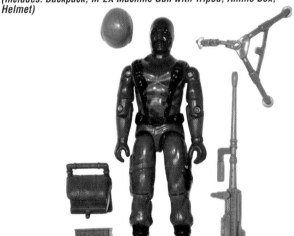

Roadblock's operative names were Steamroller, Hardball, and even the terrible, "Bubba." Roadblock was the Heavy Machine Gunner of the Joe team, and his figure's rifle is modeled after the M-2 .50 caliber Browning—a crew-served machine gun used primarily by teams of men. Roadblock holds this formidable weapon all by himself! Couple this strength with his lifelong dream to be a gourmet chef, and aspirations to attend the Escoffier school in France (a dream ruined by a recruiter who appealed to his good nature), and you've got a fantastic character. In the Sunbow cartoon, Roadblock spoke in catchy rhymes. After the original team disbanded, Roadblock became a bit of a celebrity chef, even appearing on television. He has since rejoined the Joe team.

Roadblock's helmet is a modified version of Steeler's (1982) and Zap's (1982), and it is similar to the early variant of Duke's figure (1983)—it comes without holes. His backpack is broken up into two parts, an ammo box, and a main pack that can hold his machine gun's tripod.

MOC: **$200-225**, MLC: **$15**

SPIRIT
Tracker
(Includes: Arrow Cassette Pack, Auto-Arrow Launcher, Eagle [Freedom])

On the Sunbow cartoon, Spirit Iron-Knife was the "Native American mystic warrior," of the Joe team, and was frequently pitted against Storm Shadow (1984). He and Airborne (1983) round out the first two Native American characters on the team, both mystically gifted but their economic backgrounds are as far apart as can be. Charlie Iron-Knife grew up with a family, "...so far below the poverty line that they never realized they were poor." Wanting a doctoral degree in Psychology (from his prototype file card), "he opted for the Army and the G.I. Bill, doing his initial service time during the late sixties in various parts of Southeast Asia." Spirit is a shaman and a medicine man who, along with his eagle, Freedom, has fought valiantly for the Joe team mission after mission. Spirit is currently an active member of the Joe team.

MOC: **$130**, MLC: **$15**

THUNDER

Self-Propelled Gun Artilleryman
(Includes: Helmet, Visor, Radio Headset, Monocular)
Included with the Slugger.

Thunder with full helmet gear.

Thunder came with some interesting accessories for a vehicle driver in 1983. He came with a monocular (similar to a binocular, but with one eyepiece), and a three-part helmet consisting of the helmet itself, a visor, and a radio headset. In the Marvel comic, Thunder had very few appearances altogether, and was one of the Joes killed in Trucial Abysmia by a S.A.W. Viper.

MLC: **$15** *(due to his complicated accessories)*

1984 COBRA FIGURES

BARONESS

Cobra Intelligence Agent
(Includes: Backpack, High-Density Laser Rifle)

The Baroness has acted as Cobra's primary Intelligence Agent for the past twenty plus years, and her origin is outlined in the Marvel comic. Born in 1953 to wealthy European aristocrats, Anastasia DeCobray was on Christmas holiday from her boarding school and visiting her brother, Eugen, when he was killed during the Vietnam conflict while furnishing native Vietnamese with medical supplies. Although he did not shoot the man, Snake Eyes was erroneously blamed for the death of Eugen, and the woman who would later be known as The Baroness, "graduated from student radicalism into international terrorism" (from her file card).

After becoming an infamous terrorist, she joined Cobra Command, and has been involved in many of Cobra's highest-profile missions, as "she soon became Cobra Commander's (Enemy Leader, 1982) right hand and confidant" (from the prototype file card). Her face was "severely burned" during a Cobra mission, and has undergone extensive plastic surgery. She is in love with the masked arms dealer, Destro (1983), and "her principle weakness is in the division of her loyalty between Cobra Commander and Destro. Her chief strength would seem to lie in her ability to play them against each other."

MOC: **$275**, MLC: **$25-30**

COPPERHEAD

Water Moccasin Pilot
Included with the Cobra Water Moccasin.

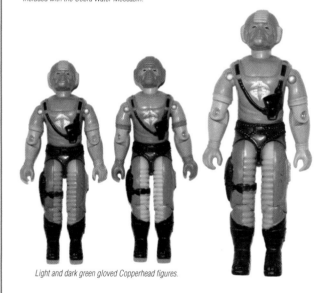

Light and dark green gloved Copperhead figures.

Copperhead had the potential to be a pretty cool Joe character, but he was never truly picked up on the cartoon or in the comic books. It is suggested that he raced high-speed boats in Monaco and Japan, and bet on his own races. After losing a bundle of money, he joined Cobra to make up his gambling losses. After paying these debts, it is rumored he recently returned to Cobra to help entrench their Navy.

MLC: *(regular uniform)* **$12-15**, *(dark green gloves)* **$20-30**

ENEMY LEADER
Cobra Commander (with hood)
(Includes: "Venom" Laser Pistol)
Mail Away Exclusive

This version of Cobra Commander, the "hooded" version, was a mail away from inserts packaged inside Joe vehicles and accessories. This portrays Cobra Commander as he was seen in Marvel Comics' *G.I. Joe #1*, and is a very common figure to find. Be careful of his gold paint applications, as they rub off easily. For a full bio, see Cobra Commander (Enemy Leader, 1982).

Mint in mailer box, mint in sealed baggie: **$30**, MLC: **$15-23**

FIREFLY
Cobra Saboteur
(Includes: Demolition Backpack, Sub-Machine Gun, Walkie-Talkie)

Firefly has become one of the favorite Cobra characters and figures. His background is shrouded in mystery and his action figure is a wonderful sculpt that comes with some unique equipment. His walkie-talkie is one of the most rare accessories in the line, and can sometimes sell for as $20 on its own. Sealed on his 1984 card, Firefly has commanded prices up to $1,000 in AFA NM-NM+ graded condition.

As a saboteur, Firefly is a respected Cobra agent whose "fees are paid into a numbered Swiss bank account and are always payable in advance. He makes no guarantees and gives no refunds. [He is] known by his work." Firefly is stealthy and world-renowned, (according to his prototype file card) "[he] served in the French Foreign Legion Paras as Michel LeClerc, in Biafra as Helmuf Knopf, [and] in Nicaragua as George Winston." Firefly's origin was revealed in the Marvel comic. He was the child of a Japanese father who was also the son of a Grand Master of Koga Ninjas. This boy was eventually adopted by ninjas, and grew up to become Firefly. He was approached by Cobra Commander (see Enemy Leader, 1982) to assassinate Snake Eyes (1982). As a ninja, Firefly infiltrated the Arashikage clan and became the "Faceless Master" (he never allowed a clear photo of himself). Upon observing Snake Eyes' fighting skills, he declined the Commander's directive and referred him to Zartan for the assassination. After this, he became a Cobra agent in earnest, engaging in a number of deadly missions. His current whereabouts are unknown.

MOC: **$400**, MLC: **$25-50**

SCRAP IRON
Cobra Anti-Armor Specialist
(Includes: RAR Pistol, Missile System with Remote Activator, 2 Missiles)

Scrap-Iron's missile system parts.

Scrap-Iron had the potential to be a fantastic character, but was rarely used in the Marvel comic and infrequently used on the Sunbow cartoon. He is, in actuality, Destro's weapons designer, "field representative and product demonstrator" (prototype file card). In other words, he creates and tests M.A.R.S.' weapons (see Destro, 1983). "To wit Scrap Iron is methodical and precise. Imperfection in any form repels and disgusts him. Perhaps that's why he wants to blow up the world." As a figure, he comes with an amazing 8-piece missile launcher (including the missiles and remote activator), and a cool-looking RAR pistol.

MOC: **$100-125**, MLC: **$15-20**

STORM SHADOW
Cobra Ninja
(Includes: Long Bow, Quiver, Two Samurai Swords, Nunchaku Sticks)

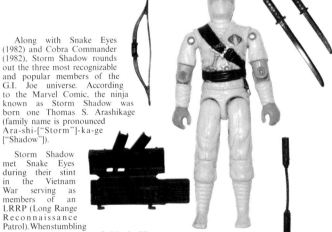

Along with Snake Eyes (1982) and Cobra Commander (1982), Storm Shadow rounds out the three most recognizable and popular members of the G.I. Joe universe. According to the Marvel Comic, the ninja known as Storm Shadow was born one Thomas S. Arashikage (family name is pronounced Ara-shi-["Storm"]-ka-ge ["Shadow"]).

Storm Shadow met Snake Eyes during their stint in the Vietnam War serving as members of an LRRP (Long Range Reconnaissance Patrol). When stumbling upon an encampment of North Vietnamese soldiers, the LRRP was hit hard and Snake Eyes went down. Thomas raced through a hail of gunfire and saved the wounded man. The two became fast friends during the war, and afterward Thomas offered Snake Eyes a position in his family's business—"they were all ninjas, of course." After Storm Shadow was blamed incorrectly for his uncle's death, he joined the ranks of Cobra in hopes of flushing out the true assassin. He found that man to be Zartan (1984), and then Storm Shadow left the Cobra organization for reasons unknown and he and Snake Eyes must once again match up against one another. From his prototype dossier, "His forefathers worked for feudal lords developing espionage and martial arts secrets that were handed down only to family members." Frequently, the action figure's bow is broken, so take care to check a loose, complete Storm Shadow's weapons.

MOC: **$300**, MLC: **$30-65** *(based on accessories and if there's any yellowing of the figure)*

THE ENEMY
Cobra Stinger Driver
Included with the Stinger.

Thankfully, this would be the last Cobra figure in the line to have the oversimplified code name "The Enemy," which was discarded in order to add more specialization to Cobra Troops. This figure is basically a repaint of the same mold as the swivel-arm Cobra Officer (The Enemy, 1983).

MLC: **$15**

WILD WEASEL
Cobra Rattler Pilot
Included with the Cobra Rattler.

Wild Weasel is the best pilot in Cobra's legions. A minor character in Cobra Command, he has a vast knowledge of military and civilian aircraft, and has a sibilant speech pattern he acquired "during a strafing run" (from his file card).

NOTE: *There is a variation of the figure where the two maps on his thighs are reversed. Neither one of these is more difficult or expensive to find than the other.*

MLC: **$15**

ZARTAN
Master of Disguise (MIB; have both f/c's–both w/ and w/out schizophrenia)
(Includes: Backpack, Face Mask, Shield, Two Knee Pads, Pistol)
Included with the Chameleon Swamp Skier.

Zartan's heat-sensitive stickers.

Zartan's chest shield and knee pad with and without heat sensitive sticker sheets.

Zartan wearing his accessories.

Zartan was sold as most smaller vehicle drivers were, packaged in a box with his Swamp Skier and its blueprints. Zartan has the distinction of being the only "vehicle driver" to be pictured on G.I. Joe card backs—a motif Hasbro usually reserved for individually carded figures without vehicles. Zartan was really the G.I. Joe universe's first foray into the realm of the supernatural, as the character and the figure would "change their skin color" in sunlight. This unique characteristic was more of a feature in the Sunbow cartoon version than in the Marvel comic, where Zartan's perception-altering capabilities were rooted in hypnotism and holography.

Zartan's military training is unknown, but it is assumed that he received "European military academy training (probably St. Cyr)." The École Spéciale Militaire de St-Cyr provides cadets with an intense and rigorous program that focuses on academics as much as military tactics, and is deeply rooted in French traditions and customs.

After completing his military training he became "a master of make-up and disguise, a ventriloquist, a linguist, an acrobatic-contortionist, and a practitioner of several mystical martial arts." With an infamous reputation, and being one of the finest archers in the world (indeed, he is a better archer than even Storm Shadow says Joe creator Larry Hama), he was approached by Cobra Commander (Enemy Leader, 1982) to assassinate Snake Eyes (1982). Snake Eyes' family perished in an automobile accident that also killed the Commander's brother (who was driving drunk). After an enlightening revelation, Zartan refused to go through with the assassination, but the Commander blackmailed the shape-changer and Zartan followed through with the hit. He arrived at the household of Storm Shadow's family, where Snake Eyes was living at the time, and mistakenly killed Storm Shadow's uncle in the melee. Zartan the assassin fled, and Storm Shadow was blamed for his own uncle's death. The young ninja then swore to find the true assassin. After forming the Dreadnoks, Zartan became an agent of Cobra and eventually he and Storm Shadow confronted one another with the death of the ninja's uncle.

Zartan is still an agent of Cobra, albeit loosely, and he has recently developed a skin condition. He and his Dreadnoks (Buzzer, Ripper, Torch, 1985) are fully operational.

NOTE: *Zartan comes with two thigh and one chest pad that included a sheet of heat-sensitive stickers. Zartan is considered complete with or without these stickers on his accessories.*

MLC: **$20-30**

1984 VEHICLES/PLAYSETS

BATTLE GEAR ACCESSORY PACK #2

Includes:

4 green Helmets (2 regular issue, 1 Airborne Helmet, 1 Doc Helmet)

2 brown Battle Stands

1 brown Marine Jungle Backpack (Gung Ho)

1 brown Helicopter Assault Trooper Backpack (Airborne/Duke)

1 brown Mine Detector Backpack with three Mines (Tripwire)

1 light gray Bazooka (Zap)

1 light gray Mortar with Stand (Short-Fuze)

1 light gray XM-76 Grenade Launcher (Gung-Ho)

1 light gray XM-16 Attack Rifle (Airborne)

1 light gray Rescue Flare Launcher (Doc)

1 light gray XMLR-3A Laser Rifle (Snow Job)

1 dark blue Rocket Launcher (Major Bludd)

2 dark blue High Density Laser Guns (Destro)

1 dark blue Laser Pistol (Cobra Commander)

1 dark blue AK-47 Attack Rifle (Cobra Officer)

1 dark blue Dragunov (SVD) Sniper Rifle (Cobra)

NOTE: *These weapons are not the same colors as the regular Joe equipment, so if you find a weapon or accessory for a Joe figure that doesn't match the colors designated in this book, then it's from the current Joe line (1997 to present), or from a Battle Gear Accessory Pack. For instance, the weapons included in the 1985 Battle Gear Accessory Pack were mainly white and dark blue in color, not the dark deep gray or black used for the weapons of the original carded figures.*

MOMC: **$15-20**, MOC: **$12**, MLC: **$8-10**

BIVOUAC
(Battle Station)

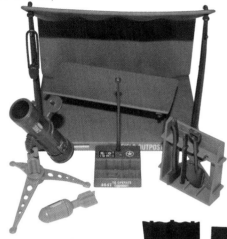

The Bivouac was a basic battle station/ accessory set to complement your G.I. Joe troops. The "forward observation post with light gear and rocket launcher" came with a cot, two cot base support legs, tent canvas, tent base, two tent support poles, (non-shooting) rocket launcher, tripod base for rocket launcher, accessory rack, field radio with removable antenna, shovel, axe, machete, 16 oz. canteen, and 98mm projectile.

MISB: **$35**, MIB: **$15**, MLC: **$10**

The Bivouac's easily lost pieces.

CHAMELEON
(Zartan's Swamp Skier)
(Includes: Zartan figure)

Like its companion figure Zartan, the Chameleon also has color-change capabilities, the ultra-violet rays from the sun turn the vehicle a darker green. The Chameleon disassembles easily in order for Zartan to pull its parts in the included towing container. Apparently, with his mask on and him towing a box full of junk, Zartan was "in disguise," a very clever concept.

Since the Chameleon could be disassembled entirely, all parts should be present for it to be considered complete.

Easily lost pieces include the frame, engine, lower faring, body, rear fork, handlebars, two rear skis, front skis, tow cable, and towing container.

NOTE: *The tow cable is usually missing and the handlebars break if too much "disassembly" occurs.*

MISB: **$150**,
MIB: **$60-70**,
MLC: *(with Zartan)* **$30-40**,
MLC: *(separate)* **$6-10**

The Chameleon's easily lost pieces.

COBRA A.S.P.
(Assault System Pod)

The Cobra A.S.P. is the first Cobra weapon system with the capacity to be towed by another vehicle (see Cobra H.I.S.S., 1983). This is a formidable weapon. The A.S.P. possesses 120mm "Eliminator" cannons, retractable stabilizers that lower and wheels that raise to make the A.S.P. stationary in order to raise the body pod to "attack" position, and a 360 degree rotation of fire.

Easily lost pieces include two shell-proof deflector shields, and the generator cover.

MISB: **$35**, MIB: **$15-18**, MLC: **$5-10**

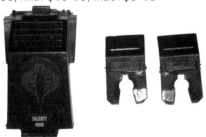

The A.S.P.'s easily lost pieces.

COBRA C.L.A.W.
(Covert Light Aerial Weapon)

The Cobra C.L.A.W. featured prominently in the Cobra arsenal, achieving fame for being the motivating factor in the most famous G.I. Joe story, Marvel Comics *G.I. Joe #21*, "Silent Interlude." An experimental weapon with nap-of-the-earth flying ability, it can go undetected by most radar devices. With retractable wing tips, two Venom missiles, a DES/28-B 750lb. Flashfire bomb (used when the aircraft is a remote, with no pilot), and fold-down wheels for landing, this vehicle is a "troop builder" for most die-hard collectors.

Easily lost pieces include two missiles, bomb, handlebars, and machine gun access shroud.

MISB: **$35**,
MIB: **$18-20**,
MLC: **$8-10**

The C.L.A.W.'s easily lost pieces.

COBRA RATTLER
(Ground Attack Jet)
(Includes: Wild Weasel figure)

The Ground Attack Jet, code-named Rattler, is the standard large aircraft of the Cobra legions. It possesses a VTOL lift off (Vertical Take-Off and Landing), and a bevy of bombs and missiles including eight cluster bombs, four short-range missiles, two "Renegade" missiles, and two ion-seeking missiles. The aircraft even had manually retractable landing gear. With a "Jawbreaker" nose cannon, a roof-mounted twin 40mm multiple fire cannons, and two "battle damage" panels, this was a child's dream, and laid waste to many a Joe squad.

As it is a large vehicle, there were many pieces to lose, but the most commonly misplaced included two damage panels, two regular panels, twelve missiles, two engine covers, machine gun (upper roof), and a turret shell.

MISB: **$150**, MIB: **$65-75**,
MLC: **$40-65**

The Rattler's easily lost pieces.

COBRA WATER MOCCASIN
(Includes: Copperhead figure)

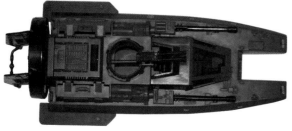

The Water Moccasin, with its two 44mm "Destructor" cannons, 20mm roof-mounted DES-20B twin machine guns, "Gator" surface torpedo, and room for troops on the exterior crew decks, certainly added to Cobra's naval prowess. The fan on the back part of the ship could spin, and the canopy for Copperhead was removable. With 580 hp and a redline at 9250 rpm, the boat could *fly*, and was showcased in a G.I. Joe commercial.

Easily lost pieces include the roof cover, torpedo, turret gun, engine cover, two fan vanes with attachments, and two storage covers.

NOTE: *Be very careful with the rear of the ship, it is easily lost. The fan and fan vanes are prone to breakage.*

MISB: **$100**, MIB: **$40-45**, MLC: **$15-25**

The Water Moccasin's easily lost pieces.

KILLER W.H.A.L.E. HOVERCRAFT
(Warrior: Hovering Assault Launching Envoy)
(Includes: Cutter figure)

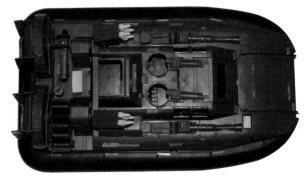

Cutter's Killer W.H.A.L.E. Hovercraft is a miracle of modern machinery and was used frequently on the Sunbow cartoon and in the Marvel comic. With six SD-30 depth charges, an HL-66 Lightweight Surveillance Cycle, a high-speed reconnaissance sled, twin diesel engines, 105mm port and starboard cannons, and twin anti-aircraft guns, this toy had a lot of special features and play value. Couple these features with a fold-down ramp for loading extra troops and you have an amazing vehicle.

Easily lost pieces include the surveillance cycle, reconnaissance sled (in two pieces, the sled and sled shroud), six depth charges, eight missiles, four steering vanes (attach to rear fans), two rear fans, two vane attachments.

NOTE: *Be careful with the fan assembly in the rear of the craft, as the assembly is very fragile.*

MISB: **$175-200**,
MIB: **$80-100**,
MLC: **$50-65**

The W.H.A.L.E.'s easily lost pieces.

MACHINE GUN DEFENSE UNIT
(Battlefield Accessories)

The Machine Gun Defense Unit was a small accessory set to complement battle scenes.

Easily lost pieces include two tripod barricades (4 parts total), machine gun (tripod should be attached), ammunition belt, ammunition box, warning restriction sign.

NOTE: *The Machine Gun Defense Unit came with two dark green battle stands that most collectors do not consider to be part of the set.*

MISB: **$20**,
MIB: **$10-15**,
MLC: **$5-8**

Easily lost pieces.

MISSILE DEFENSE UNIT
(Battlefield Accessories)

The Missile Defense Unit was a small battlefield accessory set.

Easily lost pieces: missile launcher, missile launcher base, two-piece brick wall, three missiles, two-piece missile case, "Ammunition Depot" sign.

NOTE: *There are two variations of the two-part wall, one with bullet holes, and one without. Neither is more difficult to find or more expensive than the other. Also, the Missile Defense Unit came with two gray battle stands that most collectors do not consider to be part of the set.*

MISB: **$20**, MIB: **$10-15**, MLC: **$5-8**

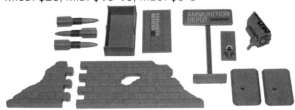

Easily lost pieces.

M.A.N.T.A.
(Marine Assault Nautical Transport; Air Driven
Mail Away Exclusive

The M.A.N.T.A. wind surfer mail-away is a fascinating bit of machinery, and is a fairly common mail away to find MISP, so it should not be treated like a holy grail. It averages around $15-20 in this condition.

It is entirely composed of easily lost pieces, including a two-piece mast, a green two-piece large surfboard, sail, green side board, two black side board attachments, backpack, rifle, sail-to-mast attachment (boom), missile, and .30 cal. machine gun.

NOTE: *The entire M.A.N.T.A. is collapsible and can fit into its included backpack for easy portability.*

MISB: *(mailer box or baggie)* **$25**, MLC: **$8-10**

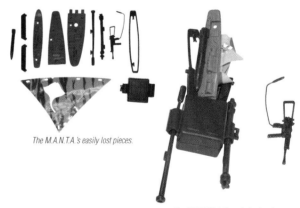

The M.A.N.T.A.'s easily lost pieces.

The M.A.N.T.A.'s items in backpack.

The M.A.N.T.A.'s variants.

MORTAR DEFENSE UNIT
(Battlefield Accessories)

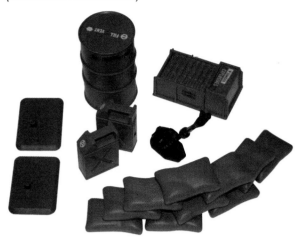

The Mortar Defense Unit was a small battlefield accessory set. The sandbags are a fantastic Joe accessory, and are popular among collectors building dioramas.

Easily lost pieces include the barrel, two gas cans, ten sandbags, mortar, and mortar projectile case.

NOTE: *The Mortar Defense Unit came with two green battle stands that most collectors do not consider to be part of the set.*

MISB: **$20**, MIB: **$10-15**, MLC: **$5-8**

The Mortar Defense Unit's easily lost pieces.

MOUNTAIN HOWITZER
(Battle Station)

The Mountain Howitzer was another small battlefield accessory set designed for the G.I. Joe team. The howitzer came with a tow hook, allowing it to be transported by Joe vehicles (see Vamp Mark II, 1984).

Easily lost pieces include the main howitzer cannon, howitzer base, shell box, three shells, howitzer shield, breach, binoculars, and tripod.

MISB: **$32**, MIB: **$15**, MLC: **$8-10**

Mountain Howitzer's easily lost pieces.

Mountain Howitzer's two-part binoculars.

S.H.A.R.C.
(Flying Submarine [Submersible High-Speed Attack and Reconnaissance Craft])
(Includes: Deep-Six figure)

Deep-Six's Flying Submarine, code named the S.H.A.R.C., is a wonderful vehicle for kids, as it has two acoustic homing torpedoes, a bellows to submerge Deep-Six (sometimes considered a figure accessory), and flip-up twin 30mm "Tidal Wave" cannons. The vehicle was used in the Marvel comic and the Sunbow cartoon, and had both underwater- and air-attack capabilities.

Easily lost pieces include two torpedoes (frequently missing), engine ventilator screen, two cannon covers.

MISB: **$150**, MIB: **$60-70**, MLC: **$15**

The S.H.A.R.C.'s easily lost pieces.

SKY HAWK
(One Man V.T.O.L. [Vertical Take-off and Landing Aircraft])

The Sky Hawk had the same VTOL (Vertical Take-Off and Landing) capability as the Cobra Rattler (1984), yet could turn on a dime. It's fast, mobile, and equipped with twin "Thunderclap" cannons and two air-to-surface rockets. Most collectors consider the Sky Hawk an "army builder" because it is inexpensive and easy to obtain.

Easily lost pieces are the two rockets, horizontal stabilizing fin (as it did not "snap" into place—it mostly rested on the Sky Hawk), and two fins.

MISB: **$60**, MIB: **$35-40**, MLC: **$10-12**

The Sky Hawk's easily lost pieces.

SLUGGER
(Self-Propelled Cannon)
(Includes: Thunder figure)

The Slugger was a fully mobile, four-wheel drive, 170mm "Slugger" Howitzer. The vehicle also came with a removable .30 caliber quick-sequence machine gun that some consider to be Thunder's accessory, but it is usually part of the vehicle itself. Some collectors consider the best part of the Slugger to be its figure hatch—a Joe can sit entirely inside the armored vehicle and be fully protected from the cannon fire. The rear bumper extends to the ground, acting as a stabilizer for the cannon when it fires.

Easily lost pieces include the removable machine gun, and engine cover.

NOTE: *The Slugger came in two versions, one regular issue with camouflage patterns, and a mail-away that lacks the camouflage paint scheme. The variant with no camouflage is more rare and more valuable.*

MISB: **$175**, MIB: **$65-70**, MLC: **$15-20**

The Slugger's easily lost pieces.

COBRA STINGER
(Cobra Night Attack 4-WD)
(Includes: The Enemy: Cobra Stinger Driver figure)

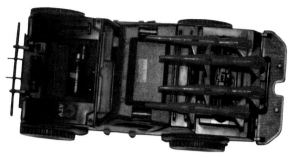

The Cobra Stinger became the standard jeep in Cobra Command's arsenal. Detailed in dark gray with a flat black molding, the Stinger is truly a Night Attack vehicle. The four pivoting ground-to-air rockets with 360-degree rotation, opening and closing gull-wing doors, a top speed of 140 mph with a range of 550 miles, and a tow-hook make this a desirable vehicle for Joe collectors.

Easily lost pieces include four rockets, roof cover, two doors, steering wheel, and rocket launcher.

MISB: **$200**, MIB: **$70-100**, MLC: **$20-30**

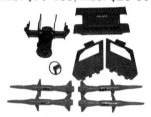

The Stinger's easily lost pieces.

VAMP MARK II
(Attack Vehicle)
(Includes: Clutch figure)

Another fine addition to the Joe arsenal, the VAMP Mark II is an updated version of the VAMP (1982) done over in desert colors. Instead of the original VAMP's machine guns, the VAMP Mark II has a missile launcher and four Stinger XK2 missiles, two water cans that snap onto the vehicle better, opening doors, and of course, a tow hook. The vehicle specifications are the same as the Cobra Stinger (1984)—a top speed of 140 mph with a range of 550 miles (they are the same model of jeep). There is a variant of the VAMP Mark II that is highly prized by collectors, as it was offered as a mail-away and was not exactly the same as the retail version. The mail-away variant's telltale signs of difference are a lighter color, gas cans (not water cans) that are similar to the original VAMP (1982), and other marked differences when examined closely.

Easily lost pieces include four missiles, roof cover, two doors, two water cans, hood blanket, and missile launcher.

MISB: **$200**, MIB: **$85-100**, MLC: **$15-25**

The VAMP's gas cans variation.

The VAMP's easily lost pieces.

WATCH TOWER
(Battle Station)

The Watch Tower was a battle station/accessory set to complement your troops. The set included a flag pole, machine gun, spotlight, two light green sandbags, ladder, watchtower floor, back wall, front wall, two side walls, and a door.

MISB: **$30**, MIB: **$15**, MLC: **$8**

Long view of the Watch Tower.

The Watch Tower's easily lost pieces.

(SERIES IV, 1985)

An excerpt from a long note attached to Larry Hama's dossier of the new 1985 character, Footloose, "Isn't this guy a do-over of Grunt [1982]? If Grunt is being phased out or to be more precise, the Grunt figure is being phased out, then why can't the character remain the same and acquire a new wardrobe just like Snake Eyes? This could give a more concrete reality to this universe."

Regardless of this note, Hasbro believed that introducing new characters would refresh the line—and it did—these new Joes sold like wildfire. 1985 would become one of the most revered of all of the years of the original line's run, and many characters (i.e. Bazooka, Flint, Dusty, Shipwreck, etc.) would endure as characters and return in newer updated uniforms later in the line's long run. Perhaps Hasbro did take Mr. Hama's comments to heart, as he goes on, "Snake Eyes is already being re-outfitted. The desert trooper, the fireman and the hostile environment trooper could all be retrained and re-outfitted Joes from the first run…"

Imagine what could have happened here to the Joe Universe. Flash could have been the 1984 Airtight, as he has experience with CBR (Chemical, Biological, and Radiological Weapons). Stalker might have been the new desert trooper, and Clutch could have driven the A.W.E. Striker. The implications are astonishing. But it was not in the cards…

The figures released in 1985 possessed a new feature, a ball-jointed head. This would be the last new physical feature added to the figures in their twelve-year run. The ball joints allowed a figure's head to move not only left to right, but also up and down. There are a few figures in Series IV, however, that did not come equipped with this new articulation—the three Dreadnoks, Tollbooth, and the re-painted "Listen 'n Fun" Tripwire. It could assumed that these few figures were designed in 1984, not 1985. All figures released in 1985 and later featured the ball joint in the figure's neck, with the obvious exception of repainted and re-cast characters (see Tiger Force [1988], Python Patrol [1989], etc.). These new ball-jointed heads accompanied swivel-arm battle grip (see 1983), and truly made these action figures a step above the norm.

File card notes: Beginning in late 1985/early 1986, the color of G.I. Joe file cards changed from the regular tan to a gray. If you purchased a few complete "troop builder" figures, and realized that one Tele-Viper file card is tan while the other is gray, the tan version is from early 1985, while the gray one is a later version.

Note on mail away vehicles: *In order to get rid of warehouse overstock (a term not in a present toy manufacturer's vocabulary), Hasbro frequently offered vehicles as mail away offers throughout the entire run of the line. Nearly every vehicle would be offered as a mail away. There may be some variant colors for mail-away vehicles, and these have been noted, but whenever possible, the most common version of the vehicle in question has been used.*

Action Stars cereal boxes with cut-outs.

The 1985 catalog.

1985 Triple Win game piece inserts, full set.

1985 G.I. JOE FIGURES

AIRTIGHT
Hostile Environment
(Includes: Compressor Pack, Sniffer, two Air Hoses)

Airtight loves his job. But his character from the Marvel comic books is a serious weirdo. He owns bizarre pets and his favorite snack is a peanut butter and tomato sandwich. Airtight frequently proves his worth as a CBR (Chemical, Biological, and Radiological Warfare) specialist. Although peculiar (he once commented that scorpions are too "crunchy"), this figure stands out as a fine specimen from the 1985 action figure line—a year often hailed by collectors as one of the Joe's best. Airtight is currently active on the Joe team.

MOC: **$55-60**, MLC: **$10**

ALPINE
Mountain Trooper
(Includes: Barretta SMG-12, Mountain Pack, Climbing Axe, GRB-88 Grappling Launch Line, Grappling Hooks)

With fantastic accessories, a great sculpt, and a well-written file card (his file name is "Albert M. Pine"), Alpine is the epitome of a mountain trooper. Alpine was an infrequent member of the Marvel comic, but made many appearances on the Sunbow cartoon—usually engaging in a tête-à-tête with his stalwart chum, Bazooka (1985). Alpine, although reluctant to return to the new Joe team initially, is currently on the roster.

MOC: **$60-70**, MLC: **$12**

BARBECUE
Fire Fighter
(Includes: Fire Axe, Foam Tanks, Nozzle Gun, Hose, Tank Bracket)

Barbecue is the first Joe firefighter character, and the figure's appearance truly does capture the essence of that occupation. Barbecue comes from a long history of firefighters in his family, and brings this template of experience to his job. His file card states that Barbecue is a real "party animal." A fun guy to have around, "he can open bottles with his teeth, pick up quarters with his ears and wrap his lips completely around the bottom of a quart Coke bottle." He is currently a reserve member of the Joe team.

NOTE: *The edge of the 1985 axe is painted silver, while the Slaughter's Marauders version (Barbecue, 1989) is not.*

MOC: **$70-100**, MLC: **$10**

BAZOOKA
Missile Specialist (w/both missile launchers)
(Includes: Helmet, M.A.T. Missile Launcher, Missile Pack)

Bazooka's missile launcher variants.

Bazooka originally came with the same missile launcher as Footloose (1985), but the launcher was soon changed to its correct version—the one pictured on his card front. A curious note on his prototype file card, where Bazooka's (alternate code names Long Shot, Rough Tackle, Heat Man, Armor Harmer, Hard Line) MOS was initially listed as a "Bazooka Soldier," states (hand written by Larry Hama), "The armies of the WORLD have not used bazookas for over THIRTY YEARS!!! They are as obsolete as the flintlock musket…"

Thus, Bazooka is a Missile Specialist. Strangely, his file card contradicts the way he was portrayed on the G.I. Joe cartoon, "Subject is a decisive fast thinker with all the instincts of a natural survivor." In the Sunbow production, he was portrayed as a dimwit. On the cartoon, Alpine is his closest friend and the two often were paired together during missions.

MOC: **$75-80**, MLC: **$8**

CRANKCASE
A.W.E. Striker Driver
(Includes: Helmet, Rifle)
Included with the A.W.E. Striker.

Crankcase's prototype file card lists his alternate names as Fast-Lane and Roll-Bar, and he was originally designated to drive the Rampage rather than the A.W.E. Striker. His character has all the qualifications of the perfect vehicle driver—he raced street machines and worked the stock car circuit until a recruiter promised him that he'd be able to drive at much faster speeds in the Army. He signed up for a "burst of four [years]" and drove many missions for the Joe team. Sadly, he was one of the Joes killed at the hands of a Cobra S.A.W. Viper in Trucial Abysmia (Marvel Comics, *G.I. Joe #108-109*).

MLC: **$8**

DUSTY
Desert Trooper
(Includes: FAMAS Assault Rifle, Bipod, Backpack)

Dusty was once falsely accused of treason in two of the most popular episodes of the Sunbow cartoons, *The Traitor* (episodes #56-57, 1985). It is rumored that the last name of Dusty's file name, Ronald W. *Tadur*, is an anagram of one of Hasbro's G.I. Joe packaging artists, Ron Rudat. As a character, Dusty became a fan favorite because of his strength of character, "Dusty loves the desert. It is clean, pure, and unforgiving." Dusty was also one of the first Joes to be "environmentally suited" for desert climates, he is a specialist like Snow Job (1983) in an arctic climate. Dusty was deployed (usually) on desert missions. Frequently missing the bi-pod to his rifle, the figure is difficult to complete, but doesn't command prices that are too high. Dusty spends his time training new recruits on the current Joe team.

MOC: **$60-70**, MLC: **$8-12**

FLINT
Warrant Officer
(Includes: Riot Shotgun I-12 Short Barrel, Backpack)

Flint is a strange character, as he was of command grade, but still a Warrant Officer. As a W.O., it was his job to communicate between officers and enlisted men. W.O.'s are a strange breed of men, and according to the U.S. Army Warrant Officer Career Corps, the rank of Warrant Officer was created to "reward enlisted men of long service and also to reward former commissioned officers of World War I who lacked either the educational or other eligibility requirements necessary for continuance in the commissioned status." Flint is a fantastic soldier, self-confident, and highly intelligent. He was a Rhodes Scholar at Oxford University where he majored in English Literature. Flint, "drafted and personally led half a dozen rescue missions in hostile territories," and participated in many Joe missions over the years. In the comic books, Flint was romantically involved with Lady Jaye (1985), and eventually the two married. Flint is an Executive Officer on the current Joe team.

MOC: **$60-80**, MLC: **$10**

FOOTLOOSE
Infantry Trooper
(Includes: M-16, M73-A1 LAWS, Helmet, Backpack)

Initially slated as a replacement for Grunt (as Grunt was fazed out the Joe line [and this was mentioned in the Marvel comic]), Footloose (alternate code names, Action, Bravo, Grunt [perhaps as a new version?])became the new Joe infantry trooper. His character was very strange, and this is reflected in his background, "[he] was valedictorian of his high school class, captain of the track team and an Eagle scout. He was going for his degree in Phys. Ed. On a [Indiana] state scholarship when he suddenly dropped out, moved out to the coast, and became quite weird for a few years." Inspiration struck and he joined the Army. Sure, the Joe team believes him to be a strange bird, but he's simply trying to "find himself." After a few important missions, it is unsure what affiliation he may currently have with the Joes.

MOC: **$60-70**, MLC: **$8-10**

FROSTBITE
Snow Cat Driver
(Includes: Rifle)
Included with the Snow Cat.

"Frostbite was born in a place where summer is a myth and a crowd consists of two people standing on the same acre," describes Frostbite's birthplace of Galen, Alaska. After working on the Alaskan pipeline, he joined the Army and eventually, the Joe team. He is always up for a challenge no matter the weather, and is currently on the Joe team's roster.

MLC: **$8**

HEAVY METAL
Mauler M.B.T. Tank Driver
(Includes: Rifle, Mouthpiece)
Included with the Mauler M.B.T. Tank.

Heavy Metal's mic. It's the most rare Joe accessory.

Heavy Metal's proposed code names were Fast Track, Road Iron, Rolling Jack, and Bogie Wheel—but Hasbro finally settled on Heavy Metal. Making sporadic appearances in the Joe universe, Heavy Metal has garnered more fame because of his action figure than his strength of character. Heavy Metal's mouthpiece/microphone is considered the most difficult domestic Joe part to find—more difficult than even Hardtop's pistol (1987). I have seen the mic sell for $125 itself, as the piece is impossible to locate, even in a sealed bag. I was lucky enough a few years back to buy a MISB Mauler Tank, and this came with a MISP Heavy Metal with mic. I opened up the figure to take this picture.

NOTE: *If you own a Heavy Metal without a darkened beard, you have a variant mail-away of the figure called Rampage (1989).*

MLC: *(with microphone)* **$120-140**, *(no mic)* **$6-8**

KEEL-HAUL
Admiral
(Includes: Pistol)
Included with the U.S.S. FLAGG.

Keel-Haul acted as the commander of the U.S.S. FLAGG aircraft carrier, and even remembers flying Navy planes (Phantom F-4's) "off of the Intrepid in the late '60s." He received the Navy Cross (an award ranked just under the Medal of Honor), is an excellent pilot, "a respected military historian, a nationally ranked chess player and possibly the world's worst clarinet player" (from his file card). This version of Keel-Haul comes with and without a patch on his right arm.

NOTE: *The figure packaged with the U.S.S. FLAGG did come with the patch, while the 1989 mail-in version of the figure did not. Strangely enough, mail-in versions of Keel-Haul after 1989 reverted back to having the patch. Some mail-in versions of the figure did not come with his pistol, a rare accessory.*

MLC: **$12**

LADY JAYE
Covert Operations
(Includes: Power Javelin, Surveillance Camera, Backpack)

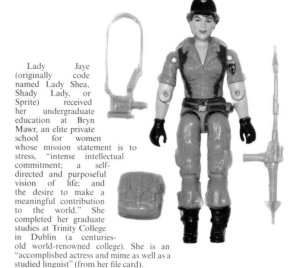

Lady Jaye (originally code named Lady Shea, Shady Lady, or Sprite) received her undergraduate education at Bryn Mawr, an elite private school for women whose mission statement is to stress, "intense intellectual commitment; a self-directed and purposeful vision of life; and the desire to make a meaningful contribution to the world." She completed her graduate studies at Trinity College in Dublin (a centuries-old world-renowned college). She is an "accomplished actress and mime as well as a studied linguist" (from her file card).

Lady Jaye's MOS was originally dubbed "Infiltrator," but was changed to the present "Covert Operations." Notes suggest that she spoke with either a "British upper-crust twang that adorns her speech" (prototype file card), or a "faint Gaelic [probably Irish Gaelic] lilt." She was romantically involved with Flint 1985, and according to the Devils' Due comic, the two married. On the Sunbow cartoon, she threw power javelins, and the figure came with a javelin-type launcher with handle.

MOC: **$60-80**, MLC: **$12**

QUICK KICK
Silent Weapons
(Includes: Nunchuka, Samurai Sword, Backpack)

The regular issue Quick Kick, and the inferior mail-away version.

Quick Kick came in two variants, the regular carded superior edition (which was offered as a mail-away later on), and a far inferior mail-away. The plastic of the inferior mail-away is of a decidedly lower quality, and the weapons included with the inferior figure were also slightly different. Quick Kick played a fairly prominent role in the Marvel comic and Sunbow cartoon as their resident martial artist and infiltration specialist.

"Too short to play basketball, Quick Kick turned to martial arts." Born in Los Angeles, he was working as a stuntman in Hollywood before signing up for the Joe team. Tragically, after a botched mission in Trucial Abysmia, Quick Kick was killed in an explosion (Marvel Comics, *G.I. Joe, #108-109*).

MOC: **$40-60**, MLC: **$6**

SGT. SLAUGHTER
Drill Instructor ("USA" logo)
(Includes: Baton)
Mail Away Exclusive

This version of Sgt. Slaughter was only offered as a mail-away in 1985, and was never available carded. Apparently, Sgt. Slaughter was a rousing success after a missed attempt to obtain the rights for Sylvester Stallone's "Rocky Balboa" character (the proposed figure was never introduced in the line). Where Rocky failed, the Sarge triumphed, and the good Sgt. became the spokesman for G.I. Joe during the cartoon show.

Collectors sit on the fence as to whether or not they accept his presence. Sgt. Slaughter was prominently featured in Sunbow's rousing *G.I. Joe: The Movie*. In the film, the Sarge was fourth in command of the team. It is assumed that the Sarge is still drilling troops to this day.

Mint in Sealed Baggie: **$20**, MLC: **$10**

SHIPWRECK
Sailor
(Includes: Percussion Pistol, Boarding Hooks w/3/8" line, Parrot)

With his raspy Jack Nicholson-like voice on the Sunbow cartoon, and his crass and crude attitude, Shipwreck found an endearing spot in Joe collector's hearts. His figure is my favorite from the 1985 line, his accessories are appropriate, and they all seem to fit nicely around his wrists and at his side. His parrot, "Polly," and his pistol clasped around his wrists and a small hook on his waist holds his boarding hooks. Shipwreck played a prominent role in both the Marvel comic and especially the Sunbow cartoon. His figure is highly desirable, and can sometimes be found with the side clasp on his waist piece broken (where he holds his boarding hooks). Watch his wrists for wear and tear on his tattoos.

MOC: **$80-100**, MLC: **$12**

SNAKE EYES
Commando
(Includes: Uzi, Wolf [Timber], Sword, Backpack)

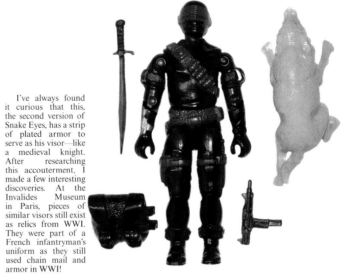

I've always found it curious that this, the second version of Snake Eyes, has a strip of plated armor to serve as his visor—like a medieval knight. After researching this accouterment, I made a few interesting discoveries. At the Invalides Museum in Paris, pieces of similar visors still exist as relics from WWI. They were part of a French infantryman's uniform as they still used chain mail and armor in WWI!

This is the first Snake Eyes that gives us a hint of his more esoteric background, for a full bio, see Snake Eyes (1982). Not surprisingly, this version of Snake Eyes is very popular with collectors and casual fans as well, perhaps because this was the figure released with Snake Eyes' first sword (well-sculpted), and his pet wolf, Timber, who, according to the Marvel comic, was befriended by Snake Eyes while he was living in a mountain cabin in the High Sierras. Timber has since passed on, but littered some pups that are being taken care of by Snake Eyes and Scarlett (1982). This version of Snake Eyes is a very expensive piece to find carded, and quite a brisk seller in mint, loose, complete condition.

MOC: **$300**, MLC: **$30-50**

TOLLBOOTH
Bridge Layer Driver
(Includes: Sledge Hammer)
Included with the Toss 'N Cross.

A very minor character in Joe lore, Tollbooth is often referred to as, "you know, the one with the sledge hammer."

NOTE: *This is one of the four figures from 1985 that did not have a ball-jointed head, suggesting that it may have been designed in late 1984. On a related note, this figure and the Toss 'N Cross vehicle were offered as an exclusive through the Sears catalog in Christmas, 1984.*

MLC: **$8**

TRIPWIRE
Mine Detector
("Listen 'n Fun" version, MOC)
(Includes: Minesweeper, Three Land Mines, Mine Detector Backpack, Cassette)

Listen 'n Fun Tripwire, MOC.

This figure is known by collectors as "Listen 'n Fun" Tripwire, as he was a special re-cast exclusive run by Hasbro in order to promote a multi-media approach to some of its toy lines. It is a common misperception that "Listen 'n Fun" Tripwire did not come with a file card, because the figure came with a small non-standard version on the card front. It read, "MINE DETECTOR: / Code Name: TRIPWIRE – Tripwire's proficient with all NATO and Warsaw Pact explosives, detonators, and blasting machines."

NOTE: *As this figure was a simple reissue of Tripwire (1982), he did not come with a ball-jointed head.*

MOC: **$50-60**, MLC: **$20-30**

1985 COBRA FIGURES

BUZZER
Dreadnok
(Includes: Diamond Toothed Chain Saw, Nunchuka Axe, Backpack, Gas Can)

With Ripper (1985) and Torch (1985), Buzzer formed the Dreadnoks—Zartan's interesting and colorful bunch of reproachable miscreants whose sole purpose in life seems to be tormenting those who are weaker than them. Buzzer is often suggested to be the leader of the team, and the three Dreadnoks figures were released in 1985. Their names reflect their specialties, Buzzer chainsaws things apart, Ripper rends things to pieces, and Torch melts them to the ground.

The file names of this triumvirate of Zartan's authority are Tom *Winken* (Torch), Dick *Blinken* (Buzzer), and Harry *Nod* (Ripper). These names are an inside joke from Larry Hama, and an allusion to Winken, Blinken, and Nod from *The Fisherman Three*—a children's mystic nursery rhyme. An important detail regarding the Dreadnoks was that Hasbro originally wanted them to be little "teddy bear" type creatures akin to the successfully marketed Ewoks from Kenner's *Star Wars: Return of the Jedi* line of figures. Mr. Hama refused to write the creatures into the Marvel comic book, on the grounds that "Good guys just can't shoot rifles at teddy bears. Parents will lose their minds! We'd better make the Dreadnoks biker thugs." And make them he did.

The Dreadnoks are cult favorites and highly collectable figures, and Buzzer's accessories are first-rate. In the Marvel comic, Buzzer was portrayed as intelligent and arrogant. He is one of the few (if not the only) of the Dreadnoks with an education, which makes him all the more dangerous.

NOTE: *Buzzer's head does not have the swivel-ball neck most 1985 figures possess, suggesting a 1984 design.*

MOC: **$60-70**, MLC: **$8-12**

EELS
Cobra Frogman
(Includes: JLS Double Harpoon with Stunner, Flippers, Air Hose, Air Tank, Jet Pack)

As the "underwater demolitions specialists of the Cobra legions" (from the file card), the Eels are the deadly Cobra divers that have undergone "a rigorous two-part training program in the warm shark and pirate-infested waters of the Cayman Islands of the Carribean and the frigid dark depths of the North Atlantic." The Eels are highly trained individuals who have encountered the Joes on various occasions, much to the American team's dismay. The Eel's equipment is excellent, and the air hose is particularly fragile and prone to breakage.

MOC: **$50-75**, MLC: **$12**

CRIMSON GUARD
Cobra Elite Trooper (with both backpack variations)
(Includes: AK48A w/Bayonet, Dress Backpack)

The Crimson Guards, or "siegies" as they came to be known ("siegie" is a phonetic pronunciation of the initials, C.G.—Cee-Gee), are "the elite shock troops of the Cobra Legions... [holding] a degree in either law or accounting as well as being in top physical condition." The siegies ushered in a new era for Cobra Command as the Crimson Guard, "dispersed about the country in deep cover, assuming apparently normal appearances and life-styles" (from the file card) and infiltrated pseudo-legitimate enterprises.

The siegies were well used in the Marvel comic and Sunbow cartoon, and are popular with collectors as troops or "army builders." Collectors view the Crimson Guard as one of the best Cobra figures ever made because of its color, design, and equipment. The Crimson Guard comes in two color variations, dark maroon, and a lighter shade of dark red. The lighter shade seems to be more difficult to find.

NOTE: *There are two versions of the Crimson Guard backpack, one has a solid inside, and the other had a hollowed-out inside. The hollow variant is quite difficult to find ($5 each).*

MOC: **$125-150**, MLC: **$15-20**

The Crimson Guard backpack variants.

LAMPREYS
Cobra Hydrofoil Pilot
(Includes: Rifle)
Included with the Moray.

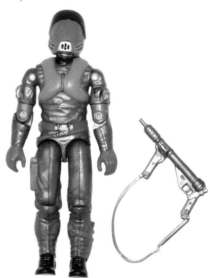

Described as "très moderne" looking by Cobra Commander (Enemy Leader, 1982) in the Marvel comic, the smartly-attired Lampreys are "the elite of the Cobra sea-arm" (from the file card). They act as Cobra Eels (1985) for the term of a year before moving on to Lamprey training. The attrition rate for acceptance includes more than a 50% wash-out. They are ranked at O-3 (Captain) or military equivalent.

MLC: **$10**

RIPPER

Dreadnok

(Includes: Power Jaws, Assault Rifle w/Metal Splitter, Hydraulic Hose, Power Pack w/Frame)

With Buzzer (1985) and Torch (1985), Ripper formed the first generation of the obnoxious Dreadnoks. "There are devils in Tasmania and Ripper is probably the meanest of them all," describes his file card, as he was "expelled from nursery school for extorting candy from his schoolmates, and spent most of his adult life in various correctional institutions." He is greedy, and dislikes all technology, "except for motorcycles."

NOTE: *Ripper's head does not have the swivel-ball neck most 1985 figure possess, suggesting a 1984 design.*

MOC: **$50-70**, MLC: **$10**

SNOW SERPENT

Cobra Polar Assault

(Includes: AK-47, Anti-Tank EK-99 Missile w/Stand, Survival Pack, Snow Shoes, Parachute Pack)

The Snow Serpent figure and equipment are well-crafted, and when he is wearing all of his equipment, he looks quite formidable. They undergo the same training procedures as the Cobra Eels (1985), but are even more deadly, as Snow Serpents then have to complete a "six month cold weather course somewhere above the Arctic Circle" (from the file card). They are involved in "airborne operations (under arctic conditions)", and other forms of cold weather fighting tactics.

MOC: **$50-70**, MLC: **$12-15**

TELE-VIPERS

Cobra Communications

(Includes: VS-11 Scanner, Communipac, Hose)

Tele-Vipers are the RTOs (Radio Telecommunications Operators) of the Cobra Legions. Because they do not come with a weapon to speak of (their hand-held accessory is a "scanner"), they are more commonly found (complete or incomplete) than other Cobra soldier figures. A microwave or laser, considered "optional transmission modes," can be added to Tele-Viper's scanner to make it a functional weapon (from the file card).

MOC: **$40-60**, MLC: **$8-10**

TOMAX

Crimson Guard Commander(s)

(Includes: Pistol, Sky Hook)
Included in a two-pack with Xamot.

Tomax and Xamot (his twin brother) have the distinction of being the only figures sold without a vehicle that were not offered on the back of the 1985 figure cards. The pair shared a file card, and are the only two figures in the line to do this. Tomax and his twin brother Xamot are characters loosely based on Alexandre Dumas' novel *The Corsican Brothers* (contemporized and romantically lampooned by the 1941 Douglas Fairbanks movie of the same name), where twin brothers share a telepathic link and feel each other's emotions. The Crimson Guard Commanders, head of the new Crimson Guard, take this theme to the furthest degree. When one is struck, only the absent twin feels the pain, and they see through one another's eyes.

The two were used frequently in the Marvel comic and on the Sunbow cartoon they headed the Extensive Enterprises organization, a corporate smokescreen to hide illegal Crimson Guard and Cobra activities. Their file card (prototype and the finalized version) suggests that they "served with the Foreign Legion Paras in Algeria before the officer's Putsch." This Putsch is in reference to the creepy and enigmatic French Foreign Legion Officers' Putsch (a putsch is an attempt by a group to overthrow the government) in 1961, when an insurgent Algerian group supported by a regiment of the Legion tried to overthrow the French government in Algiers (deGaulle tried to cover this up).

After the Legion (post-1961), the twins then became mercenaries. They grew disillusioned, and, too intelligent to keep dirtying their hands with war, became bankers in Zurich. This led to their joining with Cobra Command, heading the Crimson Guard, or "siegies" (Crimson Guard, 1985). These two evil twins will fight the Joe team with their fists in combat—or even better—in the boardroom.

MOC w/Xamot: **$75-100**, MLC: **$8**

TORCH
Dreadnok
(Includes: Acetylene Torch, BP-47 Tanks)

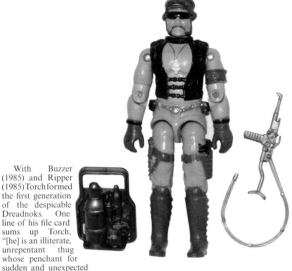

With Buzzer (1985) and Ripper (1985)Torch formed the first generation of the despicable Dreadnoks. One line of his file card sums up Torch, "[he] is an illiterate, unrepentant thug whose penchant for sudden and unexpected violence is matched only by the utter depth of his stupidity." At fourteen, he was recommended to the Borstal reform school. After Borstal, a stint in the Merchant Marine where he learned to use cutting torches, and various other attempts at incarceration, he joined the Dreadnoks in the Florida swamps feasting on grape soda, little chocolate doughnuts, and the terror the Dreadnoks inspire.

NOTE: *Torch's head does not have the swivel-ball neck most 1985 figure possess, suggesting a 1984 design.*

MOC: **$50-70**, MLC: **$8**

XAMOT
Crimson Guard Commander(s)
(Includes: Pistol)
Included in a two-pack with Tomax.

Xamot and Tomax (his twin brother) have the distinction of being the only figures sold without a vehicle that were not offered on the back of the 1985 figure cards. The pair shared a file card, and are the only two figures in the line to do this. For more background information, see Tomax (1985).

Xamot's scar has not been explained.

MOC: **$75-100**,
MLC: **$8**

Xamot's two different scar variations.

1985 VEHICLES/PLAYSETS

ACCESSORY PACK #3: BATTLE GEAR
Includes:

4 gray Helmets: 1 Duke; 1 Blowtorch; 1 Mutt; 1 Ripcord

2 green Battle Stands

1 light tan Jungle Trooper Backpack (Recondo)

1 light tan Flamethrower Backpack (Blowtorch)

1 tan Tracker Backpack (Spirit)

1 tan Heavy Machine Gunner Backpack with Ammo Box (Roadblock)

2 green Visors (Thunder)

1 red High-Density Laser Rifle (Baroness)

1 red Submachine Gun (Firefly)

1 red Walkie-Talkie (Firefly)

1 red RAR Pistol (Scrap-Iron)

1 green SLR WILI (Rip Cord)

1 green Ingram MAC-11 (Mutt)

1 green Flamethrower (Blowtorch)

1 tan Auto Arrow Launcher (Spirit)

1 green Binoculars (Duke)

1 green Monocular (Thunder)

1 green Harpoon Rifle (Torpedo)

1 light tan M-1 4E2X Rifle (Recondo)

1 green Pistol (Zartan)

MOMC: **$20**, MOC: **$12**, MLC: **$6**

NOTE: *These weapons are not the same colors as the regular Joe equipment, so if you find a weapon or accessory for a Joe figure that doesn't match the colors designated in this book, then it's from the current Joe line (1997 to present), or from a Battle Gear Accessory Pack. For example, the weapons included in the 1985 Battle Gear Accessory pack were mainly red, tan, and green in color, not the dark deep gray or black used for the weapons of the original carded figures.*

AIR DEFENSE (BATTLE STATION)

The Air Defense was one of the most simple of all G.I. Joe's battle stations. It utilized liquid propellant thrusters to fire two EE-14N long-range surface-to-air defense missiles.

The only easily lost pieces for this toy were the two huge red missiles included in the picture.

MISB: **$25**, MIB: **$10**, MLC: **$5**

AMMO DUMP UNIT (BATTLEFIELD ACCESSORY)

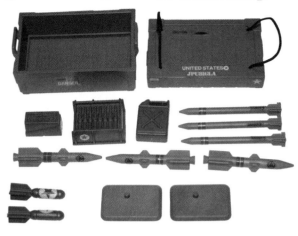

The Ammo Dump Unit was a small battlefield accessory.

Easily lost pieces include the armored grenade box, main supply case with lid, three short-range missiles, three HE-5 rockets, two mortar projectiles, a bullet-resistant gas can, and armored ammunition box. The Ammo Dump Unit came with two green battle stands that most collectors do not consider necessary for the set to be complete.

MISB: **$20**, MIB: **$10**, MLC: **$5**

ARMADILLO (MINI TANK)

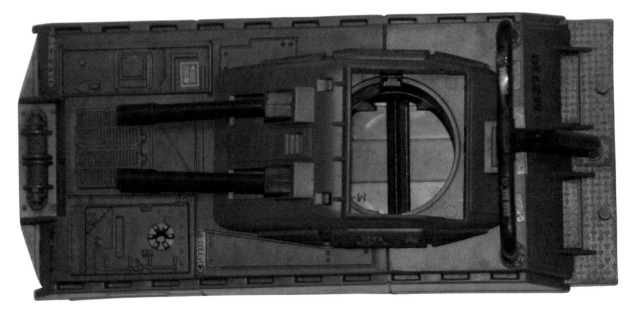

The Mini Tank Armadillo was a small all-purpose tank. It is a common piece and should not be considered rare. With 60mm synchronized variable-ranged cluster cannons and blazing speed, the Armadillo was quite popular with Joe fans.

Since it has no removable parts other than the sturdily attached roll bar, it is a quick pick-up for completionists—those collectors who require "one of everything."

MISB: **$25**, MIB: **$10**, MLC: **$5**

A.W.E. Striker (All Weather and Environment)

(Includes: Crankcase figure)

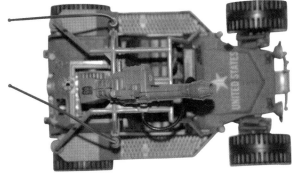

The A.W.E. Striker is an immensely popular vehicle, and with its removable engine, its 10-round 70mm automatic launcher (assumed for projectiles, not ammunition), off road tires, springing 4WD suspension, and an advanced infrared sighting/fire control camera, the vehicle has many action features. It has a few small parts that collectors should take great care not to lose, and be careful not to bend the antennae or lose the cannon's tip.

Easily lost pieces include the engine, engine cover, and cannon tip.

MISB: **$110**, MIB: **$50**, MLC: **$10-15**

The A.W.E. Striker's easily lost pieces.

Bomb Disposal Vehicle

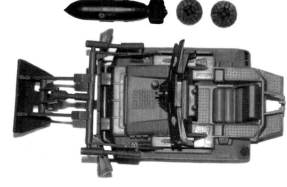

With a cast aluminum armor-piercing bomb and two high explosive antitank mines, a hydraulic claw, and a universal tow hook (for toting around the Whirlwind [1983] or FLAK [1982]), the Bomb Disposal is a fantastic utility vehicle for the Joe team with plenty of play potential. The lifting unit with claw is occasionally found broken, and the two mines are frequently missing.

Easily lost pieces include the bomb, two mines, and deflector shield.

MISB: **$25**, MIB: **$10**, MLC: **$5**

The Bomb Disposal Vehicles easily lost pieces.

C.A.T. (Motorized Crimson Attack Tank)

"A Crimson Guard Weapon"

Sears Exclusive

This rare and expensive vehicle is a tough find for collectors. The C.A.T. Tank, utilized by the Crimson Guard (1985), is a re-cast mold of the M.O.B.A.T. (see M.O.B.A.T. (1983) in black and red, and has the same basic functions. Like the M.O.B.A.T., be careful not to lose the small observation bridge cannon. The battery cover is sometimes missing, but make sure not to confuse the two battery covers, as the C.A.T.'s (a Sears Exclusive) is much more rare than the M.O.B.A.T.

Easily lost pieces include the cannon and battery cover.

MISB: **$175**, MIB: **$75**, MLC: **$50**

The C.A.T.'s easily lost piece.

Check Point Alpha

(Battle Station)

The Check Point Alpha was a small battle station/accessory set to complement a collector's Joes. It is composed of many small pieces including, four leg posts, tower top, tower bottom, entry ladder, infrared camera, submachine gun, spotlight, antenna, guard's clipboard (nearly impossible to find), gate, and road bump.

MISB: **$25**, MIB: **$10**, MLC: **$5**

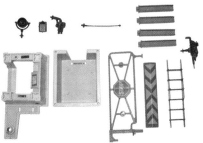

Check Point Alpha's easily lost pieces.

COBRA BUNKER
(Battle Station)

Cobra Bunker's easily lost pieces.

The Cobra Bunker was a small battle station/accessory set to complement a Cobra collection. A fascinating armored bunker that is designed to collapse with a direct hit from a G.I. Joe missile, this was a fun play set. The four-part bunker includes, base, surface-to-air missile, missile mount, and 7.8mm machine gun.

MISB: **$25**, MIB: **$10**, MLC: **$5**

COBRA FERRET

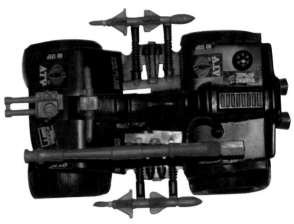

The Cobra Ferret A.T.V. (All-Terrain Vehicle) is the famed "four-wheeler" of the G.I. Joe line, and has proven immensely popular over the past twenty years—in any condition. With two laser-guided "Com-bat" missiles, synchronized .50 caliber machine guns, a six forward speed transmission, a side-slug 10-round launcher (the large cannon), and a four-cycle fender engine, collectors prize this Cobra vehicle.

Easily lost pieces include two missiles, engine cover, and hose attachment.

NOTE: *A mail-order Ferret A.T.V. was released by Hasbro Direct in the late 1980s-early 1990s that came in a brighter blue. This version is much more rare and commands a higher price than the regular retail release.*

MISB: **$45**, MIB: **$25**, MLC: **$10-15**

The Ferret's easily lost pieces.

COBRA RIFLE RANGE UNIT
(Battlefield Accessory)

The Cobra Rifle Range Unit was a small battlefield accessory set to complement your Cobra troops.

Easily lost pieces include: one high-rate M16-C5 5.56mm rifle with cartridge clip (modeled after Airborne's [1983] rifle); M16-A1 5.56mm rifle with cartridge clip (modeled after Grunt's [1982] rifle); L-88 7.65mm general purpose machine gun (modeled after Snow Job's [1983] rifle); firing embankment/bunker; two flip-down 2-piece targets (two targets plus their sandbag supports); caution sign; and rifle rack.

The Cobra Rifle Range Unit came with two blue battle stands that most collectors frequently do not consider to be part of the set.

MISB: **$25**,
MIB: **$12**, MLC: **$8**

Easily lost pieces.

FORWARD OBSERVER UNIT
(Battlefield Accessory)

The Forward Observer Unit was a small battlefield accessory set.

Easily lost pieces include: two mortar projectiles; armored ammunition box; 3-piece mortar (mortar chassis, mortar body, mortar bipod); bullet-proof micromesh tent; infrared monocular; bi-pod for monocular (commonly missing); bullet resistant radio; and a radio antenna (commonly missing).

The Forward Observer Unit came with two light green battle stands that most collectors do not consider to be part of the set.

NOTE: *The monocular does not "snap" into its base, but pivots and rest in the base, therefore, these two pieces are usually found separately.*

MISB: **$25**,
MIB: **$10**,
MLC: **$5**

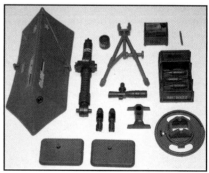

Easily lost pieces.

LISTEN 'N FUN CASSETTE (W/CARDED TRIPWIRE)

See Tripwire, Listen 'n Fun (1985). The tape is labeled "The Cobra's Revenge."

MLC: **$3**

MAULER M.B.T. TANK (MANNED BATTLE TANK)

(Includes: Heavy Metal figure)

The Mauler M.B.T. featured a more sophisticated design than the M.O.B.A.T. (1982), as the vehicle had individual moving bogie wheels, hatch covers for two drivers in the front of the vehicle, mud flaps, engine covers, storage bin covers, a tow cable, and side track skirts. The tank was also built to withstand a child's heavy play. As a motorized toy with two forward speeds, kids responded to the vehicle.

Unfortunately, collectors need some luck to find a complete Mauler, as the tank has so very many little pieces to it. The best bet is to purchase a boxed one, and you can expect a high price tag—it's rare and expensive due to Heavy Metal (1985) and his very difficult-to-find microphone.

Easily lost pieces include two hatch covers, two storage bin covers, two engine covers, tow cable, four mud flaps, antenna, meteorological antenna, and two smoke grenade attachments.

Note: *An extra bogey wheel was included w/the M.B.T. that can be placed on the remote drive control system.*

MISB: **$250**, MIB: *(w/Heavy Metal and his microphone)* **$150-160**, MIB: *(w/out Heavy Metal's mic)* **$100**, MLC: *(w/Heavy Metal's mic)* **$100-110**, *(w/out Heavy Metal's mic)* **$40-45**

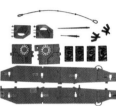

The Mauler's easily lost pieces.

MORAY (COBRA HYDROFOIL)

(Includes: Lampreys figure)

The Cobra Hydrofoil added speed and power to the Cobra naval forces. It is an intricately designed and delicate vehicle, with many small parts that are easily lost. The vehicle highlights a V-12 engine, two air-to-water missiles, and an array of .30-caliber machine guns, four smaller missiles with a pop-up launcher, a searchlight, more machine guns, and room to hold many troopers—this vehicle is a wonder of Hasbro engineering.

The long list of easily lost pieces includes: search light with lens (rarely, if ever found with loose, "complete" Morays), four smaller yellow missiles, two side missiles, two large torpedoes, two hatch openings, windshield gun (pictured on vehicle), four depth charges, two depth charge holders, engine cover, four M-30 machine guns, two small windshields.

MISB: **$110**, MIB: **$50-55**, MLC: **$30**

Cobra Hydrofoil searchlight with lens. The Hydrofoil is rarely found with this lens intact.

The Moray's easily lost pieces.

COBRA NIGHT LANDING

The Cobra Night Landing craft is the perfect infiltration device for night missions, and is quite popular with collectors. Most accessories fit into the ship loosely, and do not "snap" into place, making it difficult to find loose complete Night Landings.

Easily lost pieces include two oars, 12mm submachine gun (for mounting on the boat), entrenching knife, shovel, radio, .45-caliber machine gun, and the engine.

MISB: **$25**, MIB: **$10**, MLC: **$5**

The Night Landing's easily lost pieces.

PARACHUTE PACK
(HALO: High Altitude Low Opening)
Mail Away Exclusive

An unfolded Parachute Pack parachute.

As a mail-away, Hasbro sold thousands of these exclusives. The parachutes worked (the figure could be thrown up and float down), and could be put onto almost every Joe character. The "HALO Parachute Pack" as it is commonly referred to, is a fairly easy mail-away to obtain, but be careful that it has all of its respective parts including the mask, helmet, parachute, backpack, and strap.

MISBaggie: **$25**, MLC: **$5-7**

A boxed Parachute Pack.

SILVER MIRAGE MOTORCYCLE

The popular Silver Mirage was also aesthetically pleasing and quite an upgrade from the Joe's standard motorcycle, the RAM (1982). With its silver finish, 1200cc liquid-cooled 24-value flat-6 engine, ten round mortar launcher, driver fairing, gun operator's seat (sidecar), two ground launch missiles, and bullet resistant windshield, the Silver Mirage rounded out an already impressive array of vehicles in the G.I. Joe universe.

Easily lost pieces include two missiles, cannon, and the body fairing.

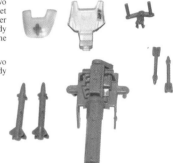

MISB: **$30**, MIB: **$12**, MLC: **$7**

The Silver Mirage's easily lost pieces.

S.M.S.
(Cobra's Sentry and Missile System, "A Crimson Guard Weapon,"—Two Parts: Cobra Missile System, Cobra Sentry)
Sears Exclusive

Many exclusive offerings were re-casts of existing vehicles in new color schemes. The S.M.S. (Sentry and Missile System) was a Sears Exclusive that saw Hasbro re-casting the Cobra H.I.S.S. (1983) with a bonus MMS (1982) for the sentry to tow. The box front suggested, as did the box front of the C.A.T. (1985), that the S.M.S. was a "Crimson Guard (1985) Weapon." Now colored red and black and painted with Cobra sigils, the hard-to-find S.M.S. has the same easily lost pieces as the Cobra H.I.S.S. and the MMS.

MISB: **$150**, MIB: **$80**, MLC: **$65-75**

The S.M.S.'s easily lost pieces.

S.N.A.K.E. (BATTLE ARMOR)
(System: Neutralizer – Armed Kloaking Equipment)

Released at retail for a very short period of time, 1985's "Blue S.N.A.K.E." as collectors refer to it, had the exact same configuration as the original Cobra S.N.A.K.E. (1983). This armor from 1985 is very hard to find, and both loose and boxed pieces command very high prices on the secondary market. The S.N.A.K.E. has the same easily lost pieces as the "White S.N.A.K.E." from 1983.

MISB: **$75**,
MIB: **$55**,
MLC: **$25-35**

SNOW CAT
(Includes: Frostbite figure)

With a 680hp direct ignition engine, five "Shockwave" missiles, two high-speed "Avalanche" ski-missiles, and room for up to ten Joes to hitch a ride, this tracked and wheeled vehicle has become one of the hallmarks of the Joe line.

Easily lost pieces include four missiles, launcher, engine cover, two ski missiles, two ski missile tracks, windshield wiper.

MISB: **$100**, MIB: **$60**, MLC: **$12**

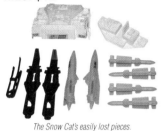
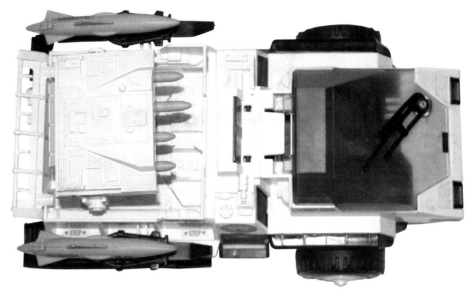

The Snow Cat's easily lost pieces.

TOSS 'N CROSS (BRIDGE LAYER)
(Includes: Tollbooth figure)
Sears Exclusive, later available at retail.

Originally offered as an exclusive from the Sears catalog, this durable and well-constructed vehicle lowers its magnesium alloy road plate to allow Joe vehicles to cross ravines. It was made available at retail stores in 1985. Couple this with two 105mm "Rap" cannons and a 1700 hp(!!!) turbine engine, and you've got a very powerful "bridge layer."

Easily lost pieces: two cannons, hydraulic fluid coupler.

MISB: **$100**, MIB: **$60**, MLC: **$20**

Bridge Layer in action.

The Bridge Layer's easily lost pieces.

TRANSPORTABLE TACTICAL BATTLE PLATFORM
(w/5 weapons on tree)

The Transportable Tactical Battle Platform was a very popular play set with kids, so collectors will be able to find it quite easily. The difficulty, however, is finding one mint, loose, and complete. This is a daunting task. In the Joe universe, the TTBP, with its surface-to-air missiles, four hydraulic platform leveling supports, munitions room, and load/unload ramp, is an effective tool for the Joe team on land or at sea.

The extensive list of easily lost pieces includes the radar dish with mount, search light, antenna, two hatch covers, four missiles, missile holder, five rifles (rarely found with the TTBP unless you buy one MISB), two heli-pad legs, windshield, heli-pad ladder, gun rack, three ladders, seat, antenna, windshield, and the crane.

MISB: **$100**, MIB: **$75-80**, MLC: **$50-60**, incomplete: **$20-30**

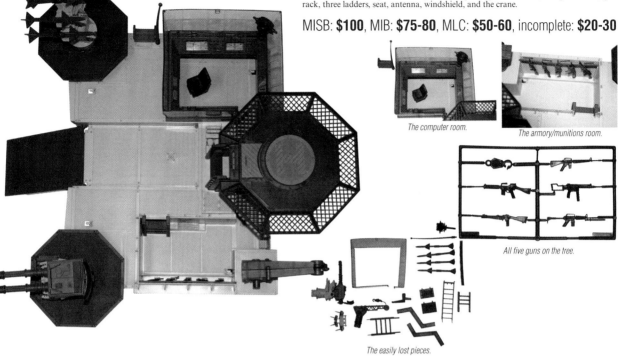

The computer room.

The armory/munitions room.

All five guns on the tree.

The easily lost pieces.

TRUBBLE BUBBLE
(Cobra Flight Pod)

Heavily utilized on the Sunbow cartoon, the Cobra Flight Pod was a favorite mode of transportation for Cobra's legions. The "Trubble Bubble" could be used as a manned aircraft, or if it was preferred, as a transport ship for the included SNK aerial mine. The ship sports a mini-cannon, two anti-tank missiles, high-thrust turbofan engine (removable), and infra-red targeting sensors.

Easily lost pieces include the mine, mine hatch, two missiles, and turbofan engine.

MISB: **$60**, MIB: **$25**, MLC: **$12-15**

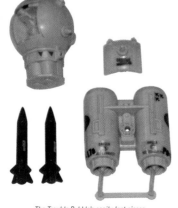

The Trubble Bubble's easily lost pieces.

WEAPON TRANSPORT VEHICLE

The G.I. Joe Weapon Transport is a fairly common vehicle to find, but is frequently incomplete. The Joes used this free-wheeling transport to remove and carry explosives, and it actually comes with a Force 1000 MK88 magnesium cased bomb, a removable shielded submachine gun, and its bomb trailer is removable. Easily lost pieces include the bomb, submachine gun, antenna, and steering wheel.

MISB: **$20**, MIB: **$12**, MLC: **$5**

The Weapon Transport's easily lost pieces.

U.S.S. FLAGG (Aircraft Carrier)
(Includes: Keel Haul)

Long hailed as the greatest toy play set ever created, the U.S.S. FLAGG was the ultimate environment for G.I. Joe. If you were lucky enough to receive one as a child, everyone on the block spent the week after Christmas at your house, Joe figures in tow.

The play set is a marvel in engineering, as Skystrikers (see Combat Jet Skytriker, 1983) fit snugly to the deck of the FLAGG, with the ship's arrestor cable snapped tightly into the aircraft's rear stabilizers. The FLAGG had many special features. Its electronic public address system could broadcast a child's voice to round up the troops, and a two-piece utility vehicle ambled around its decks that was part "low tow" tractor and part alloy armored fuel delivery trailer. If the ship was hit, the crew could jump into the "Admiral's Launch" lifeboat. The crew could man the inside decks of the command center bulkhead—replete with opening bulkhead doors, a "radio/communications" room, the admiral control room with a purge value, the helm, deck ladder, or the armory—a place to store the included missiles. Radar, missile launchers, an elevator deck, a net antenna, sea anchors, and 76mm cannons dotted the mighty ship, and kept a child happy for weeks.

To find one of these MISB will cost you over $1,200 and a mint, loose, and truly complete FLAGG will still *easily* set you back 1/2 to 3/4 of that cost. The FLAGG features many easily lost/removable items including its 9-piece main antenna, net antenna, flag, Admiral's Launch, two anchors, two-piece tractor-trailer utility vehicle (note that the fuel trailer has two gas nozzles attached to a hose, and the tractor includes an engine cover), arrestor hook, missile rack, three chairs (two green, one dark gray Admiral's chair), two bulkhead doors, four command console ladders, helm (with wheel and base), two missile control radar tips, 16 deck clips (and rarely will you see all sixteen with the FLAGG), bow ladder, fantail deck railing, six orange missiles, crane engine access cover (rarely, if ever, on the crane), stanchion (the thin white post), three deck rails, four ladders, crane, two hull doors, three chairs, two lifeboat attachments, arrestor cable with two attached deck clips, blast cover, blast cover pin, water tower housing, four hull walls, five green computer systems, lifeboat deck holder, and missile holder.

MISB: **$800-1400**,
MIB *(complete)*: **$600-750**,
MLC *(complete)*: **$400**,
(incomplete): **$250-300**

SERIES FOUR

The helm and lower computer room.

The radar.

The ladders are easily lost pieces.

Some assorted pieces.

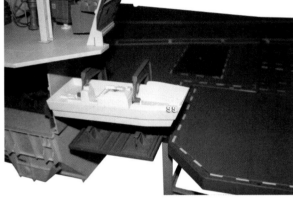

The life boat.

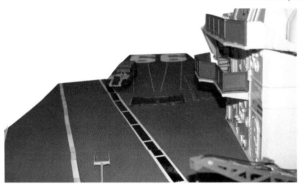

The deck facing the stern.

The fuel trailer on deck.

The deck facing the bow.

The antennas and ground maintenance vehicle.

The ground maintenance vehicle.

The sound system.

And still more easily lost pieces.

The antennas and missile system.

(Series V, 1986)

This series of Joes took them to the jungles of Brazil, and truly added support the Dreadnok forces. Due to the popularity of Zartan's band of thugs, they received some Sears exclusives, and more members to join Zartan's base in the Florida Everglades. The Joes were also now more specialized, and new members with similar MOS to still active past members emerged (Doc and Lifeline, Torpedo and Wet-Suit, Gung-Ho and Leatherneck, Dial-Tone, and Breaker). This was a point of contention with some long-time fans. Why couldn't Hasbro just re-outfit old Joes instead of changing the character completely? Regardless, the new characters were well received, and the line was more popular than ever.

G.I. Joe action figure body tattoos.

1986 Hasbro product catalog.

"Live the Adventure" game.

1986 G.I. JOE FIGURES

BEACH HEAD

Ranger
(Includes: 9mm XF-7 Wasp Submachine Gun, Utility Backpack, Ammo Case)

In the Sunbow cartoon, Beach Head was fifth in command of the Joe team. According to the DOD Dictionary of military terms, a beachhead is a "designated area on a hostile or potentially hostile shore that, when seized and held, ensures the continuous landing of troops and materiel, and provides maneuver space requisite for subsequent projected operations ashore." This certainly sums up the character's personality—potentially hostile, but steadfast and integrally important to the Joe team. His original code names (according to the prototype dossier) were Cool, Ambush, and Mr. Bones. He is currently an active member of the Joe team.

NOTE: There are two versions of Beach Head's ammo case, one made of hard plastic, and one of soft. The one with hard plastic is an earlier version of the accessory, and it was replaced with a softer plastic because the initial accessory was prone to breakage.

MOC: **$80**, MLC: **$10**

CROSS-COUNTRY

H.A.V.O.C. Driver
Included with the H.A.V.O.C.

Cross-Country comes from a family of heavy vehicle operators, and loves machinery himself. He is often portrayed with a southern accent, and has an "uncanny sense of direction [and a] fearlessness under fire" (from the file card). He is quite a popular vehicle driver in the Joe canon. Cross Country's current status is unknown.

MLC: **$8**

DIAL-TONE
Communications
(Includes: 9mm Parabellum Submachine Pistol with Silencer, Anti-Scrambler Communications Backpack with Microphone)

In his prototype dossier, Dial-Tone's operative code names were Squelch and Hot-Line. As a child, he "built his own crystal set [a rudimentary radio] when he was ten…had his own ham [wireless amateur radio] station by the time he was sixteen…[making] all his own equipment." Dial-Tone takes his job seriously, and is the Joe's primary radio man. After the team disbanded, he made a good deal of money on patents, and has since rejoined the team.

MOC: **$50**, MLC: **$8**

HAWK
G.I. Joe Commander
(Includes: Walther PPK 9mm Short Pistol, Field pack, Helmet)

The original field commander of the Joe team, this figure was the first portrayal of Hawk on the Sunbow cartoon. In this incarnation of the character, he "got his General's star and was booted upstairs to honcho the entire G.I. Joe operation."

The design of this figure was well received by collectors, as it had a distinct military flavor. For a full bio, see Hawk (1982).

MOC: **$45-55**, MLC: **$10**

ICEBERG
Snow Trooper
(Includes: XM60E3 7.62mm Machine Gun)

Along with Snow Job (1983) and Frostbite (1985), the Joes added yet another arctic operations specialist to their team. Iceberg came with only one accessory—a really big machine gun. Since Iceberg as a character grew up in a very warm place, he always wanted to escape the heat, and escape he did, to "where the mercury dips below zero." His operative code names from his prototype file card were Winter, Ice-Man, Cool Breeze, and Chill. Iceberg has recently joined missions for the Joe team.

NOTE: *The bagged Iceberg version with a Rock-Viper (1990) rifle is considered a mail-away Iceberg (1991).*

MOC: **$35**, MLC: **$6-8**

LEATHERNECK
Marine
(Includes: M-16 "Over/Under" Rifle, Field Pack)

Described in his file card as "…uncouth, opinionated and overbearing. And he has no patience at all with the indecisive, the lazy, and the dishonest. Not a man you can like, but one you can trust," Leatherneck was the second Marine recruited to the Joe team (see Gung-Ho, 1983). Some of his originally proposed code names were Gyrene, Semper-Fi, Jar-Head, and Gunny. A Marine through-and-through, he is currently on the Joe's roster.

MOC: **$45-55**, MLC: **$8**

LIFELINE
Rescue Trooper
(Includes: EMS Kit with Oxygen Mask, Browning Double-Action 9mm Pistol, Relay Backpack)

The inside of Lifeline's EMS Kit.

Lifeline, slated to be named both Angel and Last-Chance, was the pacifist rescue trooper of the Joe universe. He had a kindness and patience about him that made him an effective medic. He was a paramedic before enlistment, and entrenched his position by becoming a corpsman in the Army. Strangely enough, Lifeline was a pacifist only in the comic book and the Sunbow cartoon. He had a pistol mounted in his leg holster, and this figure actually came with a silver 9mm pistol. His carded figure is pictured holding the pistol in his right hand and according to his file card, "The troops have to know that if something really heavy comes down on them and they're in no condition to walk out of the mess, somebody is going to have the heart to wade in and extricate them. That somebody is Lifeline." Lifeline is a current member of the Joe team.

NOTE: *Lifeline figures without the pistol and holster molded on his right leg are from a later mail-away version of the figure (1991).*

MOC: **$60-70**, MLC: **$8-10**

LIFT-TICKET
Tomahawk Pilot
(Includes: Microphone)
Included with the Tomahawk.

Lift Ticket's microphone.

Lift-Ticket was a fairly popular Joe, as he came with the enormously collectable Tomahawk helicopter, and has one of the rarer G.I. Joe accessories—his small black microphone. An odd-looking figure, because the sculpt of his head with helmet on looks pretty large, Lift-Ticket joined the army "to get out of his hometown" (from the file card). On his aptitude test, he scored remarkably high and entered Flight Warrant Officer School, and discovered his love of flying. He is currently on the Joe's roster.

MLC: *(w/mic)* **$20**, *(w/out mic)* **$6**

LOW-LIGHT
Night Spotter
(Includes: 7.62mm Model 85 Sniper Rifle w/Bipod, Uzi Submachine Gun, Backpack)

With his black ski-cap, red goggles, dark gray camouflage, a sniper's rifle, and an Uzi pistol, Low-Light is a chilling figure to behold. As a child, the character was timid until "one precarious hunting expedition with his father" (from his file card). After this experience, he could hunt, shoot, and *survive.* He eventually became a marksmanship instructor in the Army. This is an outstanding figure in the 1986 line. He is currently on the Joe's roster.

MOC: **$70-80**, MLC: **$12**

MAINFRAME
Computer Specialist
(Includes: BP75E Field Transmitter Receiver Unit with Walkie Talkie and Portable Combat Ready Computer System)

With the original code names of CHIP, Big-Byte, and Rely, Mainframe was one of the few Joe figures not to come with a weapon—even though he wears his Combat Infantryman's Badge. His character spent time in the Army during Vietnam, "for the last year of hostilities" (from his file card), and then received a degree from MIT. After finishing MIT and working in Silicon Valley, he re-upped and joined the Marines, followed by a long stint with Joe team. On the team he was the resident computer specialist, but still earned respect as a combat vet. Unfortunately, Mainframe perished on a Joe mission, when he was killed in an explosion.

MOC: **$50-60**, MLC: **$8**

ROADBLOCK
Heavy Machine Gunner
(Includes: L7A21 GPMG Heavy Machine Gun and Tripod)

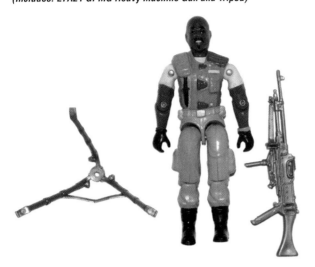

Roadblock received a new color scheme in 1986. For a full bio of this character, see Roadblock (1984).

MOC: **$50**, MLC: **$10**

SCI-FI
Laser Trooper
(Includes: XH 86 LLOM Beam Laser Rifle w/Power Source Backpack and Hose Attachment)

Sci-Fi is the second "Laser Trooper" on the Joe team. I find it strange that Hasbro didn't just name this figure Flash (1982), the original Laser Rifle Trooper of the team, and update his file card, but Sci-Fi was a cool looking figure and interesting character on his own. With the alternate code names of Hot-Spot and Red Light, Sci-Fi's file card describes him as living "in a slow motion world." He *has* to remain motionless for long periods of time in order to make shots from his laser rifle effective. Some collectors criticize this figure as being the first "neon" Joe character, but he was popular with kids at the time. Sci-Fi is currently on the Joe's roster.

MOC: **$40-45**, MLC: **$7**

SGT. SLAUGHTER
Drill Instructor
(Includes: Baton)
Included with the Triple-T Tank.

Sgt. Slaughter received a new color scheme in 1986. For a full bio on this character, see Sgt. Slaughter (1985).

MLC: **$8**

SLIP-STREAM
Conquest X-30 Pilot
Included with the Conquest X-30.

Slip-Stream was a "video game whiz and computer hacker until he discovered flying" (from his file card), and this experience enhanced his training on an airplane with computer assisted control surfaces—his Conquest X-30. He has lightning quick reflexes, is highly competitive, and is "an unrepentant practical joker and mimic." He is currently on the Joe's roster.

MLC: **$7**

THE FRIDGE
Physical Training Instructor
(Includes: Football attached to chain)
Mail Away Exclusive

The Fridge was a mail away figure only, never offered carded, and the character was directly based on William "Refrigerator" Perry, former Pro-Bowl Defensive Lineman from the Chicago Bears. This was the second real-life human being to be recruited to the Joe team (see Sgt. Slaughter, 1985). The Fridge was an exclusive mail-away you could receive with coupons packaged with Joe figures and vehicles, and by calling in to receive a special code "PTI" for Physical Training Instructor. There are still a lot of these figures floating around mint in unopened packages, as the figure was not that popular. There is a variant of the Fridge figure with differently colored belts (silver and brown) and wristbands (different patterns), but these do not affect the value of the figure.

Mint in Sealed Baggie: **$15**, MLC: **$10**

WET-SUIT
SEALS
(Includes: Underwater Sea Sled, Scuba Tanks w/Hose, Underwater Search Light, Two Flippers)

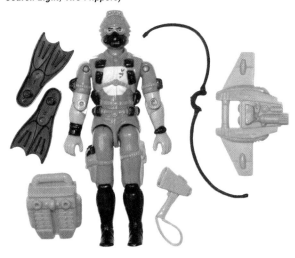

Wet-Suit was the second Joe to have his MOS as Navy SEAL (Sea, Air and Land), the elite Naval Special Operations Unit of the U.S. Navy (see Torpedo, 1983). SEALs are a respected commando force that as adaptable to any changing environment (hence the acronym) and engage in Maritime Special Operations and Counter Terrorist Operations. The character of Wet-Suit is somewhat mean, ornery, yet "quite bright, being well-read in both the classics and the standard texts of military tactics" (from the file card). His alternate code names according to his prototype dossier were Gator, Hammer-Head, and Soggy. He is currently on the Joe's roster.

MOC: **$80-90**, MLC: **$12-15**

SPECIAL MISSION BRAZIL SET
Toys 'R Us Exclusive

The Covert Operations Officer and his selected specialists set out to infiltrate the Cobra infested jungles of Brazil. Their mission was to retrieve an important military satellite concealed deep within Cobra territory. The Joes chosen for this crucial mission are the perfect representatives of the Mobile Strike Force—the masters of the game! When united, they create the absolute standard of military excellence.

[SPECIAL MISSION BRAZIL] CLAYMORE
G.I. Joe Covert Operations
(Includes: Submachine Gun [Two "Uzi" variations], Helmet)

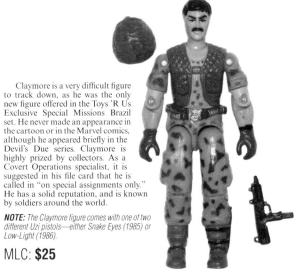

Claymore is a very difficult figure to track down, as he was the only new figure offered in the Toys 'R Us Exclusive Special Missions Brazil set. He never made an appearance in the cartoon or in the Marvel comics, although he appeared briefly in the Devil's Due series. Claymore is highly prized by collectors. As a Covert Operations specialist, it is suggested in his file card that he is called in "on special assignments only." He has a solid reputation, and is known by soldiers around the world.

NOTE: *The Claymore figure comes with one of two different Uzi pistols—either Snake Eyes (1985) or Low-Light (1986).*

MLC: **$25**

[SPECIAL MISSION BRAZIL] DIAL-TONE
Communications
(Includes: Radio Gear, Headset, Submachine Gun)

This version of Dial-Tone was included with the Special Mission Brazil set.

NOTE: *Same accessories and bio as Dial-Tone (1986).*

MLC: **$15**

[SPECIAL MISSION BRAZIL]
LEATHERNECK
Marine
(Includes: Backpack, Rifle)

This version of Leatherneck was included with the Special Mission Brazil set.

NOTE: *Same accessories and bio as Leatherneck (1986).*

MLC: **$15**

[SPECIAL MISSION BRAZIL]
MAINFRAME
Computer Specialist
(Includes: Backpack, Computer, Walkie-Talkie, Hose)

This version of Mainframe was included with the Special Mission Brazil set.

NOTE: *Same accessories and bio as Mainframe (1986).*

MLC: **$15**

[SPECIAL MISSION BRAZIL]
WET-SUIT
SEALS
(Includes: Tank, Breather Hose, Propeller Pack, Two Flippers, Light)

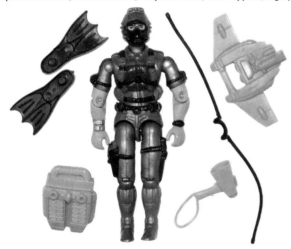

This version of Wet-Suit was included with the Special Mission Brazil set.

NOTE: *Same accessories and bio as Wet-Suit (1986).*

MLC: **$15**

Weapons bag for Special Missions Brazil. (MISB: $20)

The boxed set, front.

The boxed set, back.

MISB: (*whole set*) **$275**, MIB: **$135**, MLC: (*w/tape and all weapons*) **$90**

Flash   *Grunt*   *Rock 'N Roll*

Short-Fuze   *Stalker*   *Zap*

Major Bludd   *The Enemy*   *Airborne*   *Doc*

ORIGINAL TEAM MAIL-AWAY SET

Mail Away Exclusive

In 1986, Hasbro offered an exclusive called the "Original Team Mail-Away Set." This Hasbro Direct exclusive included the Official Collector's Display Case w/ten figures (all mint in baggies) with red-backed file cards including, Airborne (1983), Cobra Officer (The Enemy, swivel-arm, 1983), Doc (1983), Flash (swivel-arm, 1983), Grunt (swivel-arm, 1983), Major Bludd (1982), Rock 'N Roll (swivel-arm, 1983), Short-Fuze (swivel-arm, 1983), Stalker (swivel-arm, 1983), Zap (swivel-arm, 1983). All file cards have flag points attached.

NOTE: *Most G.I. Joe figures from 1986 and earlier were offered as either JC Penney or Sears catalog exclusives, or as mail-away offers from Hasbro Direct sealed in baggies with red-backed file cards. These figures sell for about three to four times more than loose samples, except for more common mail-away characters (Jinx [1987], Quick Kick [1985], Windchill [1994], etc.)*

1986 COBRA FIGURES

A.V.A.C.

Cobra Terror Drome Firebat Pilot

(Includes: Parachute)

Included with Cobra Terror Drome, Terror Drome Firebat.

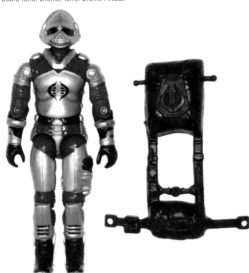

After years of discussion, it has been decided that the acronym, A.V.A.C. represents "Air Viper: Air Corps." This figure is a high-demand piece, especially if it comes with its backpack and file card. As pilots of the Firebat, the A.V.A.C.s must "be capable of complex mental calculations... [and be] absolutely fearless." Every Cobra Air Viper wants to be a Firebat pilot, and it is considered special dispensation to fly the sophisticated aircraft.

MLC: **$25**

B.A.T.S.

Cobra Android Trooper

(Includes: Backpack with Storage for Separate Laser, Torch, and Gripper Arm Attachments, Regular Hand Attachment)

With three detachable mechanical arms, the B.A.T.S. (Battle Android Troopers) are one of the most interesting Joe figures. They have a huge cult following among collectors as "army builders," and Cobra Command considered them "...the perfect Cobra Troopers" (from the file card), because they're robots—cheap to maintain, and easy to deploy. The problem is, once you "wind them up" there is no telling who they'll attack. There are two different color variants of the B.A.T.S., some have bright yellow highlights and others have orange paint highlights. Neither is more rare. These were originally dubbed "B.A.T. – Bot (Battle Android Tactical)."

MOC: **$75**, MLC: **$15-20**

DR. MINDBENDER
Master of Mind Control
(Includes: .45 cal. Pistol, Cape, Electric Prod w/Generator, Hose)

Curiously enough, Dr. Mindbender was originally called Dr ?, Professor Paine, Count Vlad the Cruel, and The Inquisitor in the prototype dossier. The prototype is fascinating, as he is described as "Two hundred pounds of nasty in a fifty pound sack." After the original mock-up sketches and descriptions were considered inappropriate, the public received Dr. Mindbender as a once, "excellent orthodontist and a very kind and honest man… [who] tinkered with electric brainwave stimulation as a means to relieve dental pain… and underwent a complete personality change…" Dr. Mindbender is currently an agent of Cobra Command and ready to hatch another nefarious plot.

MOC: **$50-55**, MLC: **$10**

Both variants of Dr. Mindbender's capes—iron-on transfer and patch.

MONKEYWRENCH
Dreadnok
(Includes: Harpoon Gun)

The fourth member of Zartan's (1984) Dreadnoks, Monkeywrench was born on Guy Fawkes Day and as such, has always had an affinity for explosions. He is rude, crude, and anti-social—a perfect fit for the Dreadnoks. His prototype code names were Hang-Fire, Blaster, Boom-Boom, and Frag-Head.

MOC: **$35-40**, MLC: **$10**

MOTOR VIPER
(Cobra STUN Pilot)
Included with the Cobra STUN.

Whether called the Cobra STUN Pilot or the Cobra STUN Driver (different MOS's are listed on Motor Viper file cards—guess not even Hasbro could figure out what the heck the STUN was), the Motor Viper is an easy figure to come across, as he has no weapons, and looks less-than-intimidating. The Motor Vipers "enjoy driving at high speeds and find amusement in danger," and it is further suggested that "danger itself" appeals to them (from the file card). These are easy to find for army builders.

MLC: **$8**

SERPENTOR
Cobra Emperor
(Includes: Ceremonial Sword, Cowl, Cape, Snake)
Included with the Air Chariot.

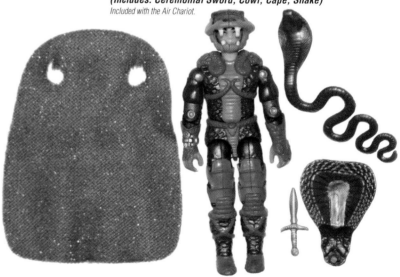

Serpentor was a very controversial figure and character in the G.I. Joe universe, and his figure is unlike any other. He has a cowl, ceremonial sword, and cape that symbolize his position as "Cobra Emperor." Originally titled King Cobra, Cobra Rex, Rama Set, or ZoR, the character is a conglomeration of the DNA of "the greatest despots in history" (from the file card). As Cobra Emperor, Serpentor is, "a master of political intrigue and a brilliant tactician," and created a rift in the Cobra organization. A note from Larry Hama to Buzz Dixon stated, "This guy should sound like John Houseman—a youthful body with an old man's voice."

MLC: **$15**

Serpentor MIP from his box.

Serpentor snake variations—mail-away brown snake and regular-issue gold snake.

STRATO-VIPER
Cobra Night Raven S3P Pilot
Included with the Cobra Night Raven S3P.

The Strato-Vipers are some of "the best secret agents in the world" who chose to work for Cobra because they pay more than national governments. They are the upper crust of the Cobra Air Vipers Corps, and undergo a strange surgical procedure "necessary to make [them] more resistant to hypoxia [oxygen deficiency], hyperventilation, and other decompression sicknesses..." Like Motor Vipers (1986), these are popular "army builder" figures, and are fairly common Cobra troops to locate.

MLC: **$8**

THRASHER
Thunder Machine Driver
(Includes: Spiked Lacrosse Stick)
Included with the Dreadnok Thunder Machine.

Another member of the Dreadnoks, Thrasher drives the mismatched Thunder Machine. Thrasher grew up a spoiled kid whose parents gave him anything he wanted. Of course, he always wanted more, and "wandered into the swamps where he could do what he wanted to living things and inanimate objects alike. It was in the swamps where he met up with Zartan and his Dreadnoks" (from the prototype file card). His alternate code names before deciding on Thrasher were Basher, Mean-Streak, Bash McFeral, and Cruncher.

MLC: **$8**

VIPER
Cobra Infantry
(Includes: Field pack, RDT-7 Assault Rifle with Grenade Launcher)

The Cobra Vipers, although not the original Cobra troopers (see The Enemy: Cobra [Soldier], 1982), quickly became the most popular standard trooper in the Cobra Legions. A note on the communiqué Larry Hama sent to Hasbro stated, "Vipers can be the generic term for all Cobra Troopers. Tele-Vipers being the comm specialists, HISS-Vipers being attached to the armored branch, Air-Vipers to flight ops, etc." Ultimately if you want to begin somewhere in the Cobra organization, you started as an infantry Viper.

MOC: **$70**, MLC: **$18-25**

ZANDAR
Zartan's Brother
(Includes: Barbed Projectile Gun with Scope, Grenade Adorned Quiver)

With the same color-changing plastic capabilities as Zartan (1984), Zandar is a "master of camouflage and covert movement" (from the file card). Zandar spent most of his life trying not to be noticed, and that education has paid off in spades. His current whereabouts are unknown.

NOTE: *Zartan's family of shape-changers raises a decades-old discussion between collectors: Are Zandar, Zarana, and Zartan mutants, or are their morphing abilities holographically-based? Larry Hama, creator of the Marvel G.I. Joe comic, elucidates this debate, "I always thought Zartan [and perhaps Zandar as well] was a mutant but that he had a somewhat limited morphing ability that was enhanced mechanically and psychologically. What the comic reader [and cartoon watcher] "sees" is not necessarily reality, but is in fact what the other characters are seeing. Zartan was just a cypher to me at first, but he sort of came alive for me when I had to start filling in the details of his back story."*

MOC: **$35-40**, MLC: **$8**

ZARANA
Zartan's Sister (w/earrings and w/out earrings)
(Includes: Razor Honed Spur Cutting Weapon, Backpack)

Zarana variants, with and without earrings. The one with earrings is more rare.

With the same color-changing capabilities that the Zartan (1984) and Zandar (1986) figures possess, their sister Zarana is "a professional assassin who gains access to her victims through skillful acting and masterful use of make up and disguise" (from her file card). Her prototype dossier goes on, "She posed as an oral hygenist for six months on one assignment and terminated her victim by swabbing his gums with poison." She is a true method actress, and is often a cruel human being. Her current activities and whereabouts are unknown.

MOC: *(w/earrings)* **$75**, MOC: *(w/out earrings)* **$25-35**,
MLC: *(w/earrings)* **$16**, MLC: *(w/out earrings)* **$8**

1986 VEHICLES/PLAYSETS

ACCESSORY PACK #4
COBRA BATTLE GEAR
Includes:

1 red Missile Backpack (Major Bludd)

1 light blue Handgun (Major Bludd)

1 red Backpack (Baroness)

1 white High-Density Laser Rifle (Baroness)

1 dark blue Armed Attache Case (Destro)

1 white High-Density Laser Gun (Destro)

1 white AK-47 Rifle (Cobra Officer)

1 white Submachine Gun (Firefly)

1 white Walkie-Talkie (Firefly)

1 dark blue Cobra Elite Backpack (Crimson Guard)

1 light blue Bayonet Rifle (Crimson Guard)

2 off-white Figure Stands

1 white RAR Pistol (Scrap Iron)

1 Missile System in 5 parts—top, bottom, 2 legs, round attachment (Scrap Iron)

1 dark blue Missile System Remote Activator (Scrap Iron)

2 dark blue Missiles (Scrap Iron)

1 light blue Dragunov SVD Sniper Rifle (Cobra)

1 light blue Laser Pistol (Cobra Commander)

MOMC: **$18**, MOC: **$10**, MLC **$6**

AIR CHARIOT
(Includes: Serpentor figure)

The Air Chariot's easily lost pieces.

Serpentor's Air Chariot is like a flying throne—it's a regal mode of transportation for the emperor. With a "Coblar" fiber reinforced battle shield, two auto-load 7.62mm attack guns, and a hover engine, this vehicle is a nice addition to the Cobra arsenal. Easily lost pieces include the serpent head and fan knob.

MISB: **$55-60**, MIB: **$35-40**, MLC: **$20-25**

COBRA HYDRO-SLED

The Cobra Hydro-Sled has two optically guided "Sunk" torpedoes, a rapid fire 9mm cannon combination "Snag" wire-guided spear gun, and a vinyl laminate reinforced hull, and these attributes make it hard to beat in naval combat. The vehicle floats, but when stationary, the vehicle is prone to capsizing due to its "flat bottomed" nature.

Easily lost pieces are its two missiles and harpoon gun.

MISB: **$25**, MIB: **$12**, MLC: **$5**

The Hydro-Sled's easily lost pieces.

COBRA NIGHT RAVEN S3P
(Includes: Strato-Viper figure)

The Cobra Night Raven S3P was based on the designs of the Blackbird SR-71 (the U.S. Air Force's Long Range Advanced Strategic Reconnaissance Aircraft—these planes are permanently retired), and is a truly gorgeous toy with its sweeping wings and high play value. The Night Raven sports two twin missile pods, a single person low radar-reflection recon jet (the "Drone"), twin 20mm cannons, dual Viper Mach 3.5 turbojet engines, and a radar-absorbing shell. Any kid (or collector) would be lucky to have this ship in his Cobra air force.

Easily lost pieces include the hydraulic airbrake, two missile pods, four missiles, two bombs, one-man drone, cockpit, cockpit bottom, left top wing, and right top wing.

MISB: **$200,** MIB: **$70**, MLC: **$45**

The undercarriage missile pod with two bombs.

The Night Raven's easily lost pieces.

COBRA STUN
(Includes: Motor Viper figure)

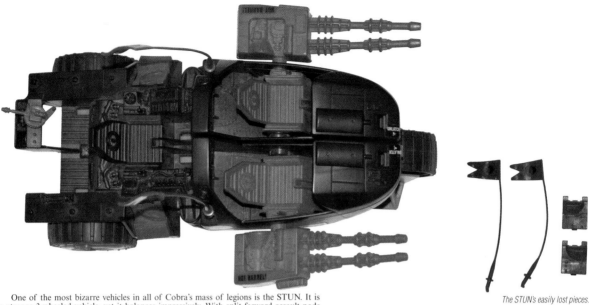

The STUN's easily lost pieces.

One of the most bizarre vehicles in all of Cobra's mass of legions is the STUN. It is a strange 3-wheeled vehicle, yet it balances impressively. With split forward assault pods (that have rotating guns), three all-terrain puncture proof tires, two "Blazer" twin rotating laser battle cannons, and a smaller 9mm machine gun, this was an excellent land vehicle to support Cobra's troops. Remember to check loose complete samples and make sure that the two included flags are not broken or missing—these are quite brittle and nearly impossible to find.

Easily lost pieces include two engine covers, two flags, and the small machine gun.

MISB: **$90**, MIB: **$45**, MLC: *(w/no broken flags)* **$18-20**

COBRA SURVEILLANCE PORT
(Battle Station)

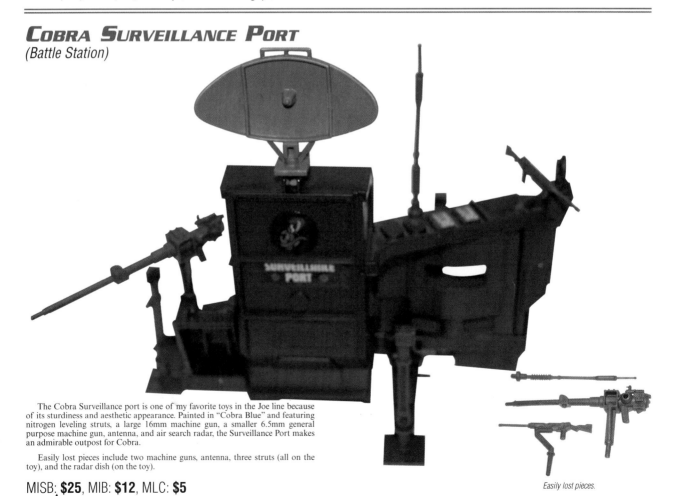

The Cobra Surveillance port is one of my favorite toys in the Joe line because of its sturdiness and aesthetic appearance. Painted in "Cobra Blue" and featuring nitrogen leveling struts, a large 16mm machine gun, a smaller 6.5mm general purpose machine gun, antenna, and air search radar, the Surveillance Port makes an admirable outpost for Cobra.

Easily lost pieces include two machine guns, antenna, three struts (all on the toy), and the radar dish (on the toy).

MISB: **$25**, MIB: **$12**, MLC: **$5**

Easily lost pieces.

COBRA TERROR DROME WITH FIREBAT
(Includes: Firebat and A.V.A.C. figure)

The Terror Drome's easily lost pieces.

The Cobra Terror Drome has an interesting back story, courtesy of the Marvel comic book. The bases were quickly produced and sold by Cobra to third world and developing nations for defense (and attack). An entire Cobra operation revolved around the profitable sale of Terror Dromes. After sales to the nation of Frusenland, the bases pumped low-frequency electronic signals into the environment, and motivated native Frusenlanders toward aggressive behavior (Marvel Comics, *G.I. Joe #67*).

The Terror Drome was the largest of the Cobra play sets. Its unique features include the fast-attack Firebat (1986) that is shot from a launch silo, a heavily armored rampart, blast-door mounted laser cannons, a projected energy field, a refueling station and service bay, and two tower-mounted "white heat" laser cannons.

Easily lost pieces include four console seats, four gunner seats, three hoses, three pumps, two red "gun door" braces, and the eight-piece silo blast shields (see images of raised Firebat).

NOTE: *The gun caps on the Terror Drome cannons have a tendency to come off. There are eight gun caps total—two for each of the four cannon units.*

NOTE: *The Terror Drome Firebat is included with the Terror Drome.*

MISB: **$500**, MIB: **$300**, MLC: **$175**

The upper computer console.

The jail doors.

The top inside gunner's station.

The fuel stations.

The gunner station.

The launch silo with blast shields closed.

The Firebat being raised with launch silo blast shields open.

The raised Firebat with launch silo blast shields open.

CONQUEST X-30
(Includes: Slip-Stream figure)

The Conquest X-30 was an interesting addition to the Joe team, and a markedly different aircraft than the Combat Jet Skystriker XP-14F (1983). With its retractable landing gear, layered/epoxy swing-wing design, twin 26k lb. thrust turbo fan engines, four "Light Sparrow" air-to-air missiles, two Mk. 3 "Drop Tanks," and laser guidance system, the Conquest put the Joe team at the forefront of battlefield technology.

Easily lost pieces include its two small wings, two large wings, four sparrow missiles, two drop tanks, underside panel, and engine cover.

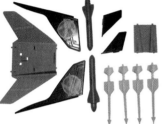

MISB: **$125**, MIB: **$50**, MLC: **$25**

The conquest X-30's easily lost pieces.

DEVILFISH

G.I. Joe's Devilfish is a one-man attack boat that, with its high-speed capability and slew of weapons, gives Cobra's forces a good fight at sea. The ship comes complete with twin 110hp "Assault" water jet motors, twin 20mm repeater cannons, two water guided Mk. 8 "Captor" torpedoes, and four laser-guided "Sea Phoenix" missiles.

Easily lost pieces include four missiles, two torpedoes, and two engine covers. The two hoses in the full vehicle image are sometimes missing as well.

MISB: **$30**, MIB: **$15**, MLC: **$8**

The Devilfish's easily lost pieces.

DREADNOK AIR ASSAULT
(Two Vehicles: Dreadnok Air Assault VTOL Copter and Dreadnok Air Assault Gyro Copter)
Sears Exclusive

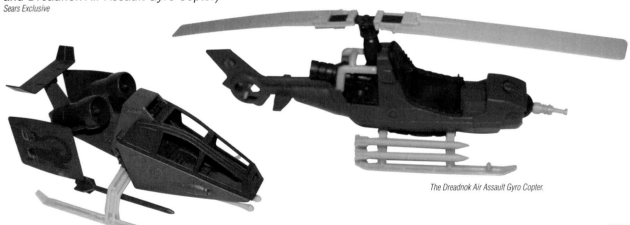

The Dreadnok Air Assault Gyro Copter.

The Sears Exclusive Dreadnok Air Assault is like nearly every other Joe exclusive, hard-to-find and expensive. Boxed specimens are quite difficult to acquire, especially with their contents sealed. The two vehicles included in the Air Assault set are really re-tooled and re-cast vehicles from earlier in the line—the VTOL Copter was the Sky Hawk (1984), while the Gyro Copter was the Cobra F.A.N.G. (1983). They share the same easily lost parts as their brother vehicles, but are cast in different colors. Both vehicles feature parts with color-change capabilities when exposed to sunlight (see Zartan, 1984).

MISB: **$350**, MIB: **$225**, MLC: **$135**

Easily lost pieces.

The Dreadnok Air Assault VTOL Copter's easily lost pieces.

DREADNOK GROUND ASSAULT

(Two Vehicles: Dreadnok Ground Assault 4WD Vehicle and Dreadnok Ground Assault Motorcycle)
Sears Exclusive

Easily lost pieces.

The Dreadnok 4WD Vehicle's easily lost pieces.

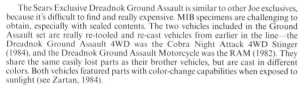

The Dreadnok Ground Assault Motorcycle.

The Sears Exclusive Dreadnok Ground Assault is similar to other Joe exclusives, because it's difficult to find and really expensive. MIB specimens are challenging to obtain, especially with sealed contents. The two vehicles included in the Ground Assault set are really re-tooled and re-cast vehicles from earlier in the line—the Dreadnok Ground Assault 4WD was the Cobra Night Attack 4WD Stinger (1984), and the Dreadnok Ground Assault Motorcycle was the RAM (1982). They share the same easily lost parts as their brother vehicles, but are cast in different colors. Both vehicles featured parts with color-change capabilities when exposed to sunlight (see Zartan, 1984).

MISB: **$400**, MIB: **$250**, MLC: **$150**

DREADNOK SWAMPFIRE

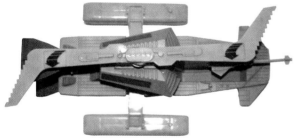

The Dreadnok Swampfire is an interesting vehicle. Its helicopter mode rotor blade can be folded back while its aluminum super-sealed gas filled pontoons could be folded down to simulate a water craft. With a "Sinker" 25mm auto-load repeating cannon, color change capabilities (like Zartan, 1984), and a reinforced carbon-mesh hull, the Dreadnok Swampfire was popular with kids and collectors.

Easily lost/broken pieces include the cannon, and the entire rotor assembly should be treated with care.

MISB: **$30**, MIB: **$18**, MLC: **$11**

The Dreadnok Swampfire's easily lost piece.

DREADNOK THUNDER MACHINE

(Includes: Thrasher figure)

The Dreadnok Thunder Machine is an immensely popular vehicle, and collectors are always on the lookout for MISB samples. The piece is fairly common to locate loose, however, the toy usually took some punishment and is known to have a few key pieces missing. The vehicle has a bevy of unique features including dual synchronized "Penetrator" Gatling guns, racing tires, an alloy ammo belt, a junked race car front grill, 21k lb. thrust turbojet engine, and plenty of armor protection.

Easily lost pieces include the lights, right door, left door, windshield, antenna, roll bar, steering wheel, two machine guns, and front grill.

MISB: **$100**, MIB: **$40**, MLC: **$20**

The Dreadnok Thunder Machine's easily lost pieces.

H.A.V.O.C.
(Heavy Articulated Vehicle Ordnance Carrier)
(Includes: Cross-Country figure)

The H.A.V.O.C. was a unique tracked vehicle for the Joes, and was a brisk seller. With a reinforced hover storage lift-off pad and reconnaissance craft, movable dual recoilless cannons, non-clogging epoxy armored tracks, and "Lancer" guidance missiles, the H.A.V.O.C. is a versatile land vehicle for the Joes.

Easily lost pieces include four missiles, two small cannons, and a reconnaissance craft.

MISB: **$85**, MIB: **$40**, MLC: **$15**

The H.A.V.O.C.'s easily lost pieces.

L.A.W.
(Laser Artillery Weapon)
(Battle Station)

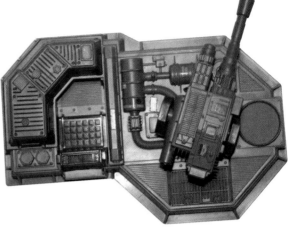

The L.A.W. battle station gives the Joe team a burst of added firepower. Its main cannon is a variable energy/uni-directional "Infinity" laser, and its entire base acts as a cooling/target acquisition/surveillance system for the weapon. There weren't any easily lost parts.

MISB: **$15-20**, MIB: **$12**, MLC: **$5**

L.C.V. RECON SLED
(Low Crawl Vehicle)

One of the oddest-looking Joe vehicles, the L.C.V. Recon Sled was an awkward machine, and had a few delicate parts that kids had to be careful with. It had off-road tires (naturally), a bullet-proof windscreen, a titanium alloy chassis, and a 96hp engine. Easily lost pieces included the plastic windshield and antenna.

MISB: **$25**, MIB: **$12**, MLC: **$5**

The L.C.V.'s easily lost pieces.

OUTPOST DEFENDER
(Battle Station)

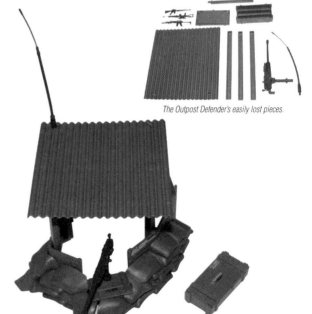

The Outpost Defender's easily lost pieces.

Another fantastic battle station that excels at capturing the essence of the best of the Joe line, the Outpost Defender was a cheap and easy play set for kids to buy. With a gun crate, gun crate top, four posts (three large, one small), antenna, mock tin roof, air-cooled heavy machine gun, and three rifles (Airborne's [1983], The Enemy's [Cobra (Soldier), 1982], Grunt's [1982] – all done in a lighter gray than the original weapons, so be wary), a kid could assemble this play set in under 15 minutes.

MISB: **$25**, MIB: **$12**, MLC: **$5**

TERROR DROME FIREBAT
(Includes: A.V.A.C. figure)
Included with the Cobra Terror Drome.

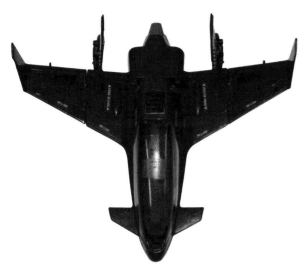

The Terror Drome Firebat, with four air-to-surface Condor bombs, two Snakeye guidance bombs, 25mm twin coaxial firing cannons, and stationary landing gear is a fantastically fast Cobra air ship. The Firebat came in its original maroon color, while some later mail-away versions came in a brighter red color. Pictured is the more common version of the Firebat.

NOTE: *The Firebat has two engine covers that are removable, six missiles, two landing gear (very fragile), and two machine guns (very fragile). For a picture of the Firebat with all of its missiles, see Cobra Terror Drome (blast shields open).*

MLC: **$30-40**

TRIPLE-T
(Tag Team Terminator)
(Includes: Sgt. Slaughter figure)

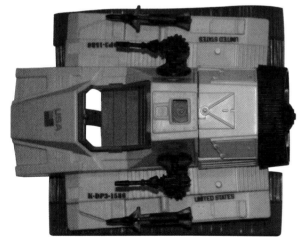

The Tag Team Terminator is a common vehicle found loose in any collection, and does not command very high prices. The favored mode of transportation for Sgt. Slaughter, it is a strange looking tank, and its special features include a reinforced inter-mesh track propulsion system, two high explosive anti-tank missiles, and a 950hp turbine engine. Easily lost pieces include the engine cover, and two missiles.

NOTE: There is a mail-away version of the vehicle that was released in 1993 with neon-colored weapons.

MISB: **$75**, MIB: **$25**,
MLC: **$8**

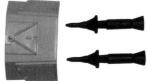

The Triple T's easily lost pieces.

TOMAHAWK
(Includes: Lift-Ticket figure)

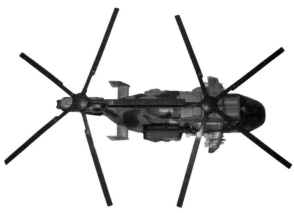

The Tomahawk has long been hailed as one of the greatest and most accurate Joe vehicles ever made. It is not overly complicated to assemble, has some great action features, and has a tremendous amount of play value. The Tomahawk comes with a cargo/ramp door that folds down in the back, working winch, five removable seats, noise reduction turbofan engines, working propeller blades, a 20mm cannon, and two laser-enhanced NVS (Night Vision System-VEH_WGIT.tif.50 caliber machine guns.

Easily lost pieces include the five removable seats, two large missiles, and six small missiles.

MISB: **$100**, MIB: **$50**, MLC: **$35**

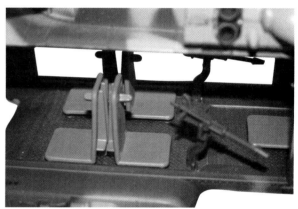

Interior seats in the Tomahawk.

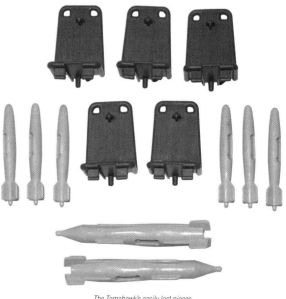

The Tomahawk's easily lost pieces.

(SERIES VI, 1987)

The sixth generation of toys added new characters to the Joe and Cobra ranks. Some characters including Falcon, Jinx, and Techno-Viper, were well received, while others including the Cobra-La figures, Raptor, and Crystal Ball, were not. This series began to branch out from its military roots and experiment more in the realm of the fantastic with its hypnotists, falconers, and a group of ancient members of a bio-mechanical cult. The premiere of *G.I. Joe: The Movie* by Sunbow Productions ensured the Real American Hero's place in the hearts of kids and collectors and Hasbro's success with the line continued.

1987 Vehicle Gear Accessory Pack #1.

1987 "Live the Adventure" game and mail away certificate.

1987 G.I. Joe catalog.

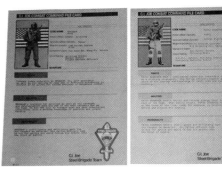

Steel Brigade file card variations, regular on the left, gold-headed on the right.

1987 G.I. JOE FIGURES

BACK-STOP
Persuader Driver
(Includes: Revolver)
Included with the Persuader.

His prototype code names were Hardball, Boxcar, and No-Guff, but Hasbro finally settled on Back-Stop—an appropriate name for a trooper who metaphorically "stops a puck." The former hockey player has broken many bones on himself and others, and "after a short career in the demolition derby" (from the file card), joined the Joes.

MLC: **$8**

CHUCKLES
Undercover
(Includes: Colt Combat Commander .45, Quick Draw Shoulder Harness)

Chuckles only made one appearance in the G.I. Joe cartoon universe, and throughout the entirety of Sunbow's *G.I. Joe: The Movie* (1987), he never uttered a single word. His character was much more compelling in the Marvel comic, where he took responsibility as the Joe's primary intelligence man. Sadly, Chuckles was killed in action by a Cobra agent, and his name was added to a memorial located at Arlington National Cemetery.

MOC: **$30**, MLC: **$8**

CRAZYLEGS
Assault Trooper
(Includes: EM-4 Assault Rifle w/Stock, Parachute Backpack)

Crazylegs "could have been the greatest organist in the world if his fingers weren't too short" (from the file card), but he still hummed classical music while parachuting into danger. Crazylegs was killed by a Cobra S.A.W. Viper while on a mission in Trucial Abysmia.

MOC: **$25-30**, MLC: **$8**

FALCON
Green Beret
(Includes: Special Forces Field Communications Pack w/Antenna, 12-Gauge Pump Shotgun, Bowie Survival Knife)

In Sunbow's *G.I. Joe: The Movie* (1987), Falcon (voiced by Don Johnson) is revealed to be the irresponsible half brother of Duke, and his lack of responsibility strangely contradicts everything written in his Hasbro file card, and personality in the Marvel comic. Falcon (or Lt. Falcon) is a "second-generation Green Beret" (from the file card) is talented with languages, and possesses a winning personality. GoArmy.com defines a Green Beret as: "mentally agile, astutely aware and physically tough, [able to] endure difficult training and face all challenges head on." Falcon is a current member of the Joe team.

MOC: **$40-50**, MLC: **$12**

FAST DRAW
Mobile Missile Specialist
(Includes: Face Mask w/Voice Activated Linkup, Blue Hose, Backpack, Two Triggers w/Hoses, Two Missiles w/Stabilizers [FAFNIR Target Acquisition and Missile Delivery System])

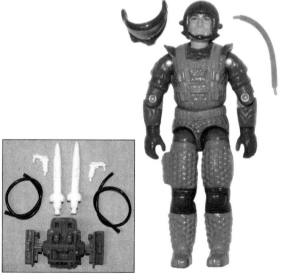

Fast Draw's FAFNIR mobile missile system.

As a figure, Fast Draw has one of the most complicated equipment systems in the G.I. Joe universe. He carries the FAFNIR (Fire and Forget Non-tube-launched Infantry Rocket) missile system, which consists of two triggers attached via hoses to the back-mounted system itself. He can take cover after the missiles launch, but prefers not to, as he "thinks of himself as an old-west gunfighter" (from the file card). His alternate prototype name was Backfire.

MOC: **$35**, MLC: **$12**

GUNG-HO
Marine Dress Blues
(Includes: [Non-Com] Dress Sabre, Dress Hat, Sticker Sheet)

This is one of the most impressive figures in the Joe universe, as it fairly accurately depicted a Marine's dress blues. With a ceremonial sword as a weapon, the figure didn't fight in many a child's battles, but he looked so very cool. For a full bio, see Gung-Ho (1983). This sticker did come with labels for his rank insignia and decorations, and most collectors consider the figure incomplete without this stickers applied.

MOC: **$35**, MLC: **$10**

HARD TOP
Crawler Driver
(Includes: Microphone and Pistol)
Included with the Defiant: Space Vehicle Launch Complex.

Hard Top's pistol and microphone.

Hard Top is one of the most difficult Joe figures to locate, and his pistol is nearly impossible to acquire. The pistol itself commands prices as high as $20-$25. His microphone is also hard to find, and sealed Hard Top figures should be considered very rare. With a MOS as Heavy Equipment Driver he drove the base of the Defiant (the Defiant's "Crawler"), and his tight-lipped character spoke only when absolutely necessary. His prototype code names were Four-Lane, Crusher, Turtle, and Slo-Mo.

NOTE: some Hard Top figures did not come with a pistol, so it is up to the individual collector as to whether or not the figure is complete or incomplete without it

MLC: (*w/pistol and mic*) **$50-75,** (*w/out*) **$15-20**

JINX
Ninja/Intelligence
(Includes: Two Ninja Swords, Naginata, Backpack)

A strange-looking figure, one who collectors refer to as having a "whipped-cream" head, Jinx is nonetheless quite popular as she is a female ninja. These two traits equal a winning combination. In Sunbow's *G.I. Joe: The Movie* (1987), she exercised a "blind fighting" technique, and in the Marvel comic she was raised by the same Arashikage family who raised Storm Shadow (1984). She is currently an active member of the Joe team.

MOC: **$50**, MLC: **$10**

LAW & ORDER
M.P. & K-9
(Includes: German Shepherd [Order], Uzi 9mm, M.P. Truncheon, Leash, Helmet)

With first-rate accessories, the Joe team finally got Law, a definitive Military policeman and his K-9 (canine) German Shepherd named, Order. This figure was snatched up by kids because of the accessories and appeal of a man and his dog. Law and Order were beat cops before joining the team, and since joining the Joes, they are frequently responsible for security detail.

MOC: **$45**, MLC: **$10**

OUTBACK
Survivalist
(Includes: Heckler and Koch G3 Rifle, Web Belt, Survival Backpack, Flashlight)

Outback is a Survivalist whose t-shirt sports the word "SURVIVAL," excerpted from the U.S. Army Ranger Handbook, which is an acronym for "S –Size up the situation, U –Undue haste makes waste, R –Remember where you are, V –vanquish fear and panic, I –Improve your situation, V –Value living, A –Act like the natives, and L –Learn basic skills." Outback's figure and character are famous for his tiny flashlight, and his H&K rifle.

MOC: **$50**, MLC: **$12**

PAYLOAD
Defiant Pilot
(Includes: Helmet, Face Shield, Backpack, Two Control Arms)
Included with the Defiant: Space Vehicle Launch Complex.

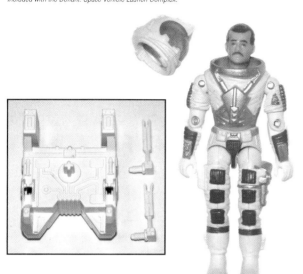

As the pilot of the Space Shuttle: Defiant, Payload is another figure popular with collectors. He grew up watching space missions blast off from Cape Canaveral (his place of birth), and joined the Air Force to "pay his dues" (from the file card) flying jets until he could sign up for the astronaut training program. He simply loves what he does.

MLC: *(w/backpack)* **$35**, *(w/out backpack)* **$15-20**

PSYCHE-OUT
Deceptive Warfare
(Includes: Variable Wave Field Projector with ELF Sonic Generator, Two "Big Ear" Sonic Receivers, .45 Assault Pistol, Backpack)

Psyche-Out has "worked on various research projects involving the inducement of paranoia by means of low frequency radio waves" (from the file card), enlisted in the Army, and pioneered work in the field of Deceptive Warfare.

MOC: **$25**, MLC: **$8**

RUMBLER
R/C Crossfire Driver
(Includes: Rifle, Helmet)
Included with the R/C Radio Control Crossfire.

Before driving the Crossfire (strangely enough, never pictured in any Joe catalog) for the U.S. Army, Earl-Bob Swilley (file name) was a revenue agent who had a "propensity toward high-speed car chases through… woods in pursuit of moonshiners and tax stamp dodgers" (from the file card). After destroying many vehicles while "doing his job," he was transferred to the Army where the vehicles could take more punishment. His prototype code names were Motor-Face, Down-Shift, Overdrive, Long-Gone, and well into production—Scrambler.

MLC: **$25**

SNEAK PEEK
Advanced Recon
(Includes: Walkie-Talkie, Binoculars, M-16A Rifle, Variable Range Optical Field Scanning Device, Multiband Radio Transponder Unit)

Owen King (file name) a.k.a. Sneak Peek was named after horror writer Stephen King's son, Owen—a huge G.I. Joe fan. Sneak Peek's hometown is even listed as Bangor, Maine.

Sneak Peek came replete with an array of different weapons and accessories, all useful for his MOS of Advanced Reconnaissance—exploring an area to obtain useful military information. Tragically, Sneak Peek was killed at the Battle of Benzheen, while saving a young child's life.

MOC: **$20-25**, MLC: **$8**

STARDUSTER
Jet Pack Trooper
(Includes: Helmet, Visor, Jet Pack JUMP, XM-76 Grenade Launcher)
Mail Away Exclusive

Starduster "origin" comics from Action Stars cereal.

One of the most sought-after figures in the Joe universe, Starduster was a mail-away initially from 1987's G.I. Joe Action Stars Cereal, and later from Hasbro Direct in different figure and vehicle inserts. Although he never made an appearance in the comics or on the cartoon, his origin was captured in some promotional comics inside boxes of Action Stars. He was a former circus acrobat who enlisted in the Airborne Rangers, was recruited by Duke, and given a JUMP Jet Pack, an accessory that sometimes was packaged with the figure. There are a few different variations of the figure, but these variations are rather minor, and do not really affect a higher cost either way. It's a hard figure to find in any condition, and with all of his accessories, is a great pick up for a collection. His origin comics are getting more difficult to find as well.

MISBaggie: **$60-80**, MLC: **$25-40**

STEAM-ROLLER
Mobile Command Center Operator
(Includes: Knife)
Included with the Mobile Command Center.

Steam-Roller was a heavy machine operator all over the continental United States before he was recruited by the Joe team. He's gutsy, persistent, and "a moose" (from his file card). His prototype code names were Tank-Trap, Pig-Iron, and Dozer.

MLC: **$15**

STEEL BRIGADE
(Regular version includes: XM-16 Attack Rifle, Assault Pack)
Mail Away Exclusive

The Steel Brigade was a clever mail-away offer by Hasbro for kids, with an ad stating, "Now, YOU can be the next Joe!" If you filled out a simple (and widely-promoted) form, checked some boxes, and provided some information, you received a generic Steel Brigade figure with backpack, rifle, a custom-made file card, and a patch. This was a great offer for kids, as they could select their own military specialties, weapons, etc., to be written up by Hasbro. Because the offer went on from 1987-1994 (frequently and infrequently), there are a few different variations of the figure, all of which are pictured. The one version of Steel Brigade that sells like wildfire is the infamous "gold headed" Steel Brigade figure, as its highlights are gold in color, and its file card, patch, backpack color, and other figure colors are noticeably different.

MLC: *(any version besides gold head)* **$15-20**

Steel Brigade gold head. MISP: $150

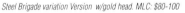

Steel Brigade variation Version w/gold head. MLC: $80-100

Steel Brigade , common variations.

TUNNEL RAT

E.O.D. (Explosive Ordinance Disposal)
(Includes: Satchel, Air-Cooled 7.62mm Machine Gun with Infrared Scope, Tunnel Floodlight System with Two Detachable Halogen Hand Lamps)

Tunnel Rat's figure is a very popular one, and was a quick sell for Hasbro. With a huge backpack, a large rifle, and removable flashlights (for ferreting out evildoers from their hidey-holes), Tunnel Rat "grew up mean on the streets of Brooklyn, got tough on the Ranger course at Fort Benning and honed his skills in Grenada" (from his file card). He then joined the Joe team, and appeared in both the Marvel comic and in *G.I. Joe: The Movie* (1987). It is rumored that Tunnel Rat's visage was modeled after Joe comic writer and dossier drafter Larry Hama. Tunnel Rat is currently a reserve member of the Joe team.

MOC: **$40-45**, MLC: **$12**

BATTLE FORCE 2000

"Battle Force 2000... The walking, breathing proving grounds for tomorrow's battlefield technology today! Highly-trained specialists entrusted with one-of-a-kind, state-of-the-art prototypes. Their mission... to support G.I. Joe and field-test experimental equipment under battlefield conditions!"

AVALANCHE

Dominator Snow Vehicle Driver
(Individually Carded and in Two-Pack)
(Includes: P-480 Sub-Zero Stun Gun, Microphone)

Avalanche spent "most of his youth in the woods with a rifle" (from the file card), and this experience prepared him for many aspects of the Army—except the discipline. His prototype names were Chill-Out, Glacier, and North-Wind. He was killed in an explosion fighting Cobra forces at the Battle of Benzheen.

NOTE: *Avalanche was also offered in a Battle Force 2000 two-pack with Blaster.*

MOC: **$20-25**, MLC: **$8**,
Avalanche/Blaster two-pack MIP: **$40**

BLASTER
Vindicator Hovercraft Diver
(Individually Carded and in Two-Pack)
(Includes: Infra-Green Laser Pistol [DK-528], Face Mask)

Blaster obsessively built hovercrafts since he was thirteen and joined the Army where he felt he would have a better chance of experimenting on the vehicles, and this led to his serving on the BF 2000 team. Sadly, he was killed in an explosion fighting Cobra forces at the Battle of Benzheen.

NOTE: Blaster was also offered in a Battle Force 2000 two-pack with Avalanche.

MOC: **$20-25**, MLC: **$8**

BLOCKER
Eliminator Four-Wheeled Vehicle Driver
(Individually Carded and in Two-Pack)
(Includes: XL-13 Light Refraction Submachine Laser, [Visor])

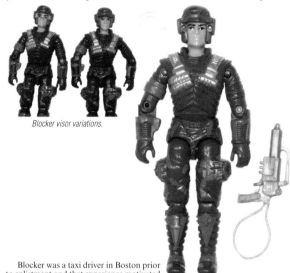

Blocker visor variations.

Blocker was a taxi driver in Boston prior to enlistment and that experience motivated him to join the Army and become qualified "to drive every wheeled vehicle in the Army inventory" (from the file card). He was killed in an explosion fighting Cobra forces at the Battle of Benzheen.

NOTE: There are two variations of the figure, as he came with and without a clear visor.

NOTE: Blocker was also offered in a Battle Force 2000 two-pack with Maverick.

MOC: **$20-25**, MLC: **$8**,
Blocker/Maverick two-pack MIP: **$40**

DODGER
Marauder Half-Track Driver
(Individually Carded and in Two-Pack)
(Includes: Ultra-Sonic Photon Rifle, Microphone)

Dodger is a tracked vehicle driver with the guts to drive by instinct and a natural talent with all the technologically advanced accouterments that accompanied these crafts. As a member of the BF 2000 team, Dodger was the only surviving BF 2000 member of the Battle of Benzheen.

NOTE: Dodger was also offered in a Battle Force 2000 two-pack with Knockdown.

MOC: **$20-25**, MLC: **$8**,
Dodger/Knockdown two-pack MIP: **$40**

KNOCKDOWN
Sky-Sweeper Anti-Aircraft Driver/Anti-Aircraft Specialist
(Individually Carded and in Two-Pack)
(Includes: Experimental Ground to Air Pistol, Helmet)

Knockdown worked at Aberdeen Proving Ground prior to his assignment to the G.I. Joe team, where his ability to repair radar systems and other complicated targeting equipment proved him a useful soldier. Tragically, he was killed in an explosion fighting Cobra forces at the Battle of Benzheen. His prototype code names were Swatter and Fly-Trap.

NOTE: Knockdown was also offered in a Battle Force 2000 two-pack with Dodger.

MOC: **$20-25**, MLC: **$8**

MAVERICK
Vector Jet Fighter Pilot
(Individually Carded and in Two-Pack)
(Includes: Semi-Automatic Machine Pistol, Helmet)

Maverick's prototype code names were Cloud-Jammer, Mach-Buster, and Vortex. He was an expert pilot who "volunteered for every experimental program that came down the line" (from the file card), which led him to serve on the BF 2000 team. He was killed in an explosion fighting Cobra forces at the Battle of Benzheen.

NOTE: *Maverick was also offered in a Battle Force 2000 two-pack with Blocker.*

MOC: **$20-25**, MLC: **$8**

SGT. SLAUGHTER'S RENEGADES
Renegade, n: an individual who rejects lawful or conventional behavior.

"There comes a time when even the Joes, with the highest standards of military discipline, must resort to 'unconventional' tactics in order to successfully complete a mission. The Renegades are the Joes' answer to offensive bullying. This highly secretive branch of G.I. Joe is made up of men who are not your typical Joe. They're tough, unruly, and most importantly, willing to take on 'secret' missions the Joes might deem 'out of character.'

"The Renegades have an eclectic variety of backgrounds including an ex-Cobra Viper, an ex-professional football star, and a gypsy acrobat from Istanbul. All are dedicated to the G.I. Joe cause but loyal only to themselves. There is no other chain of command. The Renegades are hardened, unyielding, and the tour-de-force of counter-Cobraism."

MOC: **$45-75**

MERCER
Renegade
(Includes: .45 Caliber Pistol w/Silencer, Backpack)

In *G.I. Joe: The Movie* (1987), Sgt. Slaughter's Renegades are portrayed as an organization that doesn't "answer to anyone but themselves" (from the file card). Mercer was a Cobra Viper who defected to the Joes—and lived. Initially, he wanted the riches promised by Cobra, but didn't buy into their philosophy.

MLC: **$8**

RED DOG
Renegade
(Includes: .45 Caliber Pistol, Backpack)

A former barefoot place kicker in the NFL who was "suspended for excessive roughness" (from the file card), Red Dog was a stuntman before he joined the Renegades. As a Renegade, he is a member of an organization with no restrictions, and that seems to suit Red Dog just fine.

MLC: **$8**

TAURUS
Renegade
(Includes: Pistol with Stock, Backpack)

Before joining the Renegades, Taurus was a "circus acrobat in Europe who did occasional undercover work for INTERPOL [a collaborative international intelligence agency]" (from the file card). After impressing the Joe organization with his circus act and linguistic prowess he signed on to the Renegades, or their operative name "Pentagon Pest Control."

MLC: **$8**

1987 COBRA FIGURES

BIG BOA
Cobra Trainer
(Includes: Punching Bag w/Stand, Hose, Two Boxing Gloves)

Big Boa was Cobra's first troop trainer, leading Cobra Vipers through their various exercises. He is described as a "brutal, unfeeling taskmaster... [with] a voice like a bullhorn and fists the size of frozen turkeys and the disposition of a rabid grizzly bear" (from the file card). His figure contains two boxing gloves with Cobra symbols on them (labeled with paint that wears off easily), and collectors should take care not to confuse these accessories with those of Balrog (1993) from the Street Fighter II line. His prototype code names were Snake-Charmer and "Big Bad" Boa.

MOC: **$25**, MLC: **$10**

COBRA COMMANDER (W/ BATTLE ARMOR)
(Includes: Auto Assault Pistol, Life Support Backpack, Hose)

This is the first figure in the line that actually lists this character as Cobra Commander, and not "Enemy Leader" (1982, 1984). This version of the Commander sports a sophisticated battle armor has "plate parts that can withstand a direct hit from a heavy machine-gun and the flexible parts will stop anything up to a .357 magnum." In the Marvel comic, the man who wore the battle armor was not the real Cobra Commander, but an imposter. Eventually the true Commander returned to power.

NOTE: Collectors should take care not to lose the small black hose that is usually absent from loose samples.

MOC: **$30-40**, MLC: **$12**

CROC MASTER
Cobra Reptile Trainer
(Includes: Crocodile, Binder Cable, Neuro-Lash, Hose)

Croc Master, whose prototype code name was Krawl, was a former "alligator wrestler and burglar alarm salesman" (from the file card) who used alligators to enhance home security. Eventually, his obsession led him to join the nefarious Cobra Command, where his "ravenously hungry man-eating crocodiles" could guard the waters of Cobra Island. In the Marvel comic, Croc Master perished when he was buried in a landlocked freighter.

MOC: **$25**, MLC: **$10**

CRYSTAL BALL
Cobra Hypnotist
(Includes: Reflected Light Pulse Modulator [Hypno-Shield])

Many rumors surround the creation of Crystal Ball, but it was indeed Hasbro who presented Larry Hama with a sketch of the character. Mr. Hama won't comment on the end product of the hypnotist's dossier, but here for the first time is Crystal Ball's file card as originally written by Mr. Hama:

Code Name: Trance-Master (alt. names: Prof. Id, Mesmeron, The Gazer).
A one-time theatrical hypnotist and encyclopedia sales-man, Trance Master had traveled to India to find new inspirations to spice up his act. In a remote mountain village, he was taken in by an evil band of occult priests who taught him ancient and terrible forms of hypnosis and mind control! Returning to the West, he used his new powers to subvert and take over large corporations until his activities conflicted with similar Cobra operations. Realizing that Cobra was too big for him to tackle alone, Trance-Master decided to join them rather than fight them. "If you saw a photograph of Trance-Master, you would think he was a mousy little unimposing wimp. If you met him face-to-face, you'd walk away impressed by his dynamic personality and dashing good looks. You might also find that you had purchased an encyclopedia for some unknown reason!"

MOC: **$20**, MLC: **$10**

GYRO-VIPER
Mamba Driver
(Includes: Helmet)
Included with the Cobra Mamba.

Gyro-Vipers, with the alternate code name Rotor-Vipers (from the prototype dossier), were the newest Cobra Pilots of 1987. Driving the Mamba attack helicopter in battle was "akin to operating a yo-yo with your left hand while spinning a pie plate on the tip of your right index finger while you're balancing full glasses of water on the top of your feet... [all] while riding a twelve point buck through the woods in the middle of hunting season" (from the file card). Indeed, the Gyro-Vipers are talented pilots.

MLC: **$10**

ICE VIPER
Cobra WOLF Driver
(Includes: Helmet, Two Sais)
Included with the Cobra WOLF.

Ice Vipers, often desired by collectors because of their cool weapons (and the fact that the two sais can be attached to the figure's thighs), "are the mechanized [and cold weather] branch of the Cobra Infantry" (from the file card). Their prototype code-names were Werewolves or Were-Walruses.

MLC: **$12**

RAPTOR
Cobra Falconer
(Includes: Ultralight Air Foil System, Falcon [Talon])

Raptor is one of the oddest-looking Joe figures, with his air foils system looking like faux Falcon's wings. Often criticized by collectors and casual fans alike, Raptor seemed out of place next to more military-looking Joes. His prototype code names were Peregrine, Gos, and Skree.

MOC: **$25**, MLC: **$8**

SEA SLUG
Sea Ray Navigator
(Includes: Pistol)
Included with the Sea Ray.

The Sea Slugs were formerly Cobra Eels who took additional training in three phases: "rivers and ports, deep ocean, and Arctic" (from the file card). Some 35% of the Eels undergoing the intensive trailing to become Sea Slugs wash out during the Arctic phase. Their prototype code names were Squids and Krakens.

MLC: **$8**

TECHNO-VIPER

Cobra Battlefield Technician

(Includes: Hydraulic Clamp, Forged-Steel Sledgehammer, Vario-Wrench, Phase Pulse Plasma Rifle, Backpack with Two Hookup Hoses)

A popular troop builder for those collectors who wish to amass a Cobra army, Techno-Vipers are battlefield technicians who try to repair Cobra vehicles in the field. Their array of different tools make these figures difficult to complete, but they are impressive to behold when accessorized.

MOC: **$25**, MLC: **$10**

COBRA-LA TEAM

The three members of the Cobra-La Team were packaged together.

MOC: **$45-75**

GOLOBULUS

Cobra-La Ruler

(Includes: Laser Gun)

Leader of the oft-criticized Cobra-La empire and voiced by Burgess Meredith in Sunbow's *G.I. Joe: The Movie* (1987), Golobulus was "descended from the serpent kings of pre-history," and presided over a "Bio-Mechanical cult [that] created a technology based on solely on living organisms" (from the file card). He has the strangest body construction of all Joe figures, as his bottom half is made from a semi-bendable green plastic.

MLC: **$7**

NEMESIS ENFORCER

Cobra-La Team

(Includes: Bat Wings, Tentacles)

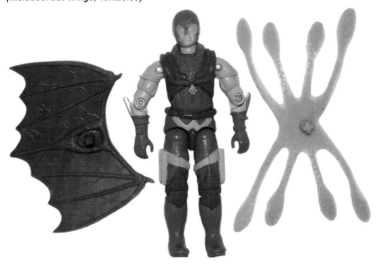

Golobulus "raised the Nemesis Enforcer from a pile of dead things… where his soul should be there is nothing but a cold emptiness" (from the file card). His accessories include bat-wings (which he wore in *G.I. Joe: The Movie* [1987]), and tentacles that, it is assumed, would attach to an enemy figure's back and "capture" them.

MLC: **$8**

ROYAL GUARD

Cobra-La Team

(Includes: Battle-Axe, Pistol, Antenna)

The Cobra-La Royal Guardsmen were bred to protect Golobulus and are covered in "organic insectoid armor" (from the file card). They are powerful, silent, and intimidating, and their antenna accessory is nearly impossible to find on a loose figure.

MLC: **$10**

W.O.R.M.S.

(Weapons Ordnance Rugged Machine Specialist)
MAGGOT Driver
(Includes: Helmet, Antenna)
Included with the Cobra MAGGOT.

W.O.R.M.S.
antenna close
up.

W.O.R.M.S. (Weapons Ordnance Rugged Machine Specialist) man the Cobra MAGGOTS, and as this is a composite vehicle, the W.O.R.M.S. specialize in one of four fields: "driver, gunner, loader, or diesel mechanic" (from the file card). To have four W.O.R.M.S. with all their accessories manning your MAGGOT toy could be quite difficult, since it is a challenge to find a W.O.R.M.S. figure complete with its antenna. Their prototype code names were Crabs, Roaches, Slugs, and Grubs.

MLC: *(w/antenna)* **$30**, *(w/out antenna)* **$8**

ZANZIBAR

Dreadnok Pirate
(Includes: Pistol)
Included with Dreadnok Air Skiff.

Zanzibar, the latest addition to Zartan's (1984) Dreadnoks, is an impressive figure as he comes with rooted hair and a nice-looking pistol. It is debatable as to whether or not the hammer and spear that came with the Dreadnok Air Skiff should be included as Zanzibar's accessories, as these two pieces have places to be mounted on the skiff. His prototype code names were Dog-Day, Top-Knot, and Keel Haul.

MLC: **$12**

1987 VEHICLES/PLAYSETS

ACCESSORY PACK #5: BATTLE GEAR

Includes:

2 brown Figure Stands
1 brown Helmet (General Hawk)
1 brown Helmet (Crankcase)
1 brown Helmet (Footloose)
1 brown Rifle (Leatherneck)
1 brown Rifle (Low-Light)
1 brown Bipod (Low-Light)
1 dark gray Pistol (Low-Light)
1 dark gray Backpack (Low-Light)
1 brown Relay Backpack (Lifeline)
1 dark gray Pistol (Lifeline)
1 dark gray Pistol (Dr. Mindbender)
1 dark gray Rifle (Iceberg)
1 dark gray Submachine Gun (Beachhead)
1 cream Backpack (Beachhead)
1 cream Pouch (Beachhead)
1 dark gray Rifle (Viper)
1 dark gray Computer (Mainframe)
1 dark gray Backpack (Mainframe)
1 cream Flashlight (Wet Suit)

MOMC: **$15**, MOC: **$10**, MLC: **$6**

COASTAL DEFENDER

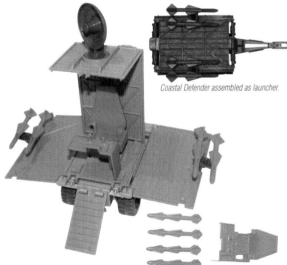

Coastal Defender assembled as launcher.

The Coastal Defender's easily lost pieces.

The Coastal Defender is possibly the strangest of all Joe weapons systems. When it is being towed it looks like a large crate, but after a few transformations it can be assembled into a coastline missile defense.

Easily lost pieces include four missiles and a chair.

MISB: **$18**, MIB: **$10**, MLC: **$5**

COBRA BUZZ BOAR

The Buzz Boar is an interesting assault vehicle that "buzzes" its way with "Boar's Teeth" specially hardened vari-pitch digging teeth, dual .50 caliber repeating machine guns, and two DAO (Destro Anti-Obstacle) side-launched missiles.

Easily lost pieces include the machine guns and two missiles.

MISB: **$25**, MIB: **$10**, MLC: **$5**

The Buzz Boar's easily lost pieces.

COBRA JET PACK

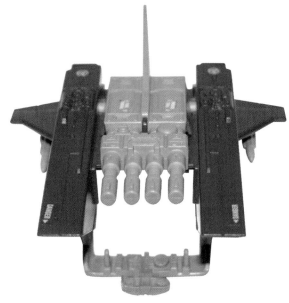

The Cobra Jet Pack is a useful mode of transportation of insertion into battle zones. With "Screener" micromesh alloy jet intakes, two "Neutralizer" air-to-air missiles, and 25mm axial-firing machine guns, this weapons puts the G.I. Joe JUMP (1982) to the test.

Easily lost pieces include the two missiles and handlebars.

MISB: **$18**, MIB: **$10**, MLC: **$5**

The Jet Pack's easily lost pieces.

COBRA MAGGOT

(Includes: W.O.R.M.S. figure)

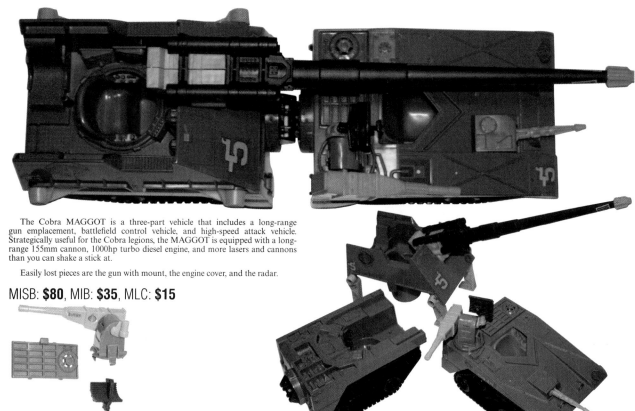

The Cobra MAGGOT is a three-part vehicle that includes a long-range gun emplacement, battlefield control vehicle, and high-speed attack vehicle. Strategically useful for the Cobra legions, the MAGGOT is equipped with a long-range 155mm cannon, 1000hp turbo diesel engine, and more lasers and cannons than you can shake a stick at.

Easily lost pieces are the gun with mount, the engine cover, and the radar.

MISB: **$80**, MIB: **$35**, MLC: **$15**

The MAGGOT's easily lost pieces.

The MAGGOT separated.

COBRA MAMBA
(Includes: Gyro-Viper figure)

The Cobra Mamba is an amazing addition to the Cobra Air Legions. This high-tech helicopter sports two detachable "Molt" (Mamba Offensive Light Tactical) attack pods armed to the teeth, "Serpentor" 9mm machine guns, and an NT-58 turboshaft engine.

Easily lost pieces include two assault pods (of course) with two missiles on each, one large bomb (almost always missing), four side missiles, and two medium-sized missiles.

MISB: **$85**, MIB: **$30**, MLC: **$20**

The Mamba's easily lost pieces.

COBRA POGO
(Ballistic Battle Ball)

Like the Cobra Buzz Boar, the Pogo is an unusual, but very popular, vehicle. It supposedly "springs" and leaps into battle on its three "Real Feel" ground sensitive landing pods, and uses infrared guidance bombs and a rotating machine gun to neutralize its opposition.

Easily lost pieces include two missiles, coolant hose, antenna, and machine gun.

NOTE: *To be considered complete, the Pogo needs its three silver hoses, but these aren't lost too frequently as they are sturdily attached to the legs of the vehicle.*

The Pogo's easily lost pieces.

MISB: **$25**, MIB: **$10**, MLC: **$5**

COBRA WOLF
(Winter Operational Light Fighting Vehicle)
(Includes: Ice Viper figure)

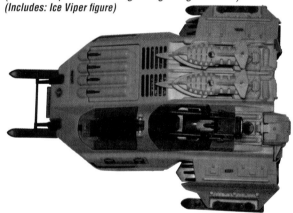

One of the most popular Cobra vehicles, the WOLF is a nice bit of Hasbro craftsmanship and has some great play value. The WOLF comes equipped with two "Snarl" ski torpedoes, four Wham-4 surface-to-air missiles, pivoting 20mm cannons, and great suspension.

Easily lost pieces include two ski torpedoes, four missiles, two skids, a machine gun, and the front skis.

MISB: **$85**, MIB: **$30**, MLC: **$20**

The WOLF's easily lost pieces.

S E R I E S   S I X

DEFIANT: SPACE VEHICLE LAUNCH COMPLEX
(Includes: Hard Top and Payload figures)

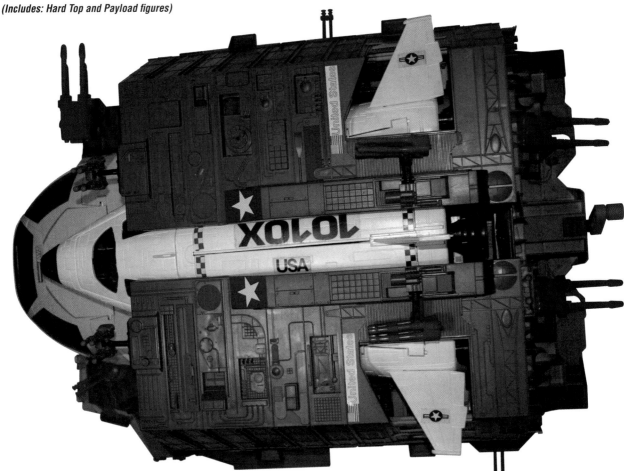

The Defiant: Space Vehicle Launch Complex is one of the three "holy grail" pieces for the G.I. Joe line (along with the Sears Cobra Missile Command Headquarters [1982], and the U.S.S. FLAGG [1985]). As such, it is quite difficult to find it either MISB, for which the piece may exceed $1,200, or to find it mint, loose, and complete at 1/2 to 3/4 of that price.

Mint, loose, complete samples are a tough find because of the vast amount of smaller parts involved in building up a Defiant. The space shuttle is broken into three different parts—the booster/space station, the shuttle itself, and the crawler/gantry. The crawler/gantry is the transportation base of the Defiant, and is driven by Hard Top (1987). The crawler/gantry features a pivoting "steel plate" gantry door, dual repeating self-generated laser cannons, surface-clearing laser cannons, and 7.62mm machine guns. Other highlights of the crawler/gantry include the launch control computer station, driver's cockpit with tinted yellow blast shields, and a crank for kids to turn in order to place the booster/space station into "blast off" position.

The booster/space station, with its primary reaction control thrusters, 65,000 lb. payload, forward rotating target lock laser cannons (some on the outside, while others swivel from hidden panels), and a cockpit protected by alum-silicate windshield glass, provides exceptional play value. As an added bonus, the booster/space station opens up to reveal a play set that boggles the imagination. With four seats to monitor computer consoles, outer hatch covers, a transporter module with sliding door, a hatch that slides open into the atmosphere, a sleeping compartment, a revolving door wall, and a cockpit entry door, this "inner" part of the booster is my favorite part of the play set.

Front view, opened Defiant.

The final part of the Defiant is the shuttlecraft itself, which features a three-station crew cockpit/operations center, cilica ceramic tiles, and an extra-vehicular activity (EVA) life support attachment. The shuttle (with retractable landing gear) opens up and reveals a claw with laser gun, a hatch that leads to outer space, and an umbilical cord you can attach to Payload's backpack for space borne missions. The entire shuttle can be mounted on the top of the booster's opened station, in order to simulate astronauts transferring from the landed shuttle to inside the booster/space station.

Easily lost pieces include (crawler/gantry): two elevators, six braces/guardrails, four laser cannons w/ studs; (booster/space station): two large thruster nozzles, four small thruster nozzles, two chairs (two other adjustable chairs are difficult to come off), transporter door, hatch, two hidden panels w/ lasers, four missiles; (shuttle craft): three large thruster nozzles, two small thruster nozzles, two-part hatch, machine gun, umbilical cord, two wings, Payload's backpack (also listed with Payload).

Defiant's easily lost pieces.

MISB: **$1000**, MIB: **$750**, MLC: **$450**, loose incomplete: **$150-250**

The left side of the gantry access, Defiant.

The outside booster, Defiant.

The right side of the gantry access, Defiant.

The interior of the booster, Defiant.

The computer area of the crawler, Defiant.

The base of the booster, Defiant.

Close up of the opened Defiant.

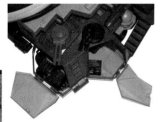

The crawler driver's seat.

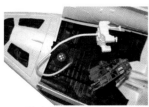

The inside of the shuttle, Defiant.

The pilot seat of the booster, Defiant.

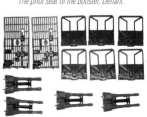

Easily lost pieces, crawler/gantry.

The cockpit of the shuttle, Defiant.

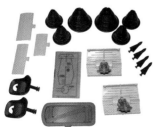

Easily lost pieces, booster/space station.

DREADNOK AIR SKIFF
(Includes: Zanzibar figure)

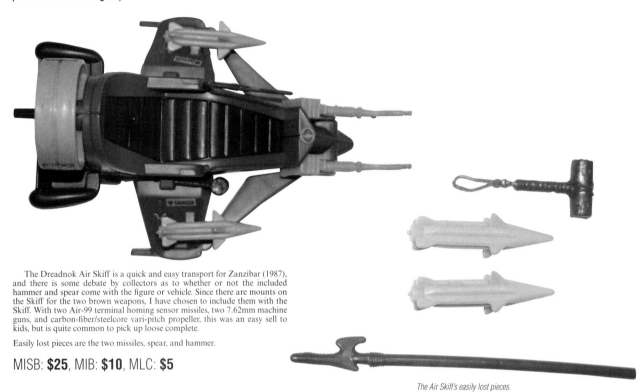

The Dreadnok Air Skiff is a quick and easy transport for Zanzibar (1987), and there is some debate by collectors as to whether or not the included hammer and spear come with the figure or vehicle. Since there are mounts on the Skiff for the two brown weapons, I have chosen to include them with the Skiff. With two Air-99 terminal homing sensor missiles, two 7.62mm machine guns, and carbon-fiber/steelcore vari-pitch propeller, this was an easy sell to kids, but is quite common to pick up loose complete.

Easily lost pieces are the two missiles, spear, and hammer.

MISB: **$25**, MIB: **$10**, MLC: **$5**

The Air Skiff's easily lost pieces.

DREADNOK CYCLE

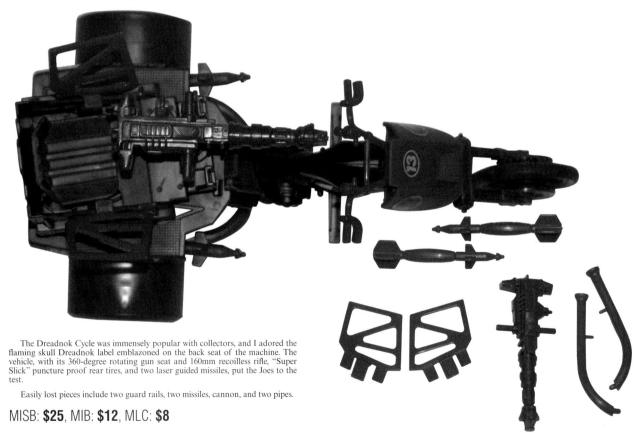

The Dreadnok Cycle was immensely popular with collectors, and I adored the flaming skull Dreadnok label emblazoned on the back seat of the machine. The vehicle, with its 360-degree rotating gun seat and 160mm recoilless rifle, "Super Slick" puncture proof rear tires, and two laser guided missiles, put the Joes to the test.

Easily lost pieces include two guard rails, two missiles, cannon, and two pipes.

MISB: **$25**, MIB: **$12**, MLC: **$8**

The Dreadnok Cycle's easily lost pieces.

MOBILE COMMAND CENTER
(Includes: Steam-Roller figure)

The G.I. Joe Mobile Command Center was as magnificent as it was unwieldy. Because it is a very delicate machine, collectors must take extra care when transporting it from place to place. Three different bays are the three main areas of the MCC: the service bay (bottom); the control station (middle); and the missile bay (upper).

The service bay features a driver's cockpit (see Steam-Roller, 1987), two lube nozzles and hoses, a three-part crane with hook, a spare engine, and a gasoline hose. The control station of the MCC sports a strategy board with map, two bunks with fold-up housings, and a sliding jail. The third section, the missile bay, comes with a helipad, an escape slide that leads to the floor, an elevator that runs the length of the MCC, a missile mount, plenty of machine guns and searchlights, and even a weapons storage rack. There are a lot of parts to the MCC, and it is very fragile, so be careful when opening the MCC and transporting it.

Easily lost pieces include twelve thin red missiles, eight small red missiles, six machine guns, four searchlights, crane, crane hook, gas hose with mount, engine, tactical board, two hoses with nozzles, two mountable machine guns, radar mount, radar, command chair, missile launcher base, two missile launcher attachments, jail cell, and small missile launcher base.

MISB: **$120**, MIB: **$65**, MLC: **$45**

MCC control station computer room w/bunk.

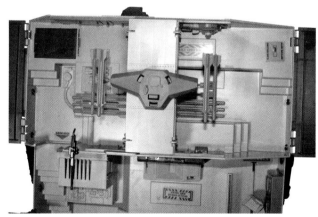
MCC missile bay.

Outer elevator for the MCC.

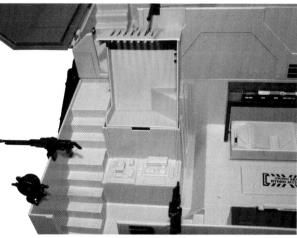
MCC control station jail cell.

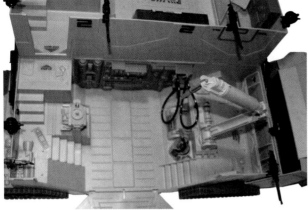

MCC service bay.

MCC's easily lost pieces.

MCC driver's seats (service bay level).

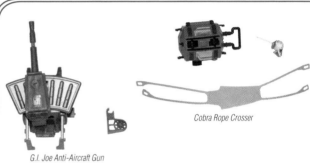

G.I. Joe Anti-Aircraft Gun

Cobra Rope Crosser

MOTORIZED ACTION PACKS

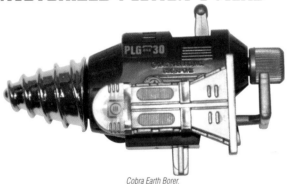

Cobra Earth Borer.

The following motorized action packs have wind-up action controlled by twisting a white knob. They are fairly easy to find MOC, but some are more rare than others. Each action pack sells for approximately

MOC: **$5-$10** each, MLC: **$3-$5** each

G.I. Joe Radar Station

G.I. Joe Helicopter

Cobra Pom-Pom Gun

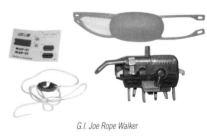

G.I. Joe Rope Walker

Cobra Mountain Climber

PERSUADER
(Includes: Back-Stop figure)

The G.I. Joe Persuader is the mobile laser cannon support for ground forces. With a "Heatwave" 10 Megawatt armor-piercing laser cannon, six "Dart" Sam-37 250 lb. missiles, and a 10-wheel drive unit axle, this vehicle gives the Joes added firepower against Cobra.

Easily lost pieces include the laser cannon, small gun, and six missiles.

MISB: **$40**, MIB: **$20**, MLC: **$10-15**

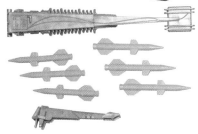

The Persuader's easily lost pieces.

R/C RADIO CONTROL CROSSFIRE
(Fast Attack Vehicle ["Alpha 27" or "Delta 49"])
(Includes: Rumbler figure)

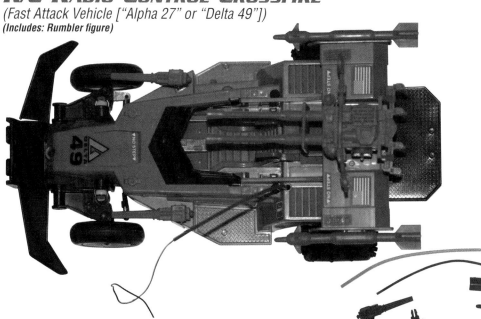

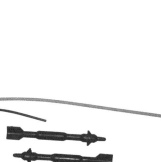

The Crossfire's easily lost pieces.

Not pictured in any regular-issue G.I. Joe catalog, the Crossfire is an amazing R/C vehicle, and has "power speed" and "high speed" controls for rough or smooth surfaces. The Crossfire also sports two "Live-Wire" Sam-19 missiles, "Pumper" 20mm cannons, and real rubber inflatable tires. (If the tires deflated, new ones could be ordered from Hasbro.)

Easily lost pieces include two missiles, two guns, thin white tube, thin red tube (both tubes for antenna—these don't necessarily need to be present for the vehicle to be considered "complete") and remote control device.

NOTE: *The R/C Crossfire came in two versions, the Alpha model and the Delta model. These two variants operated on different frequencies so that children could race them against one another. Pictured in this book is the more common Alpha model.*

MISB: **$125**, MIB: **$75**, MLC: **$40**

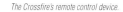

The Crossfire's remote control device.

ROAD TOAD B.R.V.
(Battlefield Recovery Vehicle)

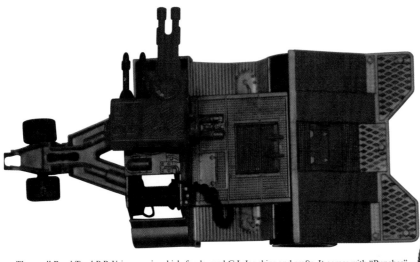

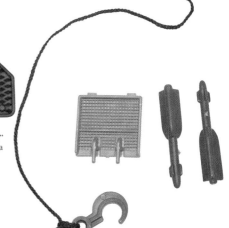

The small Road Toad B.R.V. is a repair vehicle for downed G.I. Joe ships and crafts. It comes with "Puncher" 25mm dual recoilless cannons, two "Buzz" SSM-94 wire-guided micro missiles, a powerful winch system, and a bed for towing vehicles.

Easily lost pieces include the hook and line, two missiles, and engine cover.

MISB: **$15**, MIB: **$8**, MLC: **$5**

The Road Toad's easily lost pieces.

SEA RAY
(Includes: Sea Slug figure)

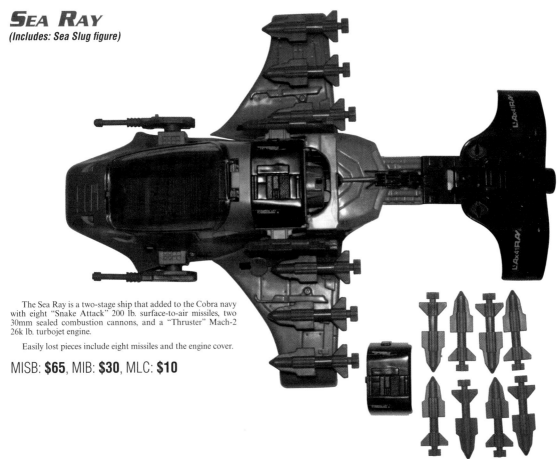

The Sea Ray is a two-stage ship that added to the Cobra navy with eight "Snake Attack" 200 lb. surface-to-air missiles, two 30mm sealed combustion cannons, and a "Thruster" Mach-2 26k lb. turbojet engine.

Easily lost pieces include eight missiles and the engine cover.

MISB: **$65**, MIB: **$30**, MLC: **$10**

The Sea Ray's easily lost pieces.

S.L.A.M.
(Strategic Long-Range Artillery Machine)

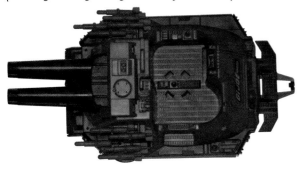

The S.L.A.M.'s missiles are quite tiny, and it is very rare to locate loose samples with all ten missiles. Its legs are hidden inside the weapon, and can be extended to stabilize it when firing. The vehicle can be towed via a tow hook.

Easily lost pieces are those ten small orange missiles.

MISB: **$15**, MIB: **$8**, MLC: **$5**

The S.L.A.M.'s easily lost pieces

[BF 2000] ELIMINATOR
(4WD)

The Eliminator's main vehicle and control unit.

The Eliminator 4WD vehicle was meant to be driven by Battle Force 2000 trooper Blocker (sold separately, 1987), and split apart into two vehicles/stations. The main body is a 4WD vehicle with missile rack in the rear, and the secondary vehicle is a control unit that could flip out four posts and become a manned laser cannon.

Easily lost pieces are the six missiles.

MISB: **$25**, MIB: **$15**, MLC: **$10**

The Eliminator's easily lost pieces.

The Eliminator.

BATTLE FORCE 2000

The following six vehicles combine to make the Battle Force 2000 "Future Fortress."

From the catalog, "Together, these 6 highly-advanced attack units form the most indestructible stronghold in the entire G.I. Joe arsenal... the BF 2000 Future Fortress!"

[BF 2000] DOMINATOR
(Snow Tank)

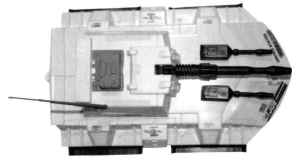

The Dominator Snow Tank was meant to be driven by Battle Force 2000 trooper Avalanche (sold separately, 1987), and split apart into two vehicles/stations. The main body is a wheeled vehicle, and the battle emplacement could flip its skis down while surrounding the main body.

Easily lost pieces are the antenna, cannon, two removable panels, and two small machine guns.

MISB: **$25**, MIB: **$15**, MLC: **$10**

The Dominator split into the main vehicle and battle emplacement.

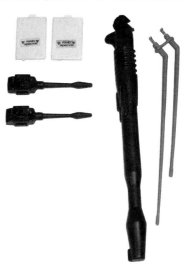

The Dominator's easily lost pieces.

[BF 2000] MARAUDER
(Motorcycle-Tank)

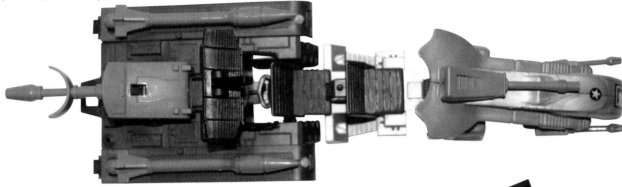

The Marauder Motor-cycle-Tank was meant to be driven by Battle Force 2000 trooper Dodger (sold separately, 1987), and split apart into two vehicles/stations. The first vehicle is a motorcycle with cannons and the second is a tank that added extra ground support.

Easily lost pieces include two missiles, radar dish, and a cannon.

MISB: **$25**,
MIB: **$15**,
MLC: **$10**

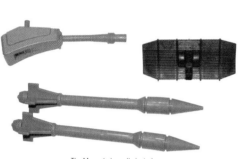

The Marauder's easily lost pieces.

The Marauder as two vehicles, the motorcycle and the tank.

[BF 2000] SKY SWEEPER
(Anti-Aircraft Tank)

The Sky Sweeper Anit-Aircaft Tank was meant to be driven by Knockdown (sold separately, 1987), and split apart into two vehicles/stations. Its main body is a fully armed battle tank and its secondary vehicle is an armored sentry post.

Easily lost pieces are four missiles and two gun attachments for the sentry post.

MISB: **$25**, MIB: **$15**, MLC: **$10**

The Sky Sweeper's easily lost pieces.

The Sky Sweeper.

The Sky Sweeper as main vehicle and sentry post.

[BF 2000] VECTOR
(Jet)

The Vector Jet as main ship and battle turret.

The Vector Jet was meant to be piloted by Maverick (sold separately, 1987), and split apart into two vehicles/stations. Its main body is a high tech jet fighter and its secondary vehicle is an armed battle turret.

Easily lost pieces include two removable panels and four missiles.

MISB: **$25**, MIB: **$15**, MLC: **$10**

The Vector Jet's easily lost pieces.

The Vector.

[BF 2000] VINDICATOR
(Hovercraft)

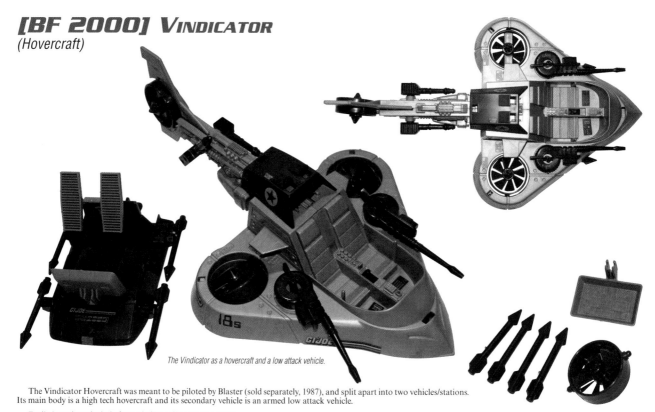

The Vindicator as a hovercraft and a low attack vehicle.

The Vindicator Hovercraft was meant to be piloted by Blaster (sold separately, 1987), and split apart into two vehicles/stations. Its main body is a high tech hovercraft and its secondary vehicle is an armed low attack vehicle.

Easily lost pieces include four missiles, tail rotor, and radar.

MISB: **$25**, MIB: **$15**, MLC: **$10**

THE BF 2000 FUTURE FORTRESS

An awkward assembly of the six Battle Force 2000 vehicles, this fortress is constructed of their secondary parts. The strange thing is that the pieces from the vehicles do not "snap" together, they merely rested next to one another with no interlocking pieces. This was perhaps my greatest disappointment in the entire Joe line as a kid—buying all these vehicles and drivers to form the fortress, and then it didn't even snap together.

MISB: **$25**, MIB: **$15**, MLC: **$10**

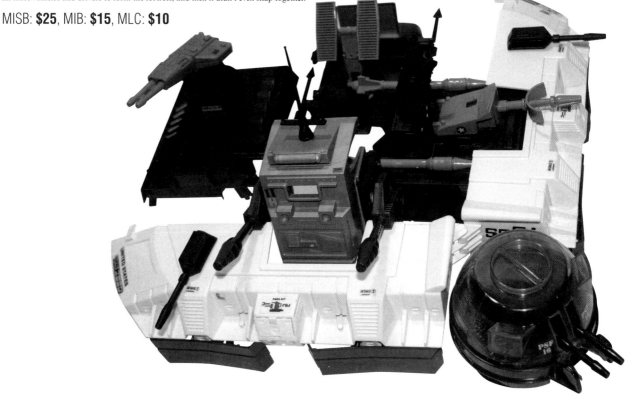

(SERIES VII, 1988)

Hasbro really branched out with its G.I. Joe line in 1988, as the theme for the year was to "re-cast" vehicles, figures, and accessories with different colors and varied paint schemes. Old figure sculpts and vehicle sculpts were done over in "Tiger Force" and the Toys 'R Us Exclusive Night Force themes. These toys did remarkably well in retail stores in 1988 and are currently highly desirable on the secondary market. Night Force pieces are especially expensive due to their exclusive nature, and the wonderful Tiger Force toys are popular because of their vibrant colors.

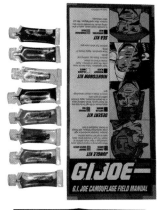

1988 G.I. Joe Camouflage insert sets, complete with Field Manual.

The Micro Figures and Micro Vehicles mail away complete sets.

The 1988 catalog.

Sgt. Slaughter 8" mail away.

The Micro Figures Poster Offer.

1988 G.I. JOE FIGURES

ARMADILLO
Rolling Thunder Driver
Included with the Rolling Thunder.

A very strange looking figure, Armadillo is a very common vehicle driver to find due to his lack of accessories and the fact that he doesn't look very much like a Joe. His character is reliable, and well-versed "in the latest land assault technologies and his experience as a vehicle driver is second to none!" (from the file card). He has little sense of humor, and is a dedicated soldier. His alternate prototype code names were Rumbler, Gila, and Sand-Turtle.

MLC: **$8**

BLIZZARD
Arctic Attack Soldier
(Includes: Helmet, Pistol, Backpack/Sled with Skis, Ice Shoes, Machine Gun)

Blizzard, the Joe's latest cold-weather trooper, has a fascinating array of weaponry. His backpack (with handle attachments—careful not to lose these) can combine with his skis to form a small attack sled, and the blue visor painted on his helmet is aesthetically pleasing. Apart from his impressive arsenal of weapons and accessories, Blizzard was one of the "hardest and meanest of the bunch" (from the file card), who, prior to joining the Joe team, led "an experimental security team" in frozen Arctic conditions. His prototype code names were Cold-Front and North Wind.

MOC: **$25**, MLC: **$15**

SERIES SEVEN

BUDO
Samurai Warrior
(Includes: Samurai Head Gear, Crimson Sword, Ornamental Sword, Sai, Pack)

In 1988, Budo was another martial artist who joined the Joe team, and has "a fifth-degree black belt in Iaido (the art of the live blade) and similar rank in three other martial arts" (from his file card). He is a fantastic swordsman, a hand-to-hand combat instructor, and loves heavy metal music and Harley-Davidson motorcycles. His character was labeled "Martial Artist" in his prototype dossier, and his alternate code-names were Katana, Daito, and Slasher.

MOC: **$25**, MLC: **$15**

CHARBROIL
Flamethrower
(Includes: Flamethrower, Flame-Retardant Hose, Pressurized Thermochemical Backpack, Thermo-Insulated Oxygenated Helmet)

Charbroil was released with two different eye colors (red and black), but neither of these variations seem to be more rare than the other. The Joe's second Flamethrower (see Blowtorch, 1984), Charbroil "was made to heat the water pipes in the family basement with a blowtorch… [and then] worked… in the Great Lakes, feeding coal into blast furnaces" (from the file card). When signing up for the Army, he chose Flame Weapons Specialist as his MOS. His prototype code names were Cinder, High-Flame, and Bunsen.

MOC: **$25**, MLC: **$15**

GHOSTRIDER
G.I. Joe X-19 Stealth Fighter Pilot
(Includes: Scarf)
Included with the Phantom X-19 Stealth Fighter.

In the Marvel comic, Ghostrider exemplified the following line from his file card, "…he's been working on not getting noticed since the second grade." Joes failed to remember his code name, forgot he was there, and passed by him with no notice whatsoever. This is a distinct advantage when flying a stealth aircraft against overwhelming odds. His list of alternate code names is quite long and includes Ghostwing, Blipless, No-Show, Silent Knight, Slinker, and Wraithwing.

MLC: **$15**

HARDBALL
Multi-Shot Grenadier
(Includes: Two-Piece Multi-Shot Grenade Launcher, Backpack)

Hardball played center field in AAA baseball until he recognized that, "big league scouts weren't interested in athletic prowess; they wanted star quality" (from the file card). He then opted to join the Joe team, because they needed "a guy who could judge distances accurately and react quickly with deliberation." His alternate code names on his prototype file card were Thumper, High-Pop, Line-Drive, and Lob-Shot.

MOC: **$25**, MLC: **$15**

HIT & RUN
Light Infantryman
(Includes: Colt 9mm Submachine Gun, Duffel Bag, Rope, Grappling Hook, Knife)

With his dark camouflage, fantastic accessories, and complicated back-story ("orphaned at the age of three by a drunken driver" [from the file card]), Hit & Run was a favorite figure from this assortment. As a character, he spent his entire life running, literally and metaphorically, but ultimately "went from the custody of the county, directly into the Army." Prototype code names for this character were Night Raid and Rope-Burn.

MOC: **$25**, MLC: **$15**

HIT & RUN TARGET EXCLUSIVE

Hit & Run was also released as a Target Exclusive with an Airborne Assault Parachute Pack. This HALO parachute and rigging are *exactly* the same as the mail away Parachute Pack mail-away (1985), except it did not come with the original Parachute Pack's gas mask. The blueprints for the Target Exclusive are much smaller in size, and *impossible* to obtain.

Hit & Run's Target Exclusive file card is orange in color, not the typical gray. The text for the Target Hit & Run with Airborne Assault Parachute Pack states, "Cobra is operating a sophisticated radar jamming station deep within the Rocky Mountains and it must be destroyed! General Hawk has ordered Hit & Run, his most experienced 'behind the lines' commando, to assault the radar station and blow it off the mountain! Wearing a camouflaged parachute pack and armed with enough explosives to ignite Manhattan Island, Hit & Run successfully parachutes to the base of the mountain. In an attempt to send Cobra's whole operation sky high, Hit & Run places high explosive mines around the station and the transmitter tower. While setting the charges to detonate in two minutes, two Vipers spot Hit & Run evacuating the area. With the cliffs only ten yards ahead, Hit & Run pulls the ripcord on his parachute pack! The Vipers are closing in fast, with only seconds remaining before the whole mountain blows up! Will Hit & Run parachute over the cliffs and parachute to safety? Or, will he be captured by the Vipers and go 'up in smoke' when the mines explode?"

NOTE: *Both the figure and parachute pack are common items, so the real value of the Hit & Run Target Exclusive is as a carded sample.*

NOTE: *Came w/same weapons as reg Hit 'n Run but w/parachute pack (1985).*

MOC: **$350**, MLC: **$25-30**

LIGHTFOOT
Explosives Expert
(Includes: Nightvision Helmet, Mine Detector Unit, Hose, Robot, Backpack)

Lightfoot was the new explosives expert for the Joe team in 1988. He has memorized many military manuals full of relevant datum to aid his MOS, and has "elevated being careful to an art form" (from the file card). He is meticulous, persistent, and acts as a demolitions expert as well as artillery coordinator. His prototype code names were Hotfoot, Nitro, and Chain-Fire.

MOC: **$25**, MLC: **$15**

MUSKRAT
Swamp Fighter
(Includes: Super 90 Shotgun, Swamp Skimmer, Machete)

As a child Muskrat spent most of his time "up to his knees in one swamp or another" (from his file card). As a result of this, "Ranger School and JWTC [Jungle Warfare Training Center] seemed like summer camp to him." The figure's accessories are interesting, especially noting his "boogie board" (swamp skimmer). His prototype code names included Swamp-Runner, Bayou, Wet Willy, Swamp Dawg, Gumbo, and Bad-Bayou.

MOC: **$25**, MLC: **$15**

MUSKRAT
Swamp Fighter
(Ultimate Enemies Target Exclusive)

"Ultimate Enemies" card front.

Voltar was also released as a Target exclusive two pack with Muskrat called "Ultimate Enemies," with the exact same weapons, but an orange file card. From the card text, "Tempers explode whenever these two 'Ultimate Enemies' clash on the battlefield! Each fearless soldier is ready to do whatever is necessary to defeat each other and achieve total victory!"

NOTE: *Both figures are common finds and the value for this Target exclusive is as a carded sample.*

MOC: **$375**, MLC: **$25-30**

REPEATER
Steadi-Cam Machine Gunner
(Includes: Machine Gun, Body Mount, Backpack)

Repeater has been in the Army more than twenty years and he never got past the grade of E-6 (Staff Sergeant). He was a fantastic soldier, but living quarters at a military post was too much for him. He is strong, tough, and dependable in the field. His prototype code names were Mower (until right before production), Graze-Fire, and Reaper-Man.

MOC: **$25**, MLC: **$15**

SGT. SLAUGHTER
Drill Instructor
(Includes: Hat)
Included with the Warthog A.I.F.V.

For a full bio, see Sgt. Slaughter (1985).

MLC: **$12**

SHOCKWAVE
S.W.A.T. Specialist
(Includes: Machine Gun, Pistol, Knife, Backpack)

Shockwave acted as the Joe's first S.W.A.T. (Special Weapons and Tactics) specialist, and his realistic design—clad in blue and urban camouflage—made him a popular Joe in this series. He was a former decorated member of the Detroit Police Department, and likes to be the soldier who is the first Joe in the door, "Shockwave is the door kicker. He's the first inside and the first to see how bad it really is." He is currently on the Joe's roster.

MOC: **$25**, MLC: **$15**

SKIDMARK
Desert Fox 6W.D. Driver
Included with the Desert Fox 6 W.D.

As a child, Skidmark was, "Annoyingly polite, maddeningly well groomed, and excruciatingly successful in his studies" (from the file card). Yet after receiving his first driver's license, he "subsequently shattered all-known records for the accumulation of speeding violations," and this led to his appointment to the Joe team. Unfortunately, this reliable reconnaissance driver perished while on a mission assaulting Cobra Island.

MLC: **$8**

SPEARHEAD & MAX
Point Man & Bobcat
(Includes: Bobcat, Rifle, Knife, Helmet, Backpack)

Spearhead, once a young and successful insurance salesman, felt the calling and one day joined the Army where he felt his winning personality would do the most good. A highly trusted soldier, this point man and his bobcat, Max, are currently on the Joe's roster. His prototype code names were Frontline and First-Wave.

MOC: **$25**, MLC: **$15**

SUPER TROOPER
(Includes: Helmet, Shield, M-17 Machine Gun)
Mail Away Exclusive

Paul Latimer, a.k.a. Super Trooper, "graduated at the top of his class… through a new Army school that's so secret it doesn't have a name" (from the file card). He is also a West Point graduate, is fluent in at least three languages, and "a recipient of the expert infantryman's badge." It is suggested that he joined the Joes "simply seeking adventure." His prototype code name was Hard Corps. (Inclue

MLC: **$10**

WILDCARD
G.I. Joe Mean Dog Driver
(Includes: Helmet, Machete, Backpack)

With an uncanny and "unnatural talent for breaking things" (from the file card), Wildcard put this aptitude to the test in the U.S. Army where it is considered more of a skill than a liability. His vehicle, the Mean Dog, acts "as an extension of himself… pulverizing all in its path." His current status is unknown.

MLC: **$10**

WINDMILL
Skystorm X-Wing Chopper Pilot
(Includes: Revolver)
Included with the Skystorm X-Wing/Cross Wing Chopper.

Windmill, pilot of the new and experimental Cross Wing Chopper, was a former flight instructor at the Army Flight Warrant Officers School in Fort Rucker who later engaged in piloting top-secret prototype helicopters before joining the Joes. "The X-Wing Chopper clocks at 345mph in its stopped-rotor mode and can carry a bigger payload than a Dragonfly" (from the file card). He is on their current roster. His prototype code names were X-Terminator, Cyclone, Xyclone, Cool-Breeze, and Chill.

MLC: **$8**

(NIGHT FORCE) CRAZYLEGS
Assault Trooper
(Includes: EM-4 Assault Rifle w/Stock, Parachute Backpack)

Packaged together with Night Force Outback. For a full bio on the character, see Crazylegs, (1987).

MOC: *(w/Night Force Outback)* **$80-100**, MLC: **$30-35**

(NIGHT FORCE) LT. FALCON
Green Beret
(Includes: Special Forces Field Communications Pack w/Antenna, 12-Gauge Pump Shotgun, Bowie Survival Knife)

Packaged together with Night Force Sneak Peek. For a full bio on the character, see Falcon, (1987).

NOTE: *The character's code name has been changed from "Falcon" to "Lt. Falcon."*

MOC: *(w/Night Force Sneak Peek)* **$80-100**,
MLC: **$30-35**

(NIGHT FORCE) OUTBACK
Survivalist
(Includes: Heckler and Koch G3 Rifle, Web Belt, Flashlight, Survival Backpack)

Packaged together with Night Force Crazylegs. For a full bio on the character, see Outback, (1987).

MOC: *(w/Night Force Crazylegs)* **$80-100**, MLC: **$30-35**

(NIGHT FORCE) PSYCHE-OUT
Deceptive Warfare
(Includes: Variable Wave Field Projector with ELF Sonic Generator, Two "Big Ear" Sonic Receivers, .45 Assault Pistol, Backpack)

Packaged together with Night Force Tunnel Rat. For a full bio on the character, see Psyche-Out, (1987).

MOC: *(w/Night Force Tunnel Rat)* **$80-100**, MLC: **$30-35**

(NIGHT FORCE) SNEAK PEEK
Advanced Recon
(Includes: Walkie Talkie, Binoculars, M-16A Rifle, Variable Range Optical Field Scanning Device, Multiband Radio Transponder Unit)

Packaged together with Night Force Lt. Falcon. For a full bio on the character, see Sneak Peek, (1987).

MOC: *(w/Night Force Lt. Falcon)* **$80-100**, MLC: **$30-35**

(NIGHT FORCE) TUNNEL RAT
EOD
(Includes: Satchel, Air-Cooled 7.62mm Machine Gun with Infrared Scope, Tunnel Floodlight System with Two Detachable Halogen Hand Lamps)

Packaged together with Night Force Psyche-Out. For a full bio on the character, see Tunnel Rat, (1987).

MOC: *(w/Night Force Psyche-Out)* **$80-100**, MLC: **$30-35**

(TIGER FORCE) BAZOOKA
Tiger Force Missile Specialist
(Includes: Helmet, M.A.T. Missile Launcher, Missile Pack)

For a full bio, see Bazooka, (1985).

MOC: **$25-35**, MLC: **$10**

(TIGER FORCE) DUKE
Tiger Force First Sergeant Squad Leader
(Includes: Binoculars, Helmet, Assault Pack, M-3 Submachine Gun)

For a full bio, see Duke, (1983).

MOC: **$30-40**, MLC: **$10**

(TIGER FORCE) DUSTY
Tiger Force Desert Trooper
(Includes: FAMAS w/Bipod, Backpack)

For a full bio, see Dusty, (1985).

MOC: **$25-35**, MLC: **$10**

(TIGER FORCE) FLINT
Tiger Force Warrant Officer Special Forces
(Includes: Short Barrel Shotgun, Backpack)

For a full bio, see Flint, (1985).

MOC: **$25-35**, MLC: **$10**

(TIGER FORCE) FROSTBITE
Tiger Cat Driver
(Includes: Rifle)
Included with the Tiger Cat.

For a full bio, see Frostbite, (1985).

MLC: **$12**

(TIGER FORCE) LIFELINE
Tiger Force Medic
(Includes: EMS Kit w/Oxygen Mask, Browning Double-Action Relay Pistol, Relay Backpack)

For a full bio, see Lifeline, (1986).

MOC: **$25-35**, MLC: **$10**

(TIGER FORCE) RECONDO
Tiger Fly Pilot
(Includes: Cross Country Backpack, M-1 4E2X Rifle)
Included with the Tiger Fly.

Recondo has moved from the stygian quagmires of the jungles to the freedom of air recon. It suggests in his file card that he'd been "flying prop jets and helicopters since he was 17 years old"—new information that seemed a bit out of character for a former infantryman. Since his last incarnation, he attended Flight School and joined the Tiger Force team. For a full bio, see Recondo, (1984).

MLC: **$12**

(TIGER FORCE) ROADBLOCK
Tiger Force Heavy Machine Gunner
(Includes: Backpack, M-2X Machine Gun w/Tripod, Ammo Box, Helmet)

For a full bio, see Roadblock, (1984).

MOC: **$25-35**, MLC: **$10**

(TIGER FORCE) SKYSTRIKER
Tiger Rat Pilot
(Includes: Helmet, Visor, Radio Headset)
Included with the Tiger Rat.

The Tiger Rat pilot, code named Skystriker (no relation to the Skystriker Combat Jet [1983]), grew up enthralled with fighter jets. Because of this obsession, he joined the Air Force and the ranks of the Joes, flying the Conquest X-30 during attacks on Cobra Island. Because of his "fearless attitude in the face of danger," he was assigned to the Tiger Force team.

MLC: **$15-25**

(TIGER FORCE) TRIPWIRE
Tiger Force Mine Detector
(Includes: Mine Sweeper, Three Landmines, Mine Detector Backpack)

For a full bio, see Tripwire, (1983).

MOC: **$25-35**, MLC: **$10**

1988 COBRA FIGURES

ASTRO-VIPER
Cobranaut
(Includes: Jet Pack, Two Guns, Two Hoses, Two Control Arms, Helmet)

The Cobra Astro-Vipers are used to repair Cobra satellites on-site, and are "capable of withstanding repeated high-G [gravity] launchings and enduring long terms in orbit" (from the file card). They are former Night Raven Pilots (see Strato-Viper, 1986) who are "conditioned" for outer space maneuvers. His prototype code names were Cosmo-Viper and Star-Viper.

MOC: **$25-35**, MLC: **$10**

DESTRO
(Includes: Ceremonial Sword)
Included with Destro's Despoiler.

This version of Destro, clad in a gold battle mask with cape and ceremonial sword, showcases him as the leader of the new Iron Grenadiers (his organization of handpicked personal bodyguards, see 1988) and highlights his growing interest in unstable countries ripe for weapons sales. Destro and his Iron Grenadiers became fan favorites, and the Marvel comic intricately explored James McCullen Destro's Scottish background. For a full bio, see Destro (1983).

MLC: **$10**

FERRET
Iron Grenadier D.E.M.O.N. Drivers
Included with the D.E.M.O.N.

Ferrets, members of Destro's Iron Grenadiers (1988) organization, are "backbones of … [the] armored assault squadrons" (from the file card). They are exceedingly positive soldiers, whose motto should be, "Don't look back!" If they and their D.E.M.O.N.s are attacked from behind, the troopers and vehicles are left vulnerable to enemy fire.

MLC: **$8**

HYDRO-VIPERS (DEMON OF THE DEEP)
Cobra Underwater Elite Trooper
(Includes: Regulator helmet, Dagger, Harpoon Gun, Scuba Pack, Fathom Fins, Devil Ray, Two Hoses)

The left hand on the figure does not hold a weapon, as its molded fingers are fully extended to show the webbing between them—an unusual feature for a Joe figure. A fascinating figure, the Hydro-Vipers (Demons of the Deep) are Cobra's new breed of underwater soldiers who "volunteer to be surgically altered to withstand nitrogen narcosis and other side effects of deep diving" (from the file card). They have synthetic webs placed between their fingers, and have been grafted with extra fat for added insulation. This process has been described as "psychologically destabilizing," but makes them formidable opponents in the open seas. These characters were initially dubbed, "Deep Demons" on the prototype dossier.

MOC: **$25-35**, MLC: **$10**

IRON GRENADIERS
Destro's Elite Troopers
(Includes: Machine Gun, Sword, Pistol)

The Iron Grenadiers [a grenadier is a soldier who is a member of a special corps or regiment] are Destro's (1988) new elite troopers who act as "agents, provocateurs, saboteurs, or… terrorists, [who] impel an unsuspecting country toward chaos and turmoil" and carefully craft new markets for Destro's (see 1982) M.A.R.S. armaments organization. They are a popular army builder figure with most collectors. These characters were first called, "The Nameless Legion, Stainless Steel Brigade, and The Hard Corps" on the prototype dossier.

MOC: **$25-35**, MLC: **$10**

NULLIFIER
Iron Grenadiers A.G.P. Pilot
(Includes: Visor)
Included with the A.G.P.

The Nullifier action figure is the downright strangest of all Joes (with the exception of the Lunartix Empire Star Brigade figures, see 1994). He looks like he just stepped out of a time machine from ancient Egypt, as there are hieroglyphs adorning his uniform. The Nullifier functions as a durable high-endurance pilot of the sophisticated Iron Grenadiers A.G.P., a vehicle that can turn most drivers to mush, except for the temperamental and physically formidable Nullifier. Their prototype MOS was "Destro's Destroyers."

MLC: **$7**

ROAD PIG
Dreadnok
(Includes: Spiked Battle Shield, Cinderblock Hammer, High-Powered Crossbow, High-Intensity Impact Pads)

Named after Donald Deluca, a former Hasbro designer, Road Pig has become one of the more popular of Zartan's (1984) Dreadnoks, and one of the most reprehensible. Ugly, cruel, dishonorable, and even a bit stinky, Road Pig's uniform (replete with "anarchy" tattoo) and accessories speak to his outlandish yet thick as a cinder block character. In the Marvel comic, Road Pig was suffering from a multiple-personality disorder, switching between the thuggish and abrasive Road Pig and sweet and considerate Donald DeLuca (his file name).

MOC: **$25-35**, MLC: **$10**

SECTO-VIPER
Cobra BUGG Driver
(Includes: Clear Helmet, Laser Pistol)
Included with the Cobra BUGG.

The Cobra Secto-Vipers patrol the coastline of Cobra Island, and are "unique specialists in amphibious operations and marine surveillance" (from the file card). They are careful and meticulous soldiers, with an intimate knowledge of their specific plot of Cobra shore. They are difficult figures to find complete, as their clear helmet is often missing.

MLC: **$12**

STAR-VIPER
Cobra Stellar Stiletto Pilot
Included with the Cobra Stellar Stiletto.

The Cobra Star-Viper was once a Strato-Viper (1986) who had an "electro-magnetic shunt [low-resistance connection] surgically implanted in the right side of his brain" (from the file card) in order to increase his reflexes and response time as a pilot. This electromagnetic shunt adversely affects these soldiers in their off-duty hours, however...

MLC: **$8**

STORM SHADOW
Ninja
(Includes: Sword, Claw, Bow, Backpack)

NOTE: *I list Storm Shadow in the Cobra section, because that is where most collectors will look for him, not knowing at this point in the Marvel comic in 1988, that he defected to the Joes.*

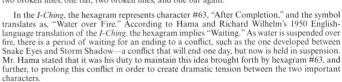

Besides the ultra cool and appropriate weapons included with this figure, a comment must be made about his *I-Ching* tattoo/hexagram—a symbol of his Arashikage ninja clan (see Storm Shadow, 1984 for further info). The Chinese *I-Ching* characters have been a method of divination (prediction; an augury) for more than 3,000 years. The tattoo, prominently displayed on the figure's right wrist, is a topic of debate for many die-hard Joe fans.

After sitting down with Larry Hama, the man who placed the tattoo on Storm Shadow and Snake Eyes' (see 1982) wrists, and discussing the symbol, a grand scheme unfolded (see Marvel Comics *G.I. Joe Issue #21*). The tattooed hexagram was originally chosen by creating contributor Hama because of its symmetry, "Heck, it was easy to remember and to draw ... if I had to draw something repeatedly, then it better be something memorable—two broken lines, one bar, two broken lines, and one bar again."

In the *I-Ching*, the hexagram represents character #63, "After Completion," and the symbol translates as, "Water over Fire." According to Hama and Richard Wilhelm's 1950 English-language translation of the *I-Ching,* the hexagram implies "Waiting." As water is suspended over fire, there is a period of waiting for an ending to a conflict, such as the one developed between Snake Eyes and Storm Shadow—a conflict that will end one day, but now is held in suspension. Mr. Hama stated that it was his duty to maintain this idea brought forth by hexagram #63, and further, to prolong this conflict in order to create dramatic tension between the two important characters.

MOC: **$35-50**, MLC: **$15-20**

TOXO-VIPER
Cobra Hostile Environment Trooper
(Includes: Pistol, Environmental Helmet, Backpack, Air Hose)

If you are "busted down" to the rank of a Toxo-Viper in the Cobra organization, you must have done something bad. The task of serving as a Toxo-Viper is "meted out as a punishment for major offenses," as these troops wear suits that are only "moderately air tight and resistant to most solvents." Therefore, being a member of the "leaky suit brigade" is an occupation few desire to pursue. Originally dubbed "Stinkbugs" on their prototype file cards, some other alternate code names were Heavy-Breathers and Gas-Vipers.

MOC: **$25-35**, MLC: **$10**

VOLTAR
Destro's General
(Includes: Condor, High Freq. Comm. Pack, Modified Uzi Submachine Gun)

Voltar, the "peg-warmer" [a collector's term for a slow selling action figure that sits on the toy pegs] of this series of Joes, has an interesting file card, but the design of the figure was perhaps a bit too fantastic. Clad in a striking scarlet and gold combination, the general of Destro's Iron Grenadiers (1988) was hired by the Scottish lord because of three attributes, he was skillful, lucky, and a winner. His figure is quite commonly found carded or loose. Voltar was also released as a Target Exclusive two pack with Muskrat called "Ultimate Enemies," with the exact same weapons, but a differently colored file card—it was orange. From the card text, "Tempers explode whenever these two 'Ultimate Enemies' clash on the battlefield! Each fearless soldier is ready to do whatever is necessary to defeat each other and achieve total victory!" (see Muskrat, 1988). This character was called Kondor until just before production began, and some other prototype names included Graf Kondor, Lord Kondor, Madagascar, and Field Marshall Null.

MOC: **$15-20**, MLC: **$7**

1988 VEHICLES/PLAYSETS

ACCESSORY PACK #6: BATTLE GEAR
Includes:
1 blue Chain Axe (Buzzer)
1 brown Rifle (Buzzer)
1 brown Stunrod (Dr. Mindbender)
1 silver Generator (Dr. Mindbender)
1 silver Pistol (Dr. Mindbender)
1 brown Gun (Monkeywrench)
1 brown Rifle (Zandar)
1 brown Missile (Snow Serpent)
1 brown Missile Pod (Snow Serpent)
2 blue Snow Shoes (Snow Serpent)
1 blue Backpack (Snow Serpent)
1 blue Backpack (Tele-Viper)
1 brown Gun (Tele-Viper)
2 Hoses (assorted users)
1 blue 2-part Backpack (Eels)
1 blue Speargun (Eels)
1 blue Respirator (Eels)
2 blue Flippers (Eels)
1 silver Backpack (Zarana)
1 silver Rifle (Zarana)
1 silver Pistol (Cobra Commander)
2 black Hoses
2 brown Figure Stands

MOMC: **$15**, MOC: **$10**, MLC: **$5**

A.G.P.
(Anti-Gravity Pod)
(Includes: Nullifier figure)

The A.G.P., with 106mm recoilless cannons, pivoting "Anti Grav" VTOL (Vertical Take Off and Landing) ability, and six "STUNG" (Silent Running Titanium Under-Radar Negative Gravity) missiles, is the first ship launched for Destro's new Iron Grenadiers (1988).

Easily lost pieces are the four missiles.

MISB: **$35**, MIB: **$25**, MLC: **$12-15**

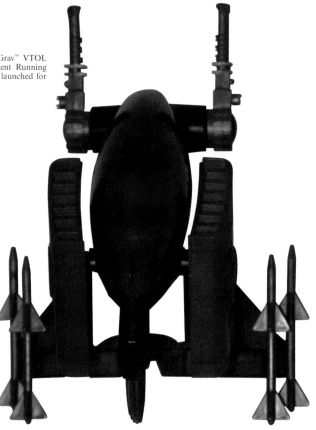

The A.G.P.'s easily lost pieces.

COBRA ADDER

The Cobra Adder functioned as a missile-carrying vehicle for the Cobra Legions. It sports two huge White Heat II SSM (surface-to-surface) missiles that can be set to firing positions to add needed ordnance to the Cobra ground forces.

Easily lost pieces are the two large missiles.

MISB: **$15**, MIB: **$8**, MLC: **$5**

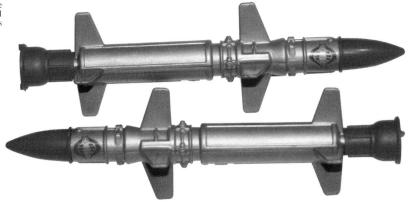

The Adder's easily lost pieces.

COBRA BATTLE BARGE

The Cobra Battle Barge comes in two variations: one with clear labels (retail) and one with white labels (mail-away). It is a funny-looking addition to the Cobra Legions, as it rests quietly in the water but carries a mass of three machine guns, and has an added magnetic array detection radar.

Easily lost pieces include the three machine guns and radar.

MISB: **$15**, MIB: **$8**, MLC: **$5**

The Battle Barge's easily lost pieces.

COBRA IMP

The Cobra IMP carries a heavy payload of three Infrared Imaging Programmable (IMP) missiles that deliver eight removable mines upon impact. Each missile contains eight mines secured around the connecting part of the "two stage" bombs.

Easily lost pieces include the three two-part missiles, and 24 mines (eight mines per missile).

MISB: **$15**, MIB: **$8**, MLC: **$5**

The IMP's easily lost pieces.

COBRA BUGG

(Includes: Secto-Viper)

The Cobra BUGG is a fascinating vehicle, and one of my favorite Cobra toys. A bevy of action features add to its play value, including pressurized doors and canopies, surface-to-air side mounted missiles, "Strike" VT-60 Flow-Through design alcohol powered torpedoes, and even .50-caliber machine guns mounted on its bottom hull. Besides two deploying jet skis (absolutely awesome) with missiles, the driver's pod is detachable and even has a moving rudder. A wonderful vehicle that still can be found (oddly enough) MISB for under $120!

Easily lost pieces include two jet skis with fold-up handles for portability (sporting two removable missiles each), turret, four missiles, and two torpedoes.

MISB: **$100**, MIB: **$55**, MLC: **$35**

An opened side panel showcasing one of the two portable jet skis.

Opened rear door for troop transport.

The BUGG's easily lost pieces.

COBRA STELLAR STILETTO

(Includes: Star-Viper figure)

The Cobra Stellar Stiletto was piloted by the arrogant Star-Viper (from the Marvel comic), and the craft is capable of exit and re-entry into Earth's atmosphere because of its reinforced carbon-carbon heat resistant nose cone, alum-glass heat resistant canopy, and liquid fuel dual "Stellar" main propulsion engines. Its tail can be maneuvered so that the Stiletto can achieve the semblance of a VTOL (Vertical Take Off and Landing) launch.

Easily lost pieces include the cannon, four missiles, and tail piece.

MISB: **$40**, MIB: **$20**, MLC: **$12**

The Stellar Stiletto's easily lost pieces.

D.E.M.O.N.

(Dual Elevating Multi-Ordnance Neutralizer)
(Includes: Ferret figure)

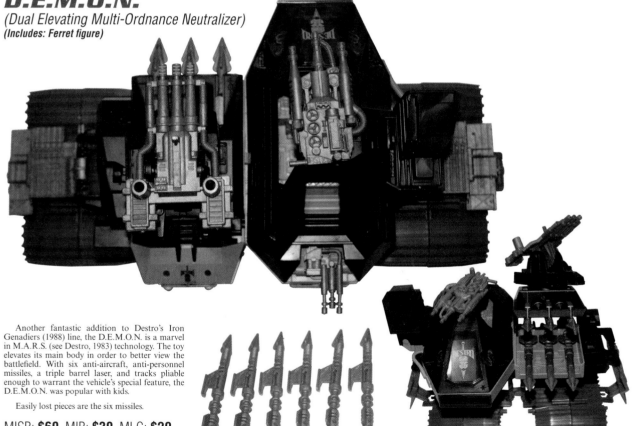

Another fantastic addition to Destro's Iron Genadiers (1988) line, the D.E.M.O.N. is a marvel in M.A.R.S. (see Destro, 1983) technology. The toy elevates its main body in order to better view the battlefield. With six anti-aircraft, anti-personnel missiles, a triple barrel laser, and tracks pliable enough to warrant the vehicle's special feature, the D.E.M.O.N. was popular with kids.

Easily lost pieces are the six missiles.

MISB: **$60**, MIB: **$30**, MLC: **$20**

The D.E.M.O.N.'s easily lost pieces.

D.E.M.O.N. in attack mode.

DESERT FOX 6W.D.
(Includes: Skidmark figure)

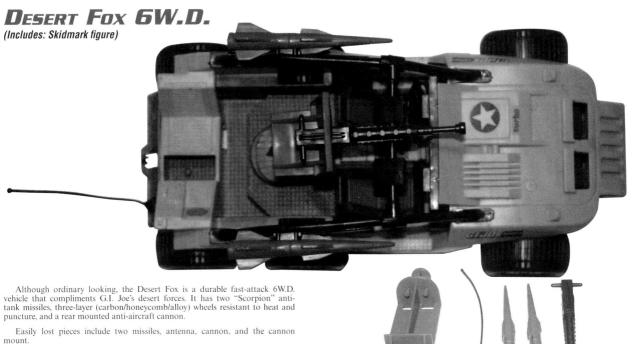

Although ordinary looking, the Desert Fox is a durable fast-attack 6W.D. vehicle that compliments G.I. Joe's desert forces. It has two "Scorpion" anti-tank missiles, three-layer (carbon/honeycomb/alloy) wheels resistant to heat and puncture, and a rear mounted anti-aircraft cannon.

Easily lost pieces include two missiles, antenna, cannon, and the cannon mount.

MISB: **$50**, MIB: **$25**, MLC: **$10**

The Desert Fox's easily lost pieces.

DESTRO'S DESPOILER
(Includes: Destro figure)

Destro's Despoiler was the aircraft manned by Destro (1983, 1988) himself to survey the progress of his Iron Grenadiers (1988) on the battleground.

Easily lost pieces include two missiles and front-mounted 20mm repeating cannons.

MISB: **$30**, MIB: **$20**, MLC: **$12**

The Despoiler's easily lost pieces.

MEAN DOG
(Includes: Wildcard figure)

The Mean Dog is a fun vehicle and toy, and is surprisingly popular with collectors and casual fans alike. Like the Cobra Maggot (1987) it is a three-part vehicle consisting of the main body, cannon, and fast attack scout car. Its main feature is a removable cannon—a M200 "Spitfire" 20mm automatic cannon that fires 2000 rounds per minute. A fast-attack vehicle with a pivoting .50-caliber machine gun, and a main body vehicle with tow hook and thick armor plating complement the cannon.

Easily lost pieces include two missile launchers, ten missiles, cannon tip (nearly impossible to find on loose samples), cannon ring, and four cannon stands that mount on the cannon ring for sturdiness when it is used as its own battle station.

The Mean Dog's easily lost pieces.

MISB: **$70**, MIB: **$35**, MLC: **$20**

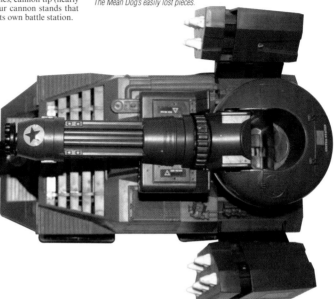

===

MOTORIZED ACTION PACKS

The Motorized Action Packs are the second generation (see 1987) of these wind-up toys, and are fairly easy to locate, though a few more difficult acquisitions are noted.

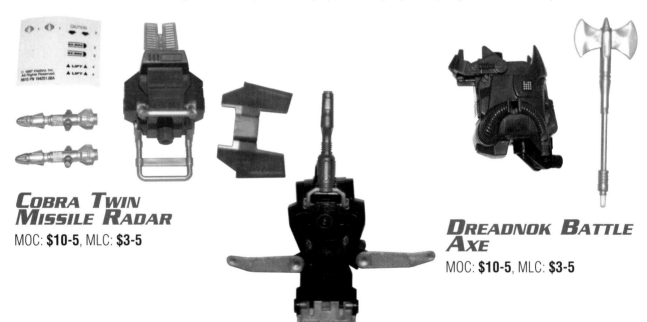

COBRA TWIN MISSILE RADAR
MOC: **$10-5**, MLC: **$3-5**

COBRA MACHINE GUN NEST
MOC: **$10-5**, MLC: **$3-5**

DREADNOK BATTLE AXE
MOC: **$10-5**, MLC: **$3-5**

G.I. Joe Double Machine Gun
MOC: **$10-5**, MLC: **$3-5**

G.I. Joe Mine Sweeper
MOC: **$10-5**, MLC: **$3-5**

G.I. Joe Mortar Launcher
(hard-to-find)
MOC: **$10-5**, MLC: **$3-5**

Motorized Vehicle Packs

Cobra Gyrocopter
MOC: **$10-5**, MLC: **$3-5**

Cobra Rocket Sled
MOC: **$10-5**, MLC: **$3-5**

G.I. Joe A.T.V.
(hard-to-find)
MOC: **$10-5**, MLC: **$3-5**

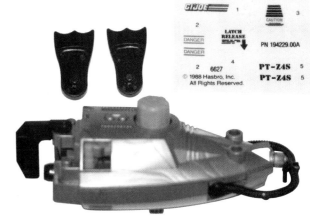

G.I. Joe Tank Car
(hard-to-find)
MOC: **$10-5**, MLC: **$3-5**

G.I. Joe Scuba Pack
The most difficult vehicle pack to acquire, perhaps because the flippers are usually missing.
MOC: **$10-5**, MLC: **$3-5**

PHANTOM X-19 STEALTH FIGHTER
(Includes: Ghostrider figure)

The Phantom X-19 is a beautiful craft that has a few fragile pieces that can be quite frustrating to pose and play with because of their delicate nature. (The mechanism of the flip-out guns on the wings is delicate to say the least, and I must have assembled the darned thing ten times whenever playing with it). The cockpit assembly is also tricky and must be opened and closed gently, so as not to take the canopy off of its guide rails. Apart from these minor gripes, the ship itself is of a marvelous design, replete with two "Bullseye II" computer-aided low-altitude terrain hugging missiles, retractable landing gear, two opening wings with flip out laser cannons, and twin BY-106 "Little Guy" long range air-to-air missiles.

Easily lost pieces include two seat belts, two "hugging" missiles with skids, two smaller missiles, and two lasers.

MISB: **$100**, MIB: **$65**, MLC: **$30-40**

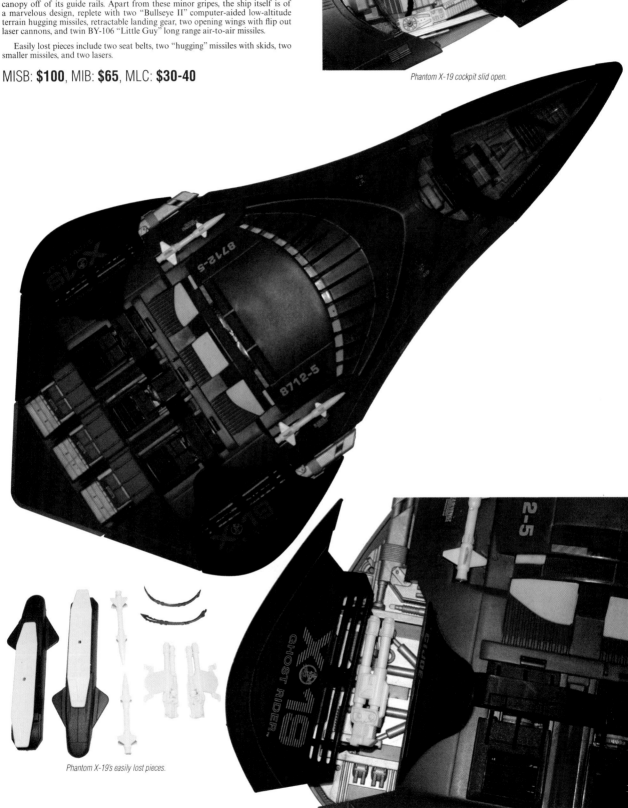

Phantom X-19 cockpit slid open.

Phantom X-19's easily lost pieces.

Phantom X-19 gun mount open.

ROLLING THUNDER
(Includes: Armadillo figure)

The Rolling Thunder impressed me as a child because it seemed to have a single purpose—deliver the payload of two huge (the largest in the entire Joe universe) missiles with "Double Team" solid propellant quad thruster rockets with six roll out "Firefly" free fall cluster bombs a piece. These missiles were cleverly hidden in the housing of the Rolling Thunder itself, and could be set into launch position, or retraced into the shell of the vehicle when transporting these monsters. With a six-wheel ATSV (all terrain scout vehicle), tons of missiles, many laser cannons, and a turret-mounted short barrel 90mm "Short Throw" main battle cannon, this vehicle had a ton of firepower.

Easily lost pieces include four seats (with four seat belts and attached support cannons), ATSV, two-part missile launcher base, three large orange missiles, six small orange missiles, six long yellow missiles, two antennas, two large white missiles with two clear shields, and six tiny yellow cluster bombs each.

MISB: **$75-100**, MIB: **$60**, MLC: **$45**

Rolling Thunder w/missile silos up.

The Rolling Thunder's easily lost pieces.

Rolling Thunder side view of weaponry.

R.P.V.
(Remote Piloted Vehicle)

The R.P.V. should be used as a remote vehicle, although the box painting shows Hardball (1988) in the driver's seat. With a sophisticated missile, a remote "Little Brother" radar station with cord, and a hydraulically operated missile rack elevation drive unit, this was a basic and functional toy.

Easily lost pieces include the seat belt, hose, radar with dish, and propulsion unit for missile.

MISB: **$20**, MIB: **$12**, MLC: **$7**

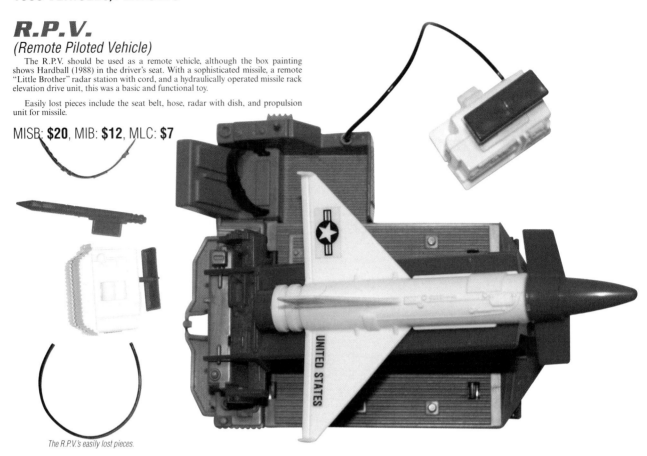

The R.P.V.'s easily lost pieces.

SKYSTORM X-WING/CROSS WING CHOPPER
(Includes: Windmill figure)

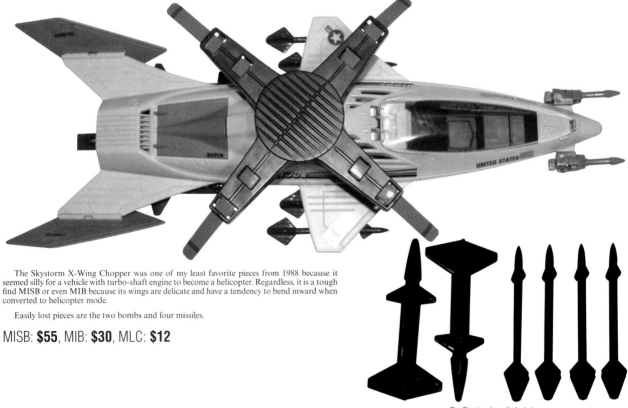

The Skystorm X-Wing Chopper was one of my least favorite pieces from 1988 because it seemed silly for a vehicle with turbo-shaft engine to become a helicopter. Regardless, it is a tough find MISB or even MIB because its wings are delicate and have a tendency to bend inward when converted to helicopter mode.

Easily lost pieces are the two bombs and four missiles.

MISB: **$55**, MIB: **$30**, MLC: **$12**

The Skystorm's easily lost pieces.

SWAMPMASHER

The Swampmasher, dolled up in bright green and purple, is bemoaned by some collectors as one of the first "neon" vehicles in the Joe line—heralding a future based on the neon premise. With a 4.3 liter 350 hp engine, strange tri-wheeled tracks, and magnetic array detector bombs, the swamp vehicle could navigate rough terrain.

Easily lost pieces are the cannon and two bombs.

MISB: **$20**, MIB: **$12**, MLC: **$6**

WARTHOG A.I.F.V.
(Amphibious Infantry Fighting Vehicle)
(Includes: Sgt. Slaughter figure)

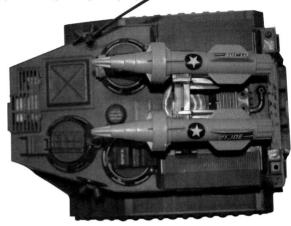

The oddly decorated Warthog was popular with kids, and Hasbro sold quite a few units of the tracked vehicle. It featured two large yellow MGM-59 "Lance" surface-to-surface dual thrust liquid propellant missiles (with flight stabilizing rings), an interior bay to hold extra troops, and a welded aluminum specially-hardened armored hull. These features, and the inclusion of the ever-popular Sgt. Slaughter, made the Warthog a durable and fun vehicle for kids and collectors alike.

Easily lost pieces are the two missiles.

MISB: **$70**,
MIB: **$35-40**,
MLC: **$15**

The Warthog's easily lost pieces.

NIGHT FORCE

Together, these 5 vehicles carry out top secret, nighttime missions aimed at eliminating Cobra's worldwide terrorist activity! Night Force vehicles are extremely rare and great care should be taken with MISB and MIB samples. Even loose samples of the larger, harder-to-complete vehicles sell for quite a bit of money, as casual fans and collectors alike understand that these pieces are hard to find. None of these vehicles included a driver.

(NIGHT FORCE) NIGHT BLASTER

The Night Blaster is based on the design of the 1987 Cobra Maggot and shares similar easily lost pieces.

MISB: **$150**, MIB: **$75**, MLC: **$45**

Three stations for the Night Blaster.

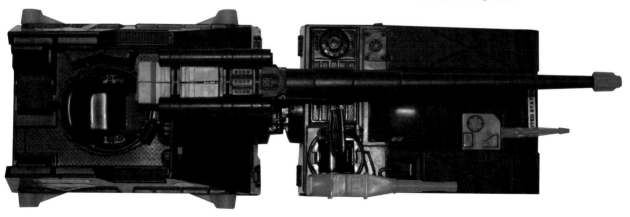

(NIGHT FORCE) NIGHT RAIDER

The Night Raider is based on the design of the 1986 Triple "T" and shares similar easily lost pieces.

MISB: **$45-50**, MIB: **$35**, MLC: **$20**

The Night Raider's easily lost pieces.

(NIGHT FORCE) NIGHT SHADE

The Night Shade is based on the design of the 1983 S.H.A.R.C. and shares similar easily lost pieces. This vehicle did not include bellows, as the S.H.A.R.C. did for Deep-Six (see Deep-Six's "bellows," 1984).

MISB: **$45-50**, MIB: **$35**, MLC: **$20**

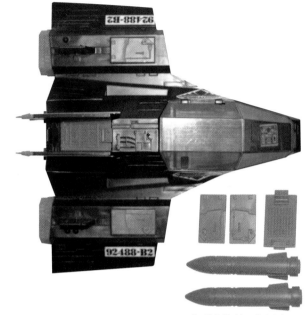

The Night Shade's easily lost pieces.

(NIGHT FORCE) NIGHT STORM

The Night Storm is based on the design of the 1987 Persuader and shares similar easily lost pieces.

MISB: **$75-80**, MIB: **$40-45**, MLC: **$30**

The Night Storm's easily lost pieces.

(NIGHT FORCE) NIGHT STRIKER

The Night Striker is based on the design of the 1984 W.H.A.L.E., and shares similar easily lost pieces. This vehicle is considered (along with the Night Boomer [1989] and Night Ray [1989]) one of the most difficult vehicles to find in the entire line, MISB, MIB, or mint, loose, complete.

MISB: **$300**, MIB: **$230**, MLC: **$200**

The Night Striker's easily lost pieces.

(TIGER FORCE) TIGER CAT
(Includes: Frostbite figure)

The Tiger Cat is based on the design of the 1985 Snow Cat and shares similar easily lost pieces.

MISB: **$65**, MIB: **$35**, MLC: **$25**

The Tiger Cat's easily lost pieces.

(TIGER FORCE) TIGER FLY
(Includes: Recondo figure)

The Tiger Fly shares the same design as the 1983 Dragonfly Assault Copter and shares similar easily lost pieces.

MISB: **$90**, MIB: **$45**, MLC: **$25**

The Tiger Fly's easily lost pieces.

(TIGER FORCE) TIGER PAW

The Tiger Paw shares the same design as the 1985 Cobra Ferret and shares similar easily lost pieces.

MISB: **$45**, MIB: **$30**, MLC: **$12-15**

The Tiger Paw's easily lost pieces.

(TIGER FORCE) TIGER RAT
(Includes: Skystriker figure)

The Tiger Rat shares the same design as the 1984 Cobra Rattler and shares similar easily lost pieces.

MISB: **$125**, MIB: **$60**, MLC: **$25-35**

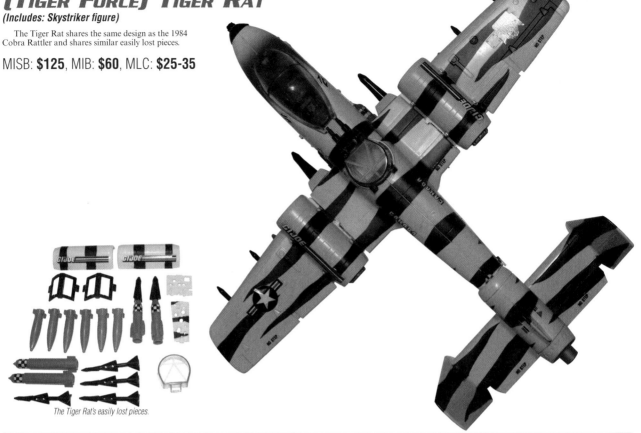

The Tiger Rat's easily lost pieces.

(TIGER FORCE) TIGER SHARK

The Tiger Shark shares the same design as the 1984 Cobra Water Moccasin and shares similar easily lost pieces.

MISB: **$55**, MIB: **$35**, MLC: **$20-25**

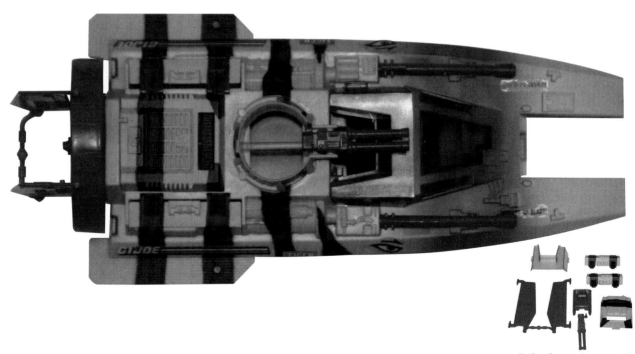

The Tiger Shark's easily lost pieces.

(SERIES VIII, 1989)

To continue in the vein that Hasbro began in 1988, the company extended its Tiger Force and Night Force lines, and added two new lines of re-cast figures and vehicles, Slaughter's Marauders and Python Patrol. New characters were released to complement the already massive armada of Joe and Cobra figures and vehicles. The line still sold well, and the figures were popular with kids and collectors.

1989 catalog.

OFFICIAL DISPATCH FROM G.I. JOE® HEADQUARTERS

Steeler™, one of G.I. Joe's top-notch infantrymen, has been re-assigned overseas and is no longer a member of the Special Mission Drivers' team. He is currently leading an assault against Cobra™ forces somewhere in the Persian Gulf. To fortify your forces, Rampage™, the heavy-duty, hard hitting tank driver, has been called in to replace him. This monster of muscle is an expert in the field and unbeatable in battle! Deploy him well.

Hawk

General Hawk™
G.I. Joe Commander

12620 p/n 41470200
©1989 Hasbro, Inc. All Rights Reserved.

Rampage mail order form.

1989 G.I. JOE FIGURES

BACKBLAST
Anti-Aircraft Soldier
(Includes: Two-Piece Triple Launcher Missile System, Three Missiles, Monocular, Knife, Bandolier)

Backblast's missile system.

Growing up right next door to a bust airport, Backblast hated hearing the loud noises of jets landing and taking off at night. He put this obsession to the test and joined the Army, where he was well rewarded for knocking enemy aircraft out of the sky. He is currently on the Joe's roster.

MOC: **$12-15**, MLC: **$8**

COUNTDOWN
Astronaut
(Includes: Backpack, Grappling Hook w/Rope, Helmet, Gun)

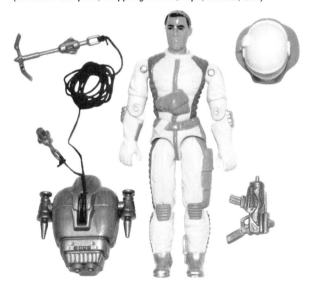

Countdown was the second astronaut to join the Joe team (see Payload, 1987). Since "the battlefield of tomorrow will surely extend into the upper atmosphere… the G.I. Joe team is ready with its own specialist" (from the file card). A former pilot and NASA astronaut, Countdown is a popular figure with collectors, as his design and accessories are first-rate.

MOC: **$12-15**, MLC: **$8**

DEE-JAY
Battle Force 2000 Comm-Tech Trooper
(Includes: Comm Tech Station, Laser Rifle, Antenna, Loudspeaker Backpack)

Formerly a popular disc jockey in Boston, Dee-Jay enlisted and became the Battle Force 2000's radio man (1987). As a figure, Dee-Jay was less than famous with strange looking accessories and an interesting costume. In toy stores, the figure was a "peg warmer," and today is easy to find loose (although usually without his antenna). His character was killed at the Battle of Benzheen along with nearly all the members of the Battle Force 2000 team.

MOC: **$10-12**, MLC: **$5**

DEEP SIX
Deep Sea Diver
(Includes: Buoy, Air Hose, Gun, Helmet, Backpack)

This version of Deep Six is more mobile and poseable than his original figure (for a full bio and reference shot, see Deep-Six, 1984), and is quite popular with collectors because of the design of his outfit and his well-crafted accessories. He is currently on the Joe's roster.

MOC: **$12-15**, MLC: **$8**

DOGFIGHT
Mudfighter Pilot
(Includes: Pistol)

Dogfight possesses an "uncanny depth perception, precise hand/eye coordination, and [a] powerful throwing arm" that makes him an asset to the Joes, and a perfect pilot for the Mudfighter.

NOTE: *Dogfight was included with the Mudfighter, and with the Benny's Exclusive Mudfighter/HISS II 2-pack w/Track Viper.*

MLC: **$8**

DOWNTOWN
Mortar Man
(Includes: Three-Piece Mortar, Six Mortar Shells, Helmet, Tri-Pod, Gun, Backpack)

Strangely enough, Downtown could just as easily have been called Short-Fuze (1982), and collectors would have been quite satisfied with an updated version of the latter character. Like Hardball (1988), Downtown can judge distances, range, and trajectory at a glance and that makes for a very effective mortar man. He is currently on the Joe's roster.

NOTE: *There are two variant versions of the Downtown figure, one has flesh-colored hands, and the other has yellow-toned hands.*

MOC: **$12-15**, MLC: **$8**

HOT SEAT
Raider Driver
(Includes: Helmet)
Included with the Raider.

Hot Seat was a contending prizefighter until he considered the toll boxing would take on his central nervous system. Possessing a fine tactical mind, he joined the Joes and became the driver of the Raider.

MLC: **$8**

LONG RANGE
Thunderclap Driver
(Includes: Helmet, Pistol)
Included with the Thunderclap.

As a child, Long Range couldn't fathom simple math problems, but was in his element when given sophisticated trigonometric and calculus equations. This made him a very effective driver for the heavily armed Thunderclap. Collectors should take care not to lose his pistol, as it is a very small accessory.

MLC: **$10**

PAYLOAD
Astronaut
(Includes: Helmet, Face Shield, Backpack, Two Control Arms)
Included with the Crusader Space Shuttle with Avenger Scout Craft.

Payload's gray backpack with control arms.

For a full bio on this character, see Payload, (1987). Note that the backpack associated with Payload and his Crusader Shuttle are colored light gray, not the brighter white of the one complementing the original version of Payload (1987) and the Defiant (1987).

MLC: *(w/backpack)* **$20**, *(w/out backpack)* **$8**

RAMPAGE
Mauler M.B.T. Tank Driver
(Includes: Rifle)
Mail Away Exclusive

Rampage was a re-cast Heavy Metal (1985) figure without beard or microphone. He is a fairly difficult figure to obtain MISBaggie with his file card, as he replaced Steeler at the last minute in a Hasbro Direct vehicle drivers mail-away.

MISBaggie: **$20**

RECOIL
L.R.R.P.
(Long Range Recon Patrol, pronounced "Lurp")
(Includes: Backpack, Rifle, Mine Case, Antenna, Pistol)

Recoil is the Joe's first member whose specialty is specifically L.R.R.P. (Long Range Reconnaissance Patrol). Like Sneak Peek (1987), this is a recon man, using his strength, size, and stealth to sneak out into the field and gather important information vital to Joe missions. Recoil is an excellent intelligence-gatherer and is a dedicated and hard working soldier. His current status is unknown.

NOTE: *Recoil's figure came with a thin- or thick-handled mine case.*

MOC: **$12-15**, MLC: **$8**

ROCK 'N ROLL
Gatling Gunner
(Includes: Two Gatling Guns, Rifle, Ammo Feeding Backpack, Two Bandoliers)

This version of Rock 'N Roll is popular with collectors as his excellent accessories include two belt-fed Gatling guns, bandoliers, etc. Constantly updating his weapons systems, Rock 'N Roll has proven himself an invaluable member of the Joe team, where he is currently a field commander. For a full bio, see Rock 'N Roll, (1982).

MOC: **$15-20**, MLC: **$8**

SCOOP
Combat Information Specialist
(Includes: Hi-Tech Camera, Pistol, Helmet, Hose, Antenna, Satellite Relay Station)

Another Joe character based upon an actual person, Scoop was modeled after NBC television news reporter, Mike Leonard. The character was even given the "real" name "Leonard Michaels." Scoop acted as the Joe's cameraman on a few missions in the Marvel comic, and earned their respect with his protection of vital combat information. Prior to enlistment, he gave up a promising future as a member of a network news crew in order to actually *be* where the news was made. His current status on the Joe team is unknown.

MOC: **$12-15**, MLC: **$8**

SNAKE EYES
Commando
(Includes: Backpack, Uzi, Three-Piece Nunchaku, Sword, Blow Gun)

This updated version of Snake Eyes hints again at his esoteric background, while his file card suggests that the character, "was Ranger qualified and graduated from Recondo School in Nha Trang [a beach-laden city in Southeastern Vietnam; Vietnamese translation is, "white house"] prior to his service with a Long Rage Reconnaissance Patrol in South East Asia." For a full bio, see Snake Eyes, (1982).

MOC: **$30-40**, MLC: **$20**

STALKER
Tundra Ranger
(Includes: Kayak, Paddle and Machine Gun, Rifle, Mask, Knife, Backpack)

Lonzo Wilkinson (Stalker's file name) served in the same L.R.R.P. (Long Range Reconnaissance Patrol) as Snake Eyes and Storm Shadow in South East Asia, and with this updated figure, his character's MOS has changed from "Ranger" to "Tundra Ranger." His file card (PMS or SMS) does not suggest any further schooling in Arctic combat, so it is suggested that this was a minor figure re-vamp. For a full bio, see Stalker, (1982).

MOC: **$18-25**,
MLC: **$8**

Stalker's Kayak.

WINDCHILL
Arctic Blast Driver
(Includes: Rifle, Two Skis)

Windchill was a "ski-mobiler and hunter before he discovered the Biathlon" (from the file card) where he was greeted by Blizzard (1988) and asked to join the Joe team. Upon enlistment, he discovered the thrill of driving heavily-armed Arctic vehicles, and that became his MOS.

MLC: **$10**

(NIGHT FORCE) CHARBROIL
Flamethrower
(Includes: Flamethrower, Flame Retardant Hose, Pressurized Thermo-chemical Backpack, Thermo-Insulated Oxygenated Helmet)

Packaged together with Night Force Repeater. For a full bio on the character, see Charbroil, (1988).

MOC: **$90-110**, MLC: **$35-45**

(NIGHT FORCE) LIGHTFOOT
Explosives Expert
(Includes: Nightvision Helmet, Mine Detector Unit, Hose, Robot, Backpack)

Packaged together with Night Force Shockwave. For a full bio on the character, see Lightfoot, (1988).

MOC: **$90-110**, MLC: **$35-45**

(NIGHT FORCE) MUSKRAT
Swamp Fighter
(Includes: Super 90 Shotgun, Swamp Skimmer, Machete)

Packaged together with Night Force Spearhead & Max. For a full bio on the character, see Muskrat, (1988).

MOC: **$90-110**, MLC: **$35-45**

(NIGHT FORCE) REPEATER
Steadi-Cam Machine Gunner
(Includes: Machine Gun, Body Mount, Backpack)

Packaged together with Night Force Charbroil and later on, with the Rapid Deployment Force (1993). For a full bio on the character, see Repeater, (1988).

MOC: **$90-110**, MLC: **$35-45**

(NIGHT FORCE) SHOCKWAVE
S.W.A.T. Specialist
(Includes: Machine Gun, Pistol, Knife, Backpack)

Packaged together with Night Force Lightfoot and later on, with the Rapid Deployment Force (1993). For a full bio on the character, see Shockwave, (1988).

MOC: **$90-110**, MLC: **$35-45**

(NIGHT FORCE) SPEARHEAD & MAX
Point Man & Bobcat
(Includes: Bobcat, Rifle, Knife, Helmet, Backpack)

Packaged together with Night Force Muskrat. For a full bio on the character, see Spearhead & Max, (1988).

MOC: **$90-110**, MLC: **$35-45**

SLAUGHTER'S MARAUDERS

"Slaughter's Marauders lead G.I. Joe's latest land offensive against Cobra! Shielded by their camouflage and armed with the heaviest artillery, the Marauders are prepared to defeat Cobra anywhere in the world!" Collectors appreciate the Slaughter's Marauders toys because of the figures' tasteful camouflage and the vehicles' upgraded weapons systems.

(SLAUGHTER'S MARAUDERS) BARBECUE
Firefighter
(Includes: Fire Axe, Foam Tanks, Nozzle Gun, Hose, Tank Bracket)

For a full bio on the character, see Barbecue, (1985).

MOC: **$15-25**, MLC: **$10**

(SLAUGHTER'S MARAUDERS) FOOTLOOSE
Infantry Trooper
(Includes: M-16, M73-A1 LAWS, Helmet, Backpack)

For a full bio on the character, see Footloose, (1985).

MOC: **$15-25**, MLC: **$10**

(SLAUGHTER'S MARAUDERS) LOW-LIGHT
Night Spotter
(Includes: 7.62mm Model 85 Sniper Rifle w/Bipod, Uzi Submachine Gun, Backpack)

For a full bio on the character, see Low-Light, (1986).

MOC: **$15-25**, MLC: **$10**

(SLAUGHTER'S MARAUDERS) MUTT
Animal Control/Utilization Technician
(Includes: Dog [Junkyard], Ingram Mac-11 w/Silencer, Night Stick, Leash, Face Mask, Helmet)

The helmet included with the Slaughter's Marauder's Mutt was not the same design as the original Mutt, but a black molded helmet based on the designs of the 1982 Joe figure helmets (see Breaker, 1982).

The Slaughter's Marauder's version of Junkyard does not have the brown underbelly that the original Junkyard came with (see Mutt, 1984). For a full bio on the character, see Mutt, (1984).

MOC: **$15-25**, MLC: **$10**

(SLAUGHTER'S MARAUDERS) SGT. SLAUGHTER
Slaughter's Marauders Commander
(Includes: Baton)

For a full bio on the character, see Sgt. Slaughter, (1985).

MOC: **$15-25**, MLC: **$10**

(SLAUGHTER'S MARAUDERS) SPIRIT
Tracker
(Includes: Arrow Cassette Pack, Auto-Arrow Launcher, Eagle [Freedom])

For a full bio on the character, see Spirit, (1984).

MOC: **$15-25**, MLC: **$10**

1989 COBRA FIGURES

AERO-VIPER
Condor Z25 Pilot
(Includes: Helmet)
Included with the Cobra Condor Z25.

As pilots of Cobra's hottest new aircraft, the Condor Z25, Aero-Vipers are not surgically enhanced like Hydro-Vipers (1988), Star-Vipers (1988) or Strato-Vipers (1986), so they compensate by lifting weights and *taking* the pain (from the file card). It is suggested that the stress on their bodies and minds provides these pilots with frequent O.B.E. (out of body) experiences.

MLC: **$15**

ALLEY VIPER
Cobra Urban Assault Trooper
(Includes: Shield, Face Shield, Gun, Backpack w/Grappling Hook)

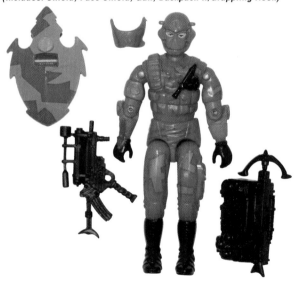

One of the most popular Joe figures in the run, the Alley Vipers are Cobra's equivalent to a S.W.A.T. team and formed "the spearhead of Cobra's inner-city invasion forces" (from the file card). They are brutal, ruthless, strong, and use "various forms of treachery to achieve their objectives." The figures are fist-rate troop builders, as most collectors like to obtain as many Alley Vipers as possible for their Cobra army.

MOC: **$28-35**, MLC: **$12**

ANNIHILATOR
Destro's Elite Trooper
(Includes: Machine Gun, Hand Gun, Helicopter Backpack)

The tenacious and ruthless Annihilators are high-ranking and well trained members of the Iron Grenadiers (1988) who act as "Destro's personal bodyguards and elite airborne assault troops" (from the file card). These soldiers descend like a plague of locusts onto enemy troops with use of their heli-packs and sleek designs.

MOC: **$15-20**, MLC: **$10**

DARKLON
Evader Driver
(Includes: Rifle)
Included with Darklon's Evader.

A distant "cousin to the Destro [1988, 1983] clan" (from the file card), he was urged by Destro himself to "lead his [Destro's] legions in his bid to take over Cobra." Darklon is a strange-looking figure, and not a very popular one with collectors.

MLC: **$12**

FRAG-VIPER
Cobra Grenade Thrower
(Includes: Cesta, Gun, Three Grenades, Two Hoses, Backpack)

As their main weapon, Frag-Vipers carry manual hurling baskets or "cestas," those scoop-shaped wicker baskets used to catch and throw a ball in the intense Basque sport of Jai Alai. Frag-Vipers, however, don't use hardened rubber balls—they chuck *grenades*. A popular figure because of their unique weapons, the Frag-Vipers are difficult to obtain complete because of their many small parts.

MOC: **$28-35**, MLC: **$10-12**

GNAWGAHYDE
Dreadnok Poacher
(Includes: Rifle, Bipod, Boar, Bow, Backpack, Shin Knife, Wrist Machete, Hat)

Gnawgahyde "could have single-handedly decimated all the endangered species in Africa" (from his file card) if his fellow poachers hadn't run him off for being a card cheat and too foul smelling even for them. Of course, he found a home with the Dreadnoks "at an all night donut and grape soda shop," the favorite Dreadnok repast.

MOC: **$15-20**, MLC: **$10**

Gnawgahyde's weapons.

H.E.A.T. VIPER
Cobra Bazooka Man
(Includes: Bazooka, Six Bazooka Shells, Backpack, Hose, Eye Piece)

H.E.A.T. Vipers are the latest "generation of Cobra anti-tank specialists" (from the file card), and the figure's arsenal of weapons is quite impressive. All of the figure's bazooka shells fit snugly around the tabs around his boots. For the character, the sights on the bazooka are fiber-optically linked to his helmet, and these Vipers would be terrific troop builders if they weren't so difficult to find mint, loose, and complete.

MOC: **$22-25**, MLC: **$10**

NIGHT-VIPER
Cobra Night Fighter
(Includes: Night Vision Goggles, Gun w/Night Scope, Backpack)

Pegs on the side of Night-Viper's legs are for his rifle. A fascinating figure, the Night-Viper's accessories are the most impressive of the 1989 figures. A scope fits onto the visor, the rifle snaps into the thigh, and the backpack looks like it has the butt of a knife sticking out! With sophisticated weaponry and equipment that functions to lower the wearer's infrared signature, these troops are hard to beat.

MOC: **$28-35**, MLC: **$12**

T.A.R.G.A.T.
Trans Atmospheric Rapid Global Assault Trooper
(Includes: Laser Gun, Shell, Joystick, Hose, Face Shield)

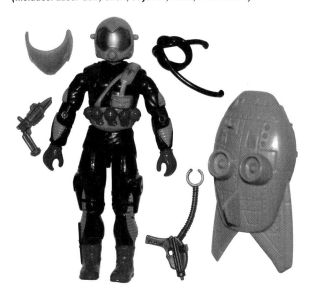

Destro's assault troopers are fascinating pieces of technology, as they can be deployed to any location around the globe, or dropped from a space shuttlecraft to hit the stratosphere like "human meteors" (from the file card).

NOTE: *The backpack contains movable wings.*

MOC: **$22-25**, MLC: **$10**

TRACK VIPER
H.I.S.S. II Driver
(Includes: Pistol)
Included with the Cobra H.I.S.S. II, and with the Benny's Exclusive Mudfighter/HISS II 2-pack w/Track Viper.

The Cobra Track Viper is "recruited from Cobra personnel who are too clumsy or too slow to fight in the infantry." But they are big and strong, and are afforded the advantage of 360-degree visibility inside the climate-controlled cockpit of the H.I.S.S. II.

MLC: **$12**

WILD BOAR
Razorback Driver
(Includes: Helmet, Hose)
Included with Destro's Razorback.

As members of the Iron Grenadiers (1988), the Wild Boars are "better trained, better equipped, and enjoy the benefits of better qualified leadership" (from the file card) than Cobra Vipers (1986). As such, they are deployed in fewer numbers than Cobra's forces. The Iron Grenadiers, and Wild Boars in particular, compensate for this disadvantage through a fierce "will to succeed."

MLC: **$8**

PYTHON PATROL

"Python Patrol is a select group of Cobra mercenaries that utilize high-tech, re-outfitted vehicles with sophisticated camouflage for venomous strikes against G.I. Joe!" This group of soldiers was originally designated under the code-name "Wraith" (from their prototype file cards), and was eventually designated, "Python Patrol."

PYTHON COPPERHEAD
Python Patrol Swamp Fighter
(Includes: M-16 "Over/Under" Rifle, Swamp Pack)

This figure is simply a repaint of the original Copperhead (1984) who has undergone the Pythonization Process, and was given a rifle and backpack. The Pythonization Process consists of "a process in which personnel and/or vehicles are outfitted with a primary layer of radar-resistant black-ball paint, then blanketed with a thermal-wave dispersal grid."

MOC: **$22-25**, MLC: **$10**

PYTHON CRIMSON GUARD
Python Patrol Elite Trooper
(Includes: AK-48A w/Bayonet, Backpack)

The Python Crimson Guard is a popular army builder, and collectors try to find as many complete versions of this figure as they can. Python Patrol Crimson Guard characters are regular "siegies" (see Crimson Guard, 1985) who have undergone extra stealth training and are often utilized by Cobra Command to spy on the troopers in their own ranks! The Pythonization Process consists of "a process in which personnel and/or vehicles are outfitted with a primary layer of radar-resistant black-ball paint, then blanketed with a thermal-wave dispersal grid."

MOC: **$22-25**, MLC: **$10**

PYTHON OFFICER
Python Patrol Officer
(Includes: Dragunov [SVD] Sniper's Rifle)

Oddly enough, the Python Officer uses the mold from the Cobra Soldier (The Enemy [1983]), yet is given the rank of "officer." He is highly trained in how to use the Pythonization Process, and other stealth skills and tactics. The Pythonization Process consists of "a process in which personnel and/or vehicles are outfitted with a primary layer of radar-resistant black-ball paint, then blanketed with a thermal-wave dispersal grid."

A handwritten note by Larry Hama in the prototype dossier's margin reads, "NOT FOR TOY PACKAGE—The nomenclature used throughout is current as to the 1987 edition of the U.S. Army Combat Leader's Guide."

MOC: **$30-40**, MLC: **$14**

PYTHON TELE-VIPER
Python Patrol Communications
(Includes: VS-11 Scanner, Hose, Communipac)

Some versions of the Python Tele-Viper came with a hose, while some did not, however, the accessory is not listed on the white "Includes" line on the figure's card front. The character of the Python Tele-Viper is similar to the Tele-Viper (1985), but uses more sophisticated technology that enhances their Pythonization Process, "a process in which personnel and/or vehicles are outfitted with a primary layer of radar-resistant black-ball paint, then blanketed with a thermal-wave dispersal grid."

MOC: **$22-25**, MLC: **$10**

PYTHON TROOPER
Python Patrol Infantry
(Includes: AK-47 Assault Rifle)

Like the Python Officer, this Python Trooper uses the mold of the original Cobra Officer (The Enemy, [1983]). The Python Troopers are similar to basic Cobras (The Enemy, [1982]), but with the benefit of the Pythonization Process and a requirement that they must be cross-trained in at least one other skill. The Pythonization Process consists of "a process in which personnel and/or vehicles are outfitted with a primary layer of radar-resistant black-ball paint, then blanketed with a thermal-wave dispersal grid."

NOTE: *Some Canadian carded versions of the figure have been found with white AK-47 rifles in their packages.*

MOC: **$22-25**, MLC: **$10**

PYTHON VIPER
Python Patrol Assault Viper
(Includes: Backpack, RDT-7 Assault Rifle w/Grenade Launcher)

Python Vipers are original Vipers (1986) enhanced with Python Patrol technology that equipped the soldiers with "stealth-like capabilities, whereby [they] can penetrate into enemy areas undetected" (from the file card). The Pythonization Process consists of "a process in which personnel and/or vehicles are outfitted with a primary layer of radar-resistant black-ball paint, then blanketed with a thermal-wave dispersal grid."

MOC: **$30-40**, MLC: **$12**

1989 VEHICLES/PLAYSETS

ARCTIC BLAST
(Includes: Windchill figure)

The Arctic Blast's easily lost pieces.

The Arctic Blast adds support to the already massive G.I. Joe arsenal of cold-weather vehicles. It comes with a progressive spring rate/independent air suspension system, two "Chain Gang" forward-mounted armor-piercing 30mm Gatling guns, two 7.62mm coaxial firing double-barreled machine guns, and side-mounted surface missiles.

Easily lost pieces include two missiles (sorry that the one pictured came factory-cut), two machine gun barrels, and a seat belt.

MISB: **$35**, MIB: **$15**, MLC: **$10**

BATTLEFIELD ROBOT RADAR RAT

The Radar Rat is a battlefield robot with a MM-15 "Flat Face" target track/guidance parabolic dishes, three down-low terminal homing/semi active radar missiles, and puncture proof tires.

Easily lost pieces include three missiles, radar mount, radar dishes, handlebars, missile mount, antenna, and seat belt.

MISB: **$15**, MIB: **$10**, MLC: **$3-5**

The Radar Rat's easily lost pieces.

EIGHT

COBRA BATTLEFIELD ROBOT DEVASTATOR

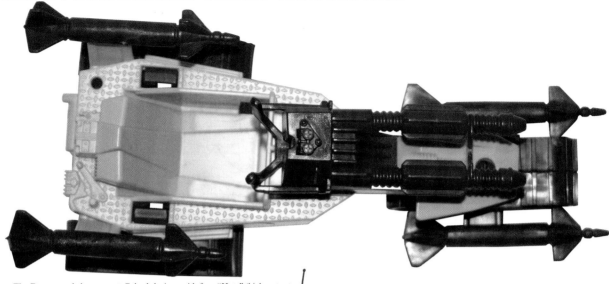

The Devastator helps support Cobra's legions with four "Hots" (high output terrain hugging system) missiles, a "Tandem-Blaster" .50-caliber machine gun, and hardened steel rotation rear tracks.

Easily lost pieces are the antenna and four missiles.

MISB: **$15**, MIB: **$10**, MLC: **$3-5**

The Devastator's seat belt.

The Devastator's easily lost pieces.

COBRA BATTLEFIELD ROBOT HOVERCRAFT

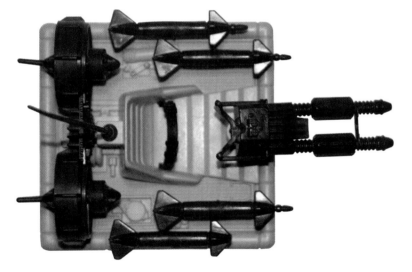

The Battlefield Robot Hovercraft is a small vehicle that has carbon-fiber high-speed rotors, a dual barreled "Crusher" internally cooled .50-caliber machine gun, and four "Sailfish" forward looking radar surface torpedoes.

Easily lost pieces are the antenna, seatbelt, machine gun, and four missiles.

MISB: **$15**, MIB: **$10**, MLC: **$3-5**

The Hovercraft's easily lost pieces.

BATTLEFIELD ROBOT TRI-BLASTER

The Battlefield Robot Tri-Blaster is a one-man four-wheel drive vehicle with a triple-barreled "Tri-Blaster" pulse fire laser cannon, digital communications array, and super-duty antenna.

Easily lost pieces are the three missiles, antenna, "Tri-Blaster" cannon, and the missile launcher rack.

MISB: **$15**, MIB: **$10**, MLC: **$3-5**

The Tri-Blaster's easily lost pieces.

COBRA CONDOR Z25
(Includes: Aero-Viper figure)

The Cobra Condor, because of its white color, is prone to discoloration over time, and because of its various small pieces, is difficult to find MISB, MIB, or loose and complete. Its wings, with their swept-back design, are reminiscent of the Conquest-X30 (1986). The Condor has two different component parts that are detachable at the press of a button—an attack "wing" and a high-speed aircraft. Other special features of the Condor included a thumb-wheel bomb-dropping mechanism, two bomb-bay door dropping mechanisms, retractable landing gear, and a gun-ring assembly with mounted dual-laser support cannons armed with 3,700 laser rounds.

Easily lost pieces include four missiles, the seven drop bombs, 14 wing bombs, and the laser cannon.

MISB: **$100**, MIB: **$75**, MLC: **$50**

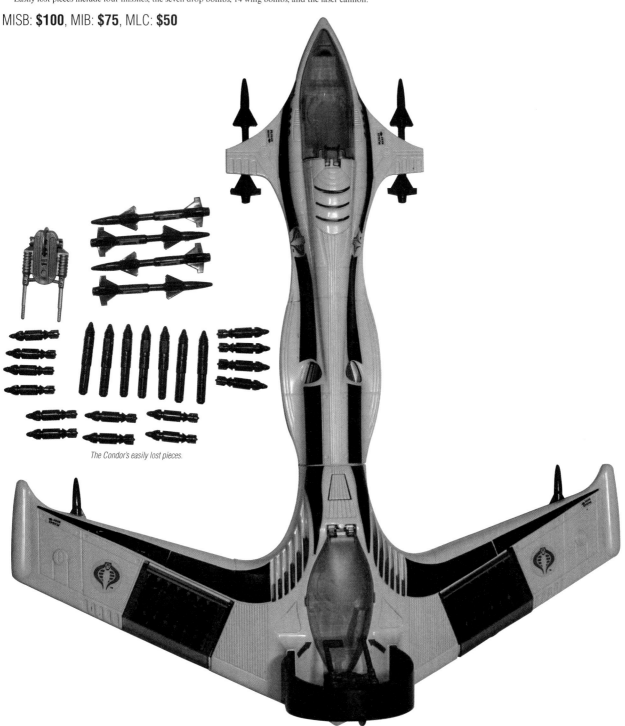

The Condor's easily lost pieces.

COBRA *FANG II*

The Cobra FANG II is an updated version of the original Cobra F.A.N.G. (1983) and its design is much different from the first version. It has rotating wings, a 20mm long range cannon, and six "AIMZ-33" air-to-air crusher missiles.

Easily lost pieces are the six missiles.

MISB: **$25**, MIB: **$15**, MLC: **$8**

The FANG II's easily lost pieces.

COBRA *H.I.S.S. II*

(Includes: Track Viper figure)

The H.I.S.S. II's easily lost pieces.

The Cobra H.I.S.S. is an updated version of the original Cobra H.I.S.S. (1983) and its design is much different from the first version. It has a hull that opens and carries Cobra troopers, a tri-barreled, thermal-propulsion XTX-a20b cannon, two 100mm armor-piercing laser machine guns, and two surface-hovering, no noise, multi-warhead "Slam" missiles.

Easily lost pieces include two guard rails, two missiles, and two seat belts.

NOTE: *The machine was also included with the Mudfighter (1989) as a Benny's exclusive "two-pack" along with both drivers, and this exclusive is rare and expensive. The Benny's II two-pack sells for more than $180 MISB, but loose samples are relegated to the vehicle's original prices.*

MISB: **$60**, MIB: **$30**, MLC: **$18-20**

CRUSADER SPACE SHUTTLE WITH AVENGER SCOUT CRAFT

(Includes: Payload figure)

The Crusader Space Shuttle is based on the design of the Defiant Shuttle (1987), but in lieu of the robot arm, the Crusader comes with the Avenger Scout Craft—a small single person low radar reflection recon jet (based on the designs of the recon jet that came with the Cobra Night Raven [1986]). The Crusader is a fun toy for those kids who couldn't afford the more expensive Defiant. Other than these few differences, the Crusader and the Defiant are remarkably similar.

MISB: **$90**, MIB: **$75**, MLC: **$55**

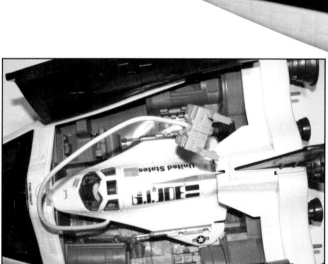

Crusader interior with umbilical cord.

The Crusader's easily lost pieces.

DARKLON'S EVADER
(Includes: Darklon figure)

Darklon's Evader is an unusual vehicle that holds Darklon (1989) and sports an "Eliminator" canopy-mounted 9mm machine gun, two "Pursurer" roof-mounted terminal-homing stinger-type missiles, and low-ride tires.

Easily lost pieces are the two missiles.

MISB: **$25**, MIB: **$15**, MLC: **$10**

The Evader's easily lost pieces.

DESTRO'S RAZORBACK
(Includes: Wild Boar figure)

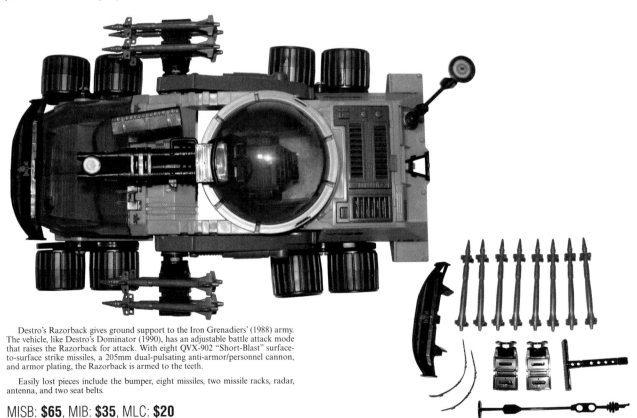

Destro's Razorback gives ground support to the Iron Grenadiers' (1988) army. The vehicle, like Destro's Dominator (1990), has an adjustable battle attack mode that raises the Razorback for attack. With eight QVX-902 "Short-Blast" surface-to-surface strike missiles, a 205mm dual-pulsating anti-armor/personnel cannon, and armor plating, the Razorback is armed to the teeth.

Easily lost pieces include the bumper, eight missiles, two missile racks, radar, antenna, and two seat belts.

MISB: **$65**, MIB: **$35**, MLC: **$20**

The Razorback's easily lost pieces.

MUDFIGHTER
(Includes: Dogfight figure)

The Mudfighter, with its AS-99's (2000 lbs. of delayed detonation air-to-surface bombs) and a 100FW 1670 lb. unducted ('propfan') propeller with forward/reverse power modes was a powerful addition to the G.I. Joe air force.

Easily lost pieces include sixteen bombs, two bomb racks, and three wheels.

NOTE: *The craft was also included with the H.I.S.S. II (1989) as a Benny's exclusive two-pack along with both drivers, and this exclusive is rare and expensive. The Benny's H.I.S.S. II two-pack sells for more than $180 MISB, but loose samples are relegated to the vehicle's original prices.*

MISB: **$50**, MIB: **$25**, MLC: **$12**

The Mudfighter's easily lost pieces.

PULVERIZER
(Battle Force 2000)

The Battle Force 2000 Pulverizer, with its composite fiber flexible HHR (High Heat Resistant) energy transport duct, can fire its "Pulverizer" adjustable laser cannon in a variety of directions.

Note: *The only easily lost part of the Pulverizer was one small black seat belt (see Battlefield Robot Devastator seat belt, 1989).*

MISB: **$18**, MIB: **$12**, MLC: **$5**

Pulverizer with full cannon extension.

RAIDER

(Includes: Hot Seat figure)

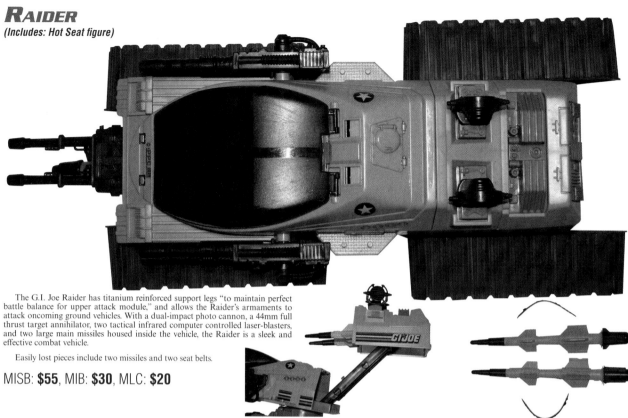

The G.I. Joe Raider has titanium reinforced support legs "to maintain perfect battle balance for upper attack module," and allows the Raider's armaments to attack oncoming ground vehicles. With a dual-impact photo cannon, a 44mm full thrust target annihilator, two tactical infrared computer controlled laser-blasters, and two large main missiles housed inside the vehicle, the Raider is a sleek and effective combat vehicle.

Easily lost pieces include two missiles and two seat belts.

MISB: **$55**, MIB: **$30**, MLC: **$20**

Raider with extension of upper attack module.

The Raider's easily lost pieces.

THUNDERCLAP

(Includes: Long Range figure)

The Thunderclap is a complicated vehicle to complete and is rather bulky to transport from place to place. The Thunderclap has three components—a tractor vehicle, a trailer vehicle, and a cannon base. The tractor vehicle has an MG-999 assault weapon as its main gun and two surface-to-surface low attack missiles. The trailer vehicle comes replete with a computer controlled blaster cannon, three surface-to-surface cruise missiles, and a ventilation exhaust system. The main piece of the Thunderclap is its cannon base, which includes the huge multi-extendable, high-powered battlefield "Annihilator" cannon, two rotary mini-cannons, and a thermal-protected missile launcher with three surface-to-surface missiles. The cannon also has four stabilizer legs to support the cannon when set up separately from the vehicle itself. The cannon also has a mechanism that holds the shells and simulates actual firing.

MISB: **$85**, MIB: **$60**, MLC: **$30**

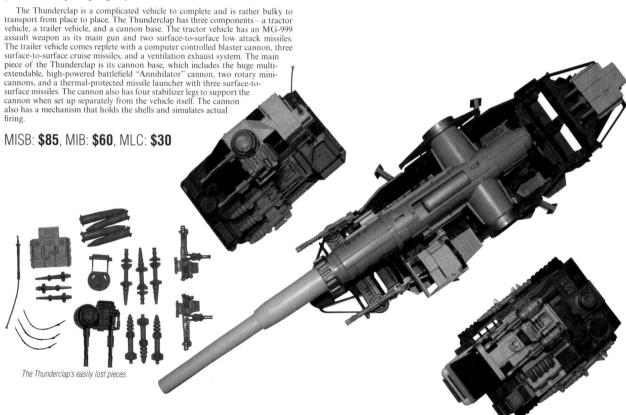

The Thunderclap's easily lost pieces.

NIGHT FORCE

Night Force vehicles are extremely rare and great care should be taken with MISB and MIB samples. Even loose samples of the larger, harder-to-complete vehicles sell for quite a bit of money, as casual fans and collectors alike understand that these pieces are hard to find. None of these vehicles included a driver.

NIGHT BOOMER

The Night Boomer shares the same design as the 1983 Combat Jet Skystriker and shares similar easily lost pieces, but the Night Boomer did not come with parachutes. This vehicle is considered (along with the Night Ray [1989] and Night Striker [1988]) one of the most difficult vehicles to find in the entire line, MISB, MIB, or mint, loose, complete.

MISB: **$350**, MIB: **$260**, MLC: **$240**

The Night Boomer's easily lost pieces.

Night Boomer with wings swept back.

NIGHT RAY

The Night Ray shares the same design as the 1985 Cobra Hydrofoil and shares similar easily lost pieces. This vehicle is considered (along with the Night Boomer [1989] and Night Striker [1988]) one of the most difficult vehicles to find in the entire line, MISB, MIB, or mint, loose, and complete.

MISB: **$275**, MIB: **$200**, MLC: **$135**

Night Ray, MISB.

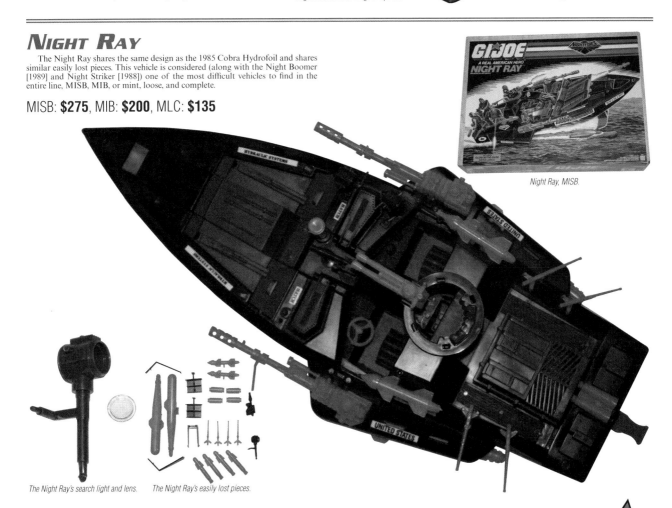

The Night Ray's search light and lens.   *The Night Ray's easily lost pieces.*

NIGHT SCRAMBLER

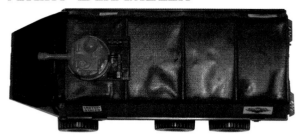

The Night Scrambler shares the same design as the APC (1983) and shares similar easily lost pieces.

MISB: **$100**, MIB: **$60**, MLC: **$35-40**

Night Scrambler, side view.

The Night Scrambler's easily lost pieces.

PYTHON PATROL

"The Python Patrol is Cobra's answer to Tiger Force! Using sleek combat color schemes, Cobra has refurbished and redecorated battled-scarred vehicles for sophisticated counter-strikes against G.I. Joe!" Each vehicle is designed with "snake skin" camouflage, for surprise attacks behind enemy lines.

PYTHON ASP

The Python ASP shares the same design as the Cobra A.S.P. (1984) and shares similar easily lost pieces.

MISB: **$45**, MIB: **$25**, MLC: **$15**

PYTHON CONQUEST (X-30)

The Python Conquest shares the same design as the Conquest X-30 (1986) and shares similar easily lost pieces.

MISB: **$65**, MIB: **$35**, MLC: **$18-25**

The Python Conquest's easily lost pieces.

PYTHON *STUN*

The Python STUN shares the same design as the Cobra STUN (1986) and shares similar easily lost pieces.

MISB: **$65**, MIB: **$40**, MLC: **$20** *(unbroken flags)*

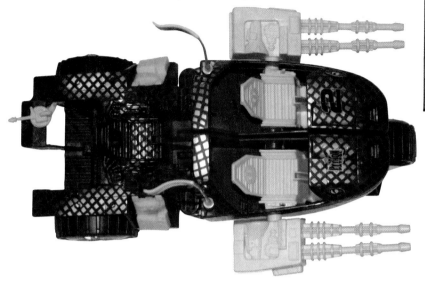

Python STUN, MISB.

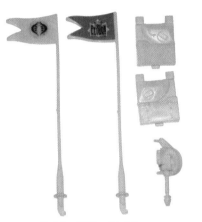

The Python STUN's easily lost pieces.

SLAUGHTER'S MARAUDERS

The Slaughter's Marauders line, unlike the Tiger Force, Night Force, and Python Patrol lines, not only borrow previous vehicle designs with which to build up and re-outfit these new vehicles, but Hasbro added newly-minted parts to enhance their camouflaged frames. These vehicles have new accessories not included with the vehicles their designs were based upon. Many collectors prize these vehicles, but they do not command Night Force prices.

(SLAUGHTER'S MARAUDERS) ARMADILLO

The Slaughter's Marauders Armadillo is based on the designs of the 1985 Armadillo Mini-Tank, yet has a newly-attached missile launcher and stabilizer for the launcher. It also comes with six missiles.

Easily lost pieces include six missiles and the missile launcher stabilizer.

MISB: **$28**, MIB: **$20**, MLC: **$15**

The Armadillo's easily lost pieces.

(SLAUGHTER'S MARAUDERS) EQUALIZER

The Slaughter's Marauders Equalizer is based on the designs of the Mauler M.B.T. (1985) but is not motorized. Instead of motorization, it has added accessories and features including a flip-up radar dish, dual missile launchers with six missiles, and dual M-80A anti-lock machine guns.

Easily lost pieces are similar to the Mauler M.B.T. (1985) except with the addition of two radar dishes and six missiles.

MISB: **$65**, MIB: **$45**,
MLC: **$25-30**

The Equalizer's easily lost pieces.

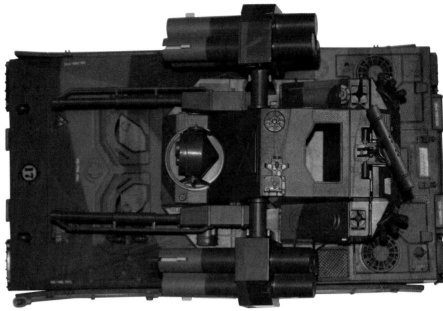

(SLAUGHTER'S MARAUDERS) LYNX

The Slaughter's Marauders Lynx is based on the designs of the Wolverine (1983). It does not have the missile launchers of the Wolverine, however, but it does come with the engine cover and tow cable. Its main offense is a huge cannon, similar to the one attached to the Mauler M.B.T. (1985).

MISB: **$45**, MIB: **$28**, MLC: **$18-20**

The Lynx's easily lost pieces.

TIGER FISH

The Tiger Fish shares the same design as the Devilfish (1986) and shares similar easily lost pieces.

MISB: **$35**, MIB: **$25**, MLC: **$15-20**

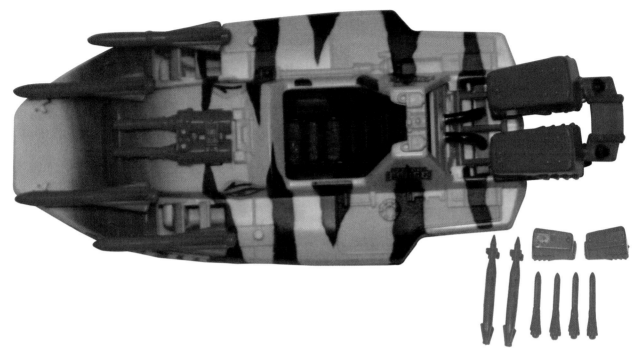

The Tiger Fish's easily lost pieces.

TIGER STING

The Tiger Sting shares the same design as the Vamp Mark II (1984) and shares similar easily lost pieces. Note that the gas cans, however, are re-cast from the original VAMP (1982).

MISB: **$55**, MIB: **$32**, MLC: **$22-25**

The Tiger Sting's easily lost pieces.

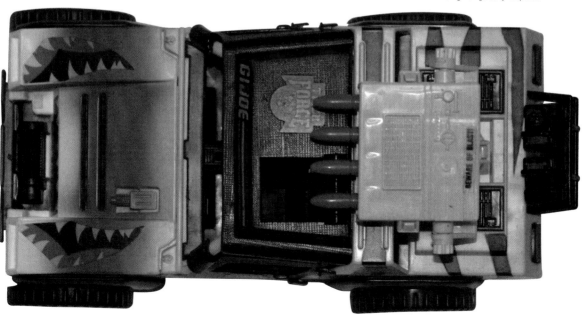

(Series IX, 1990)

The 1990 series of Joes enlists many new soldiers, with very few re-sculpted characters. In addition, a new set of re-cast vehicles—the chrome plated Sky Patrol—made its way on the scene. The troopers to man these vehicles were called "Sky Patrol" and were constructed from re-cast body parts from previous G.I. Joe figures—with newly molded heads. Yet another new sub-series for the line was dubbed "Sonic Fighters," and came with push button sound-blasting backpacks—to the consternation of many die-hard Joe collectors. This year, sales were beginning to see a downturn.

1990 catalog.

G.I. Joe Combat Command Rings.

1990 Wal-Mart file cards given away to employees. NOTE: These mock file cards were never released to the mass-market, just to Wal-Mart employees and are fun to read anyhow!

1990 G.I. JOE FIGURES

AMBUSH
Concealment Specialist
(Includes: Rifle, Tent Throw Cover, Cape, Four-Piece Lean-To Assembly, Helmet, Grenade Launcher, Backpack)

Ambush's camouflage.

With the prototype code names of Sgt. Hyde and Smokescreen, Ambush came with some of the most fascinating G.I. Joe accessories ever packaged. His bedroll and tent had real fabric that a child could actually set up—Ambush was well worth a child's hard earned $2.99. Combine the excellent accessories with the muted color scheme and a helmet that could have come out of WWII, and Hasbro had a winner.

From his prototype file card, "Ambush could sneak up and tag a second-baseman in Yankee Stadium during a capacity night game and NOBODY would know it. All anybody would notice would be a slight lumpiness in the infield that <u>almost</u> seemed to be moving."

NOTE: *At this point in the Joe crafting process, Hasbro was now heavily editing Mr. Hama's dossiers, electing to eventually write some (and indeed, toward the end of the line, most) of the file cards in-house.*

MOC: **$10-15**, MLC: **$8**

BULLHORN
Intervention Specialist
(Includes: Helmet, Three-Piece Rifle, Bullhorn, Rifle w/Scope, Backpack)

Bullhorn's original MOS from his prototype file card was "Hostage Negotiator" and "Hostage Crisis Specialist," and his prototype code names were Peacemaker, Talkdown, Wingshot, and Last-Chance. Bullhorn is quite a popular action figure, as his rifle is collapsible and its sight, stock, and barrel fit into a hard attaché case, which was one of the G.I. Joe lines most fascinating accessories. As a character, Bullhorn is charismatic and gregarious—the right type of person for his MOS.

Bullhorn's backpack. It holds his rifle perfectly.

MOC: **$12-18**, MLC: **$10**

CAPTAIN GRID-IRON
Hand-to-Hand Combat Specialist
(Includes: Pistol, Three Football Grenades, Helmet w/Visor, Machine Gun, Four Missiles, Two Blocking Pads, Backpack)

Captain Grid-Iron is one of the most reviled and maligned figures in the entire Joe line. Most collectors abhor this colorful yellow and green quarterback from West Point, yet (or perhaps, because) his accessories are interesting. The Captain comes with football-shaped grenades and elbow pads—'Nuff said.

MOC: **$10-15**, MLC: **$8**

COLD FRONT
Avalanche Driver
(Includes: Pistol, Visor, Microphone)
Included with the Avalanche.

A close-up of Cold Front's impossible-to-find microphone.

With the prototype code names of Big Chill, Cold Wave, Sub-Zero, Perma-Frost, Cold War, and Cold Steel, the character who would ultimately be known as Cold Front grew up next to Fort Knox and breathed diesel fumes until they became part of his character, "Tanks are his life" (from the file card). Collectors should take care not to lose his microphone, as it is quite difficult to locate.

MLC: *(with mic)* **$25**, *(no mic)* **$8**

FREEFALL
Paratrooper
(Includes: Assault Rifle, Hose, Helmet, Gas Mask, Backpack)

Freefall, whose prototype code name was Jumpmaster, earned his Master's Degree in Eastern Philosophy through a nose grinding work ethic and an "unparalleled degree of technical skill and seemingly boundless fonts of energy and determination." Therefore, he should have been popular with his Joe teammates. Unfortunately, his arrogance and degree of motivation frequently puts them off.

MOC: **$10-15**, MLC: **$8**

MAJOR STORM
General Commander
(Includes: Helmet, Pistol)
Included with the General.

Major Storm, originally code-named Major Foray, has "rolled" in nearly every huge machine the U.S. Army has produced for the past thirty years. Although it is immense, he thinks of his General (prototype code names of Centurion, Juggernaut, T-Wrecks, Mastodon, and Phalanx) as "just another tank, but BIGGER" (from the file card).

MLC: **$15**

PATHFINDER
Jungle Assault Specialist
(Includes: Two Machine Guns, Two Ammo Belts, Hose, Weed Eater w/Blade, Backpack)

With the prototype code names of Whacker, Bushmaster, Wildfire, Brushfire, and Wildwood, the man known as Pathfinder was a very proactive environmentalist who wished to become the Governor of Florida one day to protect his "beloved Big Cypress Swamp...from developers, poachers, and polluters" (from the prototype file card). He needed to obtain an education to accomplish this goal, and promptly signed up for the G.I. Bill joining the ranks of the Joe team shortly thereafter.

MOC: **$10-15**, MLC: **$8**

RAMPART
Shoreline Defender
(Includes: Missile Launcher, Strap, Cannon, Two Cannon Stands, Two Missiles)

As the Coastal Defender or Shoreline Defender of the G.I. Joe team, every second of Rampart's adolescence was spent in video arcades or in front of a game console. This intensive training led to his pursuit of a real challenge—the Joe team.

MOC: **$10-15**, MLC: **$8**

RAPID-FIRE
Fast Attack Expert
(Includes: Videotape, Helmet, M-17 Machine Gun)

Rapid Fire, MOC.

It was common practice for Hasbro to name and/or sculpt G.I. Joe characters after real-life individuals. For Rapid Fire, the character is named "Robbie London," after an executive at DIC Animation. Fitting, since Rapid Fire's packaging included a free video tape of a DIC G.I. Joe episode. This figure is clad in bright, bright neon.

MOC: **$25-30**, MLC: **$12**

SALVO
Anti-Armor Trooper
(Includes: Cache, Five Mines, Helmet, Five Missiles, Mine Launcher, Missile Backpack)

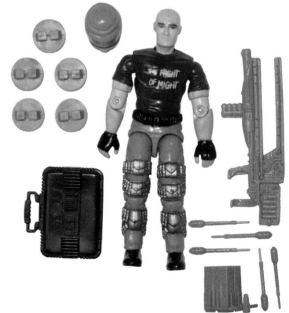

Salvo's missile launcher and missiles.

Across Salvo's t-shirt are scrawled the words "The Right of Might" and his figure did indeed look mighty. He distrusts high-tech weaponry and all its incarnations, preferring to arm himself with a bevy of conventional weapons amassed in great quantities. Overwhelming Cobra forces with mass amounts of firepower, Salvo is one tough soldier.

MOC: **$10-15**, MLC: **$8**

STRETCHER
Medical Specialist
(Includes: Microphone, Hose, Weapon, Antenna, Flying Platform, Windshield, Driving Shift, Backpack)

With the prototype code name of Hosuecall, the character known as Stretcher would be the third medical specialist on the Joe team (see Doc, 1983; Lifeline, 1986). His array of accessories is impressive and somewhat overwhelming, and there is some intricacy in putting them together. His antenna attaches to his backpack along with his microphone (attached to a black hose), his windshield and driving shift attach to his flying platform, and his microphone then attaches to a tab on his chest.

MOC: **$12-18**, MLC: **$10**

SUB-ZERO
Winter Operations Specialist
(Includes: Two-Piece Short-range Mortar, Two Snow Shoes, Four Mortar Shells, Ammo Belt, Bipod, Lightweight Machine Gun, Backpack)

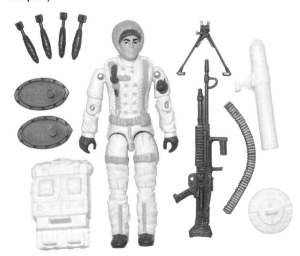

Sub-Zero was another 1990 Joe with a large set of accessories and they were some of the finest made up to this point in the line. As a character, his specialties were based on an intimate knowledge of Arctic Operations from training received at the Army Northern Warfare Training Center and as a "consultant to the Cold Regions Test Center." Both facilities were located in Fort Greeley, Alaska (from the file card). He hates the cold, which is probably what motivates him to conquer that unforgiving element whenever he can.

MOC: **$11-16**, MLC: **$10**

TOPSIDE
Navy Assault Seaman
(Includes: Submachine Gun, Helmet, Three Missiles, Missile Stand, Missile Backpack)

In an altercation with the Joes aboard a Navy transport ship, Topside popped "a can of fistfight and proceeded to mop the deck with Joes" (from the file card). He was then happily made a member of the team. His prototype code names were Barracuda, Snipe, Marlinspike, Swabbie, and Salty Dog.

MOC: **$10-15**, MLC: **$8**

UPDRAFT
Retaliator Pilot
(Includes: Helmet, Rifle)
Included with the Retaliator.

Updraft is a difficult Joe pilot to acquire, and his gun is also a hard to find accessory. As a character (with the alternate code name of "Eggbeater"), Updraft was a championship helicopter pilot and was an instructor at Flight Warrant Officer School. His talents made him a natural selection for the Joe team.

MLC: **$15**

SKY PATROL

Command of the air is crucial to determining the outcome of a battle. Sky Patrol, G.I. Joe's elite six-man airborne unit, uses advanced stealth technology and sophisticated laser weaponry to clear the sky of Cobra aerial assault crafts. The original code name for the Sky Patrol line was "F.L.A.S.H. Force," and the acronym is unknown. The Sky Patrol subset is quite popular with collectors because of the action figures' opening parachutes and muted colors.

(SKY PATROL) AIRBORNE

Sky Patrol Parachute Assembler
(Includes: Parachute, Rifle, Helmet, Backpack, Instructions)

An unfolded Sky Patrol parachute.

Airborne is not the same character as the Joe's original Helicopter Assault Trooper (see Airborne, 1983), and does not share the same file name. He is the Sky Patrol's paratrooper parachute assembler and his original prototype code name was Rigger.

MOC: **$25-35**, MLC: **$15**

(SKY PATROL) AIRWAVE

Sky Patrol Audible Frequency Specialist
(Includes: Parachute, Gun, Helmet, Face Shield, Backpack, Instructions)

Airwave is the Sky Patrol's paratrooper communications specialist.

MOC: **$25-35**, MLC: **$15**

(SKY PATROL) ALTITUDE

Sky Patrol Recon Scout
(Includes: Parachute, Helmet, Gun, Missile w/Mount, Face Shield, Backpack, Instructions)

Altitude's prototype code name was Geronimo!, and he functions as the Sky Patrol paratrooper recon scout.

MOC: **$25-35**, MLC: **$15**

(SKY PATROL) DROP ZONE

Sky Patrol Weapons Specialist
(Includes: Parachute, Helmet, Gun, Face Shield, Backpack, Instructions)

Drop Zone is the Sky Patrol's paratrooper weapons specialist.

MOC: **$25-35**, MLC: **$15**

[SKY PATROL] SKYDIVE
Sky Patrol Leader
(Includes: Parachute, Helmet, Rifle, Pistol, Backpack, Instructions)

Skydive's prototype code name was Jump Master, and he functions as the Sky Patrol's paratrooper team leader.

MOC: **$25-35**, MLC: **$15**

[SKY PATROL] STATIC LINE
Sky Patrol Demolitions Expert
(Includes: Parachute, Gun Assembly w/Harness, Gun, Helmet, Backpack, Instructions)

Static Line functions as the Sky Patrol's paratrooper demolitions specialist.

MOC: **$25-35**, MLC: **$15**

1990 COBRA FIGURES

DECIMATOR
Cobra Hammerhead Driver
(Includes: Helmet, Spear Gun)
Included with the Cobra Hammerhead.

Like the Secto-Vipers (1988), the Decimators (whose prototype code name was Panhead) guarded the beaches of Cobra Island in their Hammerheads, vehicles that were "specifically designed to function in shallow coastal waters, [and] sand and scrub vegetation" (from the file card). The Decimator's helmets are specially designed to give them a "180 degree view in almost complete darkness," like a wide-screen version of a movie.

MLC: **$15**

LASER-VIPER
Cobra Laser Trooper
(Includes: Two Barrel-Laser Guns w/Two Bases, Control Arm, Two Hoses, Helmet, Backpack)

The job of a Laser-Viper is to illuminate targets for H.E.A.T. Vipers (1989) and Cobra Condors (1989). This might force the Joes not take these troopers seriously, but Laser-Vipers are frequently supported by the vehicles they "spot" for, and this could put the Joes in peril.

MOC: **$20-30**, MLC: **$12**

METAL-HEAD
Destro's Anti-Tank Specialist
(Includes: Gun, Six Missiles, Helmet, Two Hoses, Two Leg Missile Packs, Backpack w/Frame)

Metal Head's missile system and missiles.

There are two different variations of Metal-Head's pegs on which he holds his missile launchers, some are thin and more brittle, while others are thicker and sturdier. Metal-Head's many prototype code names were Tank-Buster, Tank-Zapper, Squash-Head Harry, Salvo, and Heat-Round. He functioned as an anti-tank trooper for Destro's (1983, 1988) Iron Grenadiers (1988) and was considered to be "a walking anti-tank weapon" (from the file card) with his mass of missiles and launchers.

MOC: **$15-18**, MLC: **$12**

NIGHT CREEPER
Cobra Ninja
(Includes: Crossbow, Two Swords, Backpack)

The Night Creepers, with their prototype code names of Ghost-Tigers, Brotherhood of the Were-Tigers, and Ghost-Dragons, were the high-tech Ninjas of Cobra Command. Provided here is an excised paragraph from their prototype file card, "We caught one of these Night Creepers in a steel deadfall trap. Before we could interrogate him, he <u>willed</u> himself into a coma, causing an electro-chemical shunt that was wired into his central nervous system to auto-destruct all the weapons and equipment he was carrying! We suspect his gear included image-intensifiers, radar deflectors, infra-red dissipaters, and holographic decoy projectors, all built into bulletproof armor panels!"

MOC: **$20-30**, MLC: **$13**

OVERLORD
Dictator Driver
(Includes: Helmet, Two Claws)
Included with Cobra Overlord's Dictator.

His clever prototype code names were Braco Dracommen and Carbo Medmornac—anagrams of "Cobra Commander" (see 1982). As the Cobra Usurper (prototype MOS), the Cobra Overlord "was an officer of the... Crimson Guard [1985] who saw a golden opportunity to take control of the Cobra organization" (from the file card). In the prototype file card, it suggests that Cobra Commander was defeated by Destro (1983) and that gave the Overlord his motivation to assume command.

MLC: **$14**

RANGE-VIPER
Cobra Wilderness Troopers
(Includes: Knife, Hose, Grenade Launcher, Mortar, Two-Piece Machine Gun, Backpack)

In their prototype file cards, they were dubbed Bush Vipers, Badgers, Snake-Eaters, and Dingos, but in the end, the Range-Viper was actually the Cobra Shock Trooper and the Cobra Wilderness Trooper combined. The Range-Vipers are peculiar looking, oddly colored, and strangely attractive as wilderness troopers. As soldiers, they are cheap to operate in the field, can live on nuts and roots, can create their own shelter, and can "procure their own ammunitions" (from the file card).

MOC: **$18-30**, MLC: **$12**

ROCK-VIPER
Cobra Mountain Trooper
(Includes: Rifle, Pistol, Rope, Hose, Grappling Hook, Backpack)

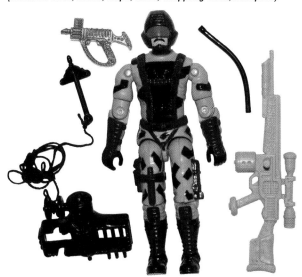

The Cobra Rock-Vipers endure unspeakable hardship on their graduation day, as the candidates "are dropped... on top of a 500 foot high, sheer sided mesa. Each candidate is has been given 250 feet of rope and is told that only 50% of the candidates will graduate." The odds are against them.

MOC: **$18-30**, MLC: **$12**

S.A.W.-VIPER (SEMI AUTOMATIC WEAPONS)
Cobra Heavy Machine Gunners
(Includes: Heavy Machine Gun, Ammo Belt, Bipod, Backpack)

The S.A.W.-Viper corps produced one of the most infamous Cobra soldiers in existence. In the Marvel comics, it was a lone S.A.W.-Viper on a mission in Trucial Abysmia that misunderstood a command to release some Joe prisoners and then proceeded to kill a large contingent of G.I. Joes. Originally called "C.L.A.W.-Vipers" (Cobra Light Automatic Weapons, from the prototype file card), the S.A.W.-Vipers action figures have one of the largest machine guns of all the Joe characters. The S.A.W.-Vipers are lethal and deadly Cobras, and the technology that supports them is highly advanced.

MOC: **$18-30**, MLC: **$12**

UNDERTOW
Destro's Frogmen
(Includes: Barracuda, Trident, Mask, Torpedo, Riding Skiff, Hose, Two Flippers)

The Undertow frogmen are members of Destro's Iron Grenadiers (1988), and function as "Underwater Destroyers" (from the prototype MOS) that will swim through anything, from murky to polluted waters. Thankfully, their wetsuits are specially treated to repel foreign elements.

MOC: **$18-30**, MLC: **$12**

VAPOR
Cobra Hurricane Pilot
Included with Cobra Hurricane V.T.O.L.

There is a rumor that Vapor action figures came with a rifle, but there have never been found any MISP samples to prove this true (I opened a MISB Hurricane myself). Akin to the Star-Vipers (1988), the Vapor contingent of the Cobra legions "have direct shunts from their optic nerves to their inboard targeting computers" (from the file card). Unfortunately, the prowess they attain from this instantaneous visual acquisition only lasts for approximately one half hour, after which the Vapor soldiers "degenerate into babbling idiots."

MLC: **$18-25**

SONIC FIGHTERS

These specially trained front line fighters blast into action, equipped with a devastating arsenal of battle-ready weapons! Take command of these front line commandos and put the sounds of battle at your fingertips! (Use your Sonic Backpack as a Hand-held Weapon!) These file cards were the first that were written in-house by Hasbro, as Mr. Hama was sent these dossiers to edit and then send back to Hasbro. Be careful to remove the batteries from the Sonic Fighter backpacks, if these are left inside the accessories, they will corrode and ruin the toys.

(SONIC FIGHTERS) DIAL-TONE

Communications

(Includes: Four Sonic Weapons—Laser Pistol, Laser Rifle, Machine Gun, Laser Gun)

For a full bio of this figure, see Dial-Tone (1986).

MOC: **$18-22**, MLC: **$10**

(SONIC FIGHTERS) DODGER

Heavy Ordnance Operator

(Includes: Four Sonic Weapons—Pistol, Machine Gun, Laser Rifle, Laser Pistol)

There are two different versions of Dodger's Sonic Backpack—one with raised edges around the buttons, one without. For a full bio of this figure, see Dodger (1987).

MOC: **$18-22**, MLC: **$10**

(SONIC FIGHTERS) LAMPREYS

Amphibious Assault Troopers

(Includes: Four Sonic Weapons—Machine Gun, Laser Rifle, Laser Pistol, Pistol)

For a full bio of this figure, see Lampreys (1985).

MOC: **$22-30**, MLC: **$10**

(SONIC FIGHTERS) LAW

M.P.

(Includes: Four Sonic Weapons—Pistol, Machine Gun, Laser Pistol, Laser Rifle)

There are two different versions of Law's Sonic Backpack—one with raised edges around the buttons, one without. For a full bio of this figure, see Law (1987).

MOC: **$18-22**, MLC: **$10**

(SONIC FIGHTERS) TUNNEL RAT
E.O.D.
(Includes: Four Sonic Weapons—Laser Pistol, Pistol, Missile Launcher, Machine Gun)

For a full bio of this figure, see Tunnel Rat (1987).

MOC: **$18-22**, MLC: **$10**

(SONIC FIGHTERS) VIPER
Cobra Infantryman
(Includes: Four Sonic Weapons—Laser Pistol, Missile Launcher, Pistol, Machine Gun)

For a full bio of this figure, see Viper (1986).

MOC: **$22-30**, MLC: **$10**

1990 VEHICLES/PLAYSETS

AVALANCHE
(Includes: Cold Front figure)

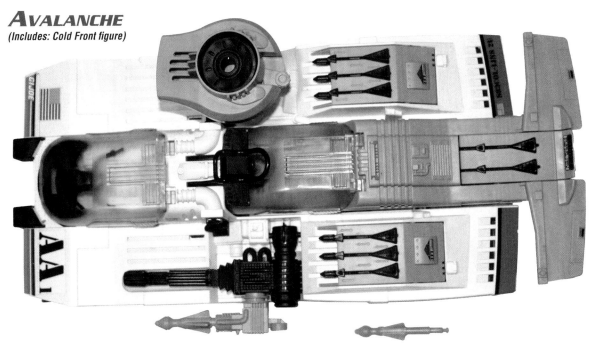

The G.I. Joe Avalanche is one of the most popular pieces in the Joe line, especially MISB samples which sell for quite a lot of money. The vehicle has a digitally accurate ice mine deployer, a side-swipe missile-firing pulse cannon, six heat-seeking high impact surface-to-air missiles, and a removable scout craft for Arctic reconnaissance.

Easily lost pieces include two white missiles, eight black missiles, and six mines.

MISB: **$75**, MIB: **$35**, MLC: **$20**

The Avalanche's easily lost pieces.

COBRA HAMMERHEAD
(Includes: Decimator figure)

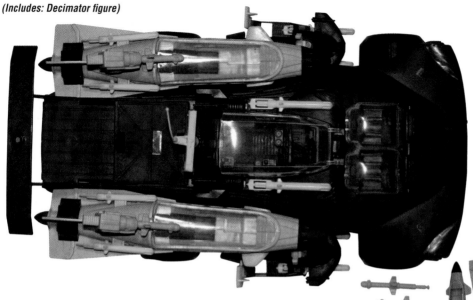

The Cobra Hammerhead is a one of Cobra's premier pieces in the 1990 line, and adds firepower and support to Cobra's naval legions. The vehicle comes equipped with two sea-net penetrating low-noise attack subs with missile firing capabilities, an air-tight self-contained control center, a pressurized decompression chamber, and an upper deck airborne/undersea command module with pivoting radar unit.

Easily lost pieces include two attack subs, command module, antenna, two machine guns, four torpedoes, two small missiles, fourteen thin green missiles, and two sea sleds with belts.

The Hammerhead's easily lost pieces.

MISB: **$60**, MIB: **$35**, MLC: **$20**

COBRA HURRICANE V.T.O.L.
(Includes: Vapor figure)

One of the most highly-demanded Cobra aircraft, the Hurricane with VTOL (Vertical Take Off and Landing) capabilities has many armaments to add to Cobra's Air legions: eleven missiles (two are on the bottom of the jet), dual fuselage underside 75mm cannons, and a VTE-490 pilotless fighter/interceptor attack drone mounted on its back.

Easily lost pieces are the ten thin yellow missiles and engine cover.

MISB: **$100**, MIB: **$70**, MLC: **$35**

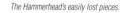

The Hurricane's easily lost pieces.

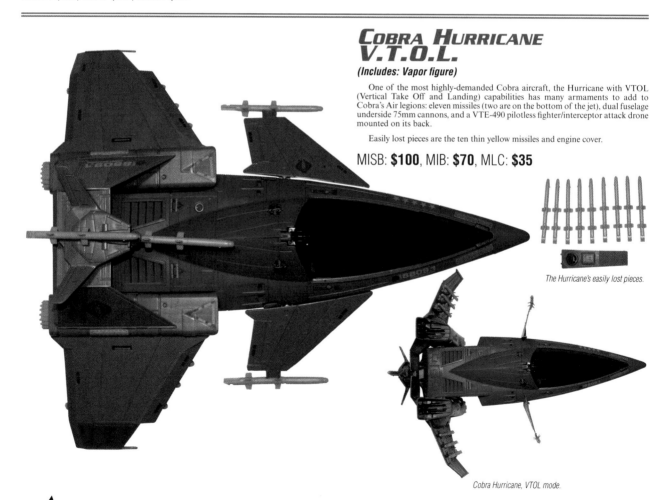

Cobra Hurricane, VTOL mode.

COBRA OVERLORD'S DICTATOR
(Includes: Overlord figure)

The Overlord's Dictator is a simple combination tracked and wheeled craft, with rapid-fire .40-caliber high impact machine guns, and low to the ground air-to-surface missiles.

Easily lost pieces are the two missiles.

MISB: **$30**, MIB: **$20**, MLC: **$12**

The Dictator's easily lost pieces.

COBRA PIRANHA

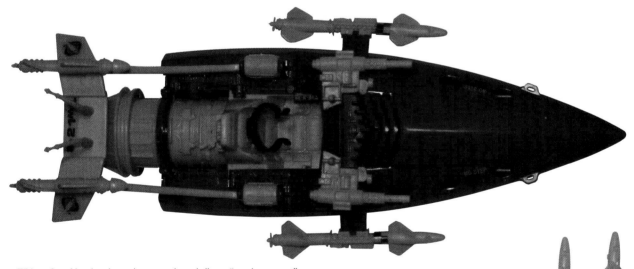

With surface-skimming, low noise concussion missiles, a "pop in, pop out" machine gun emplacement, a 12,000 horsepower hydraulically energized aqua power plant, and a high-velocity depth charge launcher, the Cobra Piranha is one of the fastest ships in the Cobra navy.

Easily lost pieces include two torpedoes, two depth charges, and four missiles.

MISB: **$25**, MIB: **$15**, MLC: **$10**

The Piranha's easily lost pieces.

COBRA RAGE

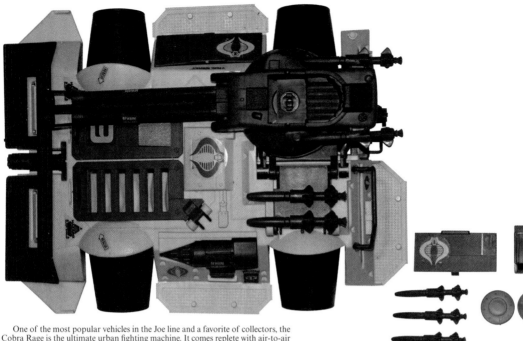

One of the most popular vehicles in the Joe line and a favorite of collectors, the Cobra Rage is the ultimate urban fighting machine. It comes replete with air-to-air full blast missiles, a 25-valve thruster engine, a long-range dual-barreled concussion cannon, and a multi-shot high-intensity machine cannon. It also has armor plating scattered about the vehicle, a movable turret, and a mine holder.

Easily lost pieces include the hatch, mine holder, four mines, and four missiles.

The Rage's easily lost pieces.

MISB: **$65**, MIB: **$35**, MLC: **$20**

DESTRO'S DOMINATOR

Yet another popular vehicle from the 1990 line, Destro's Dominator is one of the Iron Grenadier's (1988) premiere tracked vehicles. It transforms from a helicopter to a tank with its movable chopper blades and retractable tank treads. It includes a mutli-shot rapid fire 3.5mm missile pod, many missiles, and heavy armor plating.

Easily lost pieces are the four missiles.

MISB: **$50**, MIB: **$30**, MLC: **$20**

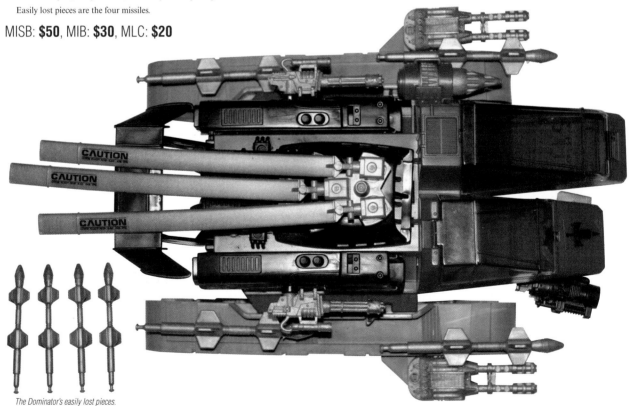

The Dominator's easily lost pieces.

GENERAL
(Includes: Major Storm figure)

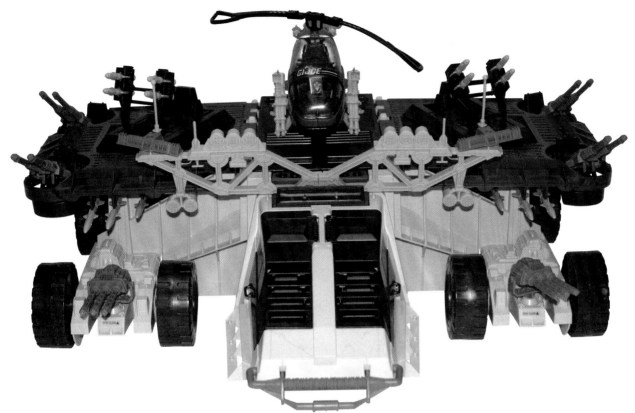

The General is an impressive vehicle and is difficult to find MISB or mint, loose, complete because of its many small accessories. The General's unique features include a recoiling front tow hook with 50,000 lb. test cable; tri-barrel machine guns that function as defensive armaments stations; ground-hugging, heat-sensitive surface-to-surface missiles; two platform air defense missile stations; a landing deck for the included Locust (a notably different vehicle from the regular 1990 version); a long range positional mortar cannon with four shells; an impressive pull-out loading ramp; and rear multi-cannon anti-attack gunnery stations.

Easily lost pieces include four mortar shells, twelve large yellow missiles, two tiny antennas (almost always missing), eight smaller thicker yellow missiles (for the air defense missile stations), a large two-part main antenna display, four green cannons (rear mounted), and four green cannons (roof mounted).

MISB: $120, MIB: $75, MLC: $50

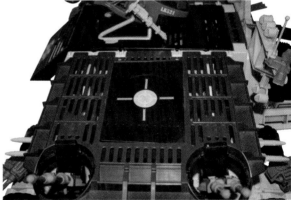

The General's side with non-active cannon.

The General's front cockpit.

The General's side with active cannon.

The General's side, completely flipped up.

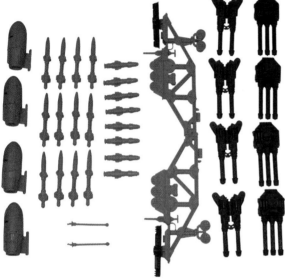

The General's hidden cannon system.

A MISB General.

The General's easily lost pieces.

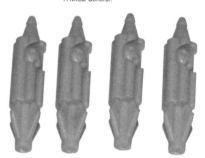

The four bombs for the General's Locust.

HAMMER

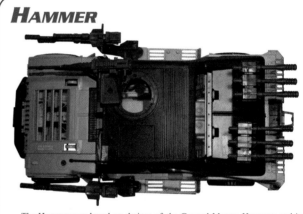

The Hammer was based on designs of the General Motors Hummer, and is hugely popular with collectors, especially MISB samples. Even loose, the Hammer has so many tiny pieces and parts that it is difficult to complete. The Hammer is ready for battle with a removable engine cover, a high-impact pulse cannon, a fully rotational computer controlled gun turret, shrapnel resistant cover, multiple launch direction missile fire stations, and quick slide rear hatches with storage ducts.

Easily lost pieces include two side cannons, one large cannon, gun turret, two sliding storage covers for the rear, antenna, gun mount, ammo case, gas can, and ammo belt—the last three parts are nearly always missing from loose Hammers.

MISB: **$50**, MIB: **$35**, MLC: **$25**

The General's Locust Helicopter.

The Hammer's easily lost pieces.

LOCUST

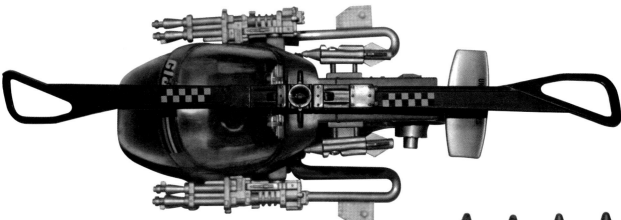

The Locust helicopter is a very popular vehicle with collectors, and is becoming more difficult to find MISB. With aerodynamic high-tech propeller blades, damage resistant landing skids, heat seeking, low-noise air-to-air missiles, a bomb-dropping inner mechanism, and a tinted blast-proof windscreen canopy, it is a great small attack craft.

Easily lost pieces are the four missiles.

NOTE: *This is a different vehicle than that included with the General.*

MISB: **$25**, MIB: **$15**, MLC: **$8-10**

The Locust's easily lost pieces.

MOBILE BATTLE BUNKER

Mobile Battle Bunker's easily lost pieces.

The Battle Bunker is one of the most unusual looking Joe vehicles, and is loaded to the gills with armaments to support the Joe team's land assault forces. With a 5,000 round capacity, laser ammunition dispenser, two double-barreled mortar cannons, and a hidden missile rack that pops out from the inside, the Battle Bunker is an interesting addition to the Joe's arsenal.

Easily lost pieces are its five missiles.

MISB: **$40**, MIB: **$20**, MLC: **$12**

Mobile Battle Bunker in assault mode.

RETALIATOR
(Includes: Updraft figure)

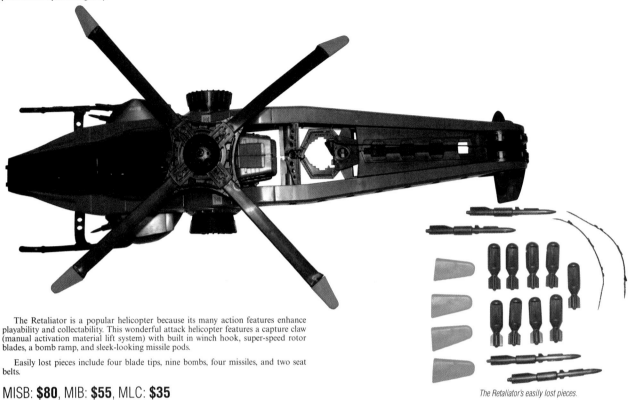

The Retaliator is a popular helicopter because its many action features enhance playability and collectability. This wonderful attack helicopter features a capture claw (manual activation material lift system) with built in winch hook, super-speed rotor blades, a bomb ramp, and sleek-looking missile pods.

Easily lost pieces include four blade tips, nine bombs, four missiles, and two seat belts.

MISB: **$80**, MIB: **$55**, MLC: **$35**

The Retaliator's easily lost pieces.

SKY PATROL

Created with a scientifically advanced radar-reflective protectant, these modified combat crafts have been refurbished and re-equipped with the latest in high-impact armaments, giving G.I. Joe total air superiority over Cobra.

SKY HAVOC

The Sky Havoc shares the same design as the HAVOC (1986) and shares similar easily lost pieces. The chrome wears easily, check its condition.

MISB: **$50**, MIB: **$28**, MLC: **$20**

The Sky Havoc's easily lost pieces.

SKY HAWK

The Sky Hawk shares the same design as the Sky Hawk (1986) and shares similar easily lost pieces. The chrome wears easily, check its condition.

MISB: **$30**, MIB: **$18**, MLC: **$12**

The Sky Hawk's easily lost pieces.

SKY RAVEN

The Sky Raven shares the same design as the Cobra Night Raven S3P (1986) and shares similar easily lost pieces. The chrome wears easily, check its condition.

MISB: **$100**, MIB: **$70**, MLC: **$40**

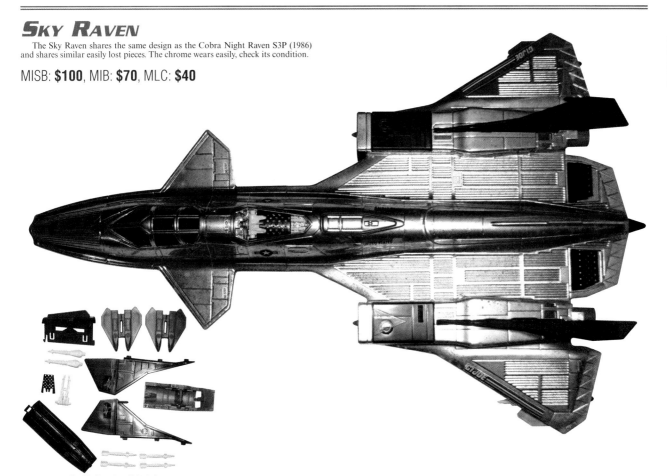

The Sky Raven's easily lost pieces.

Sky S.H.A.R.C.

The Sky S.H.A.R.C. shares the same design as the S.H.A.R.C. (1984) and shares similar easily lost pieces. The chrome wears easily, check its condition.

MISB: **$35-40**, MIB: **$22**, MLC: **$15**

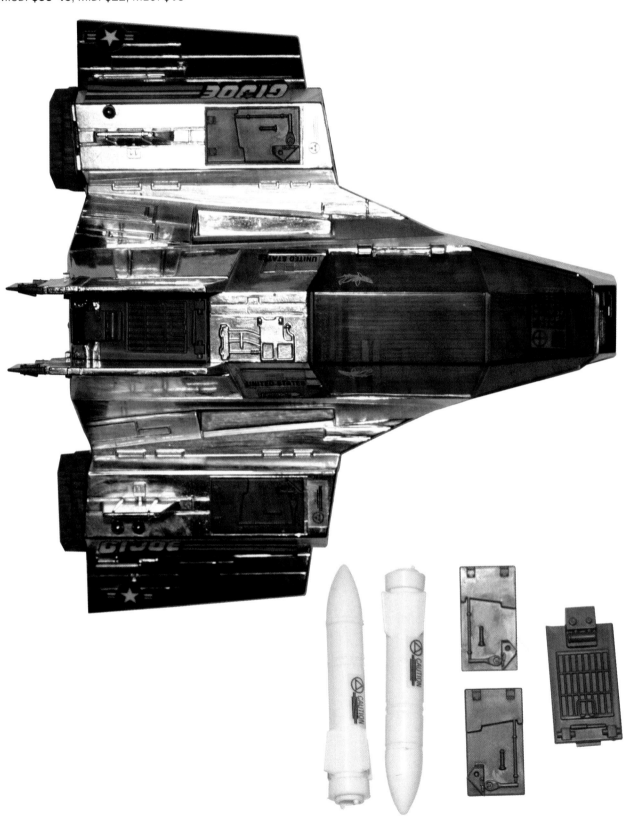

The Sky S.H.A.R.C.'s easily lost pieces.

(SERIES X, 1991)

In Series Ten, most G.I. Joe figure packages include spring-loaded weapons for the action figures, and a few even included "battle stands." Collectors feel that this was one of the last "well-done" generations of figures and vehicles before neon colors spread over the toy line. In 1991, many old characters have been re-sculpted and re-outfitted with new weapons and accessories, while most of the newer figures were pretty well designed. The Eco-Warriors line of figures and accessories were introduced this year, perhaps an attempt by Hasbro to become more environmentally conscious.

NOTE: *At one point in 1991, Iceberg (1986) was issued as a mail-away figure with a Rock-Viper rifle (1990) and square-sized gray file card. Steeler (1982-83) was also offered as a mail-away with a square gray file card, minus his headset, but including a set of Duke (1983) binoculars.*

1991 Catalog.

G.I. Joe Magnet inserts.

Samples of the super-rare gold-bordered Impel Hall of Fame trading card inserts.

1991 G.I. JOE FIGURES

BIG BEN
SAS Trooper
(Includes: Backpack, Grenade Pouch w/Strap, Two Grenades, Machine Gun, Bipod)

As the Joe's first British SAS [Special Air Service] trooper, it has been suggested that Big Ben "participated in initial recon operations in the Falklands campaign and in various covert operations" (from the file card). The qualifications to become SAS are rigorous and grueling, and Big Ben completed the training with grace and dignity. His figure comes with some excellent accessories, and he is fairly popular with collectors.

MOC: **$15-20**, MLC: **$10**

CLOUDBURST
Glider Trooper
(Includes: Rifle, Visor)
Included with the Air Commando glider.

Cloudburst "designed and built his own working" (from the file card) prototype gliders "as a teenager in San Francisco." After joining the U.S. Army, he developed "ultra-stealth gliders for military recon and special-troop insertion." He is currently the glider specialist on the Joe team. His prototype code name was Spindrift.

MLC: **$15**

Dusty & Sandstorm
Desert Trooper & Coyote
(Includes: Coyote [Sandstorm], Backpack, Pistol, Submachine Gun w/Sliding Stock)

This version of Dusty includes his coyote Sandstorm, and is a fascinating figure sculpt as his motif reflects America's 1990-1991 conflict in the Persian Gulf. With a sliding stock and fairly muted colors, his figure is a nice update of Dusty (1985). In this incarnation, Dusty is fluent in many different languages "spoken in the great desert regions of the world," and these are noted, "Arabic... Hebrew... Kazakh and Khalkha" (from the file card).

MOC: **$15-20**, MLC: **$10**

General Hawk
G.I. Joe Commander
(Includes: Jet Pack w/Movable Wings, Four Missiles, Helmet w/ Visor, Machine Gun)

This incarnation of Hawk (now called, "General Hawk") showcases a detailed jet pack and communications helmet in order for the Joe's commander to "survey the progress of battle as well as keep in constant radio contact with all the elements of his command" (from the file card). For a full bio on this character, see Hawk (1982, 1986).

MOC: **$15-20**, MLC: **$10**

Grunt
Infantry Squad Leader
(Includes: Machine Gun, Blast 'Em Rocket Launcher, Bipod, Missile, Battle Stand, Helmet)

A strange update to 1982's Grunt (see this character for a full bio), he has now been promoted to Infantry Squad Leader, and his hair color has been changed from brown to black—an inconsistency with this character. His file card shows that Grunt became reactivated with the team after taking a leave to obtain his degree in Engineering at Georgia Tech. Grunt is a stand-up soldier who, "When the smoke clears... did his job" (from the file card).

MOC: **$15-20**, MLC: **$10**

Heavy Duty
Heavy Ordnance Trooper
(Includes: Backpack w/Missile Sight, Launcher Base, Center Mount Cannon w/Two Spring-Loaded Side-Mount Missile Launchers, Two Missiles)

With more heavy machinery than you can shake a stick at, Heavy Duty became the Joe's new Heavy Ordnance Trooper, proficient with classical guitar as well as his "Man-Portable Heavy Weapons System" (from the file card). Heavy Duty became a fairly popular Joe, and in his original prototype dossier his code names were Cinder-Block, Bulwark, or Brick-Wall. Heavy Duty was a classical harpsichordist in his spare time.

Heavy Duty's assembled cannon.

MOC: **$15-20**, MLC: **$10**

LIFELINE
(Kellog's Rice Krispies Exclusive)
(Includes: Rescue Case, Backpack)
Mail Away Exclusive

For a full bio on this character, see Lifeline (1986). Note that this mail-away version from Kellogg's cereal does not have a pistol mounted on his left thigh and did not come with a pistol, as the cereal company did not wish to offer a promotional including a toy gun. Strangely, this mail-away figure is more exacting to Lifeline's Sunbow cartoon character as an avowed pacifist.

MLC: **$10**

LOW-LIGHT
Night Fighter
(Includes: Backpack, Knife, Flashlight, Helmet, Visor, Gun)

Now sporting a grizzled beard, face camouflage, and black hair (he used to have yellow hair see Low-Light, [1986]), Low-Light came with weapons appropriate to a "Night Fighter." This character is now more proficient with "image intensifiers (starlight scopes), infrared metascopes, and thermal imaging devices." For a full bio, see Low-Light (1986).

MOC: **$15-20**, MLC: **$10**

MAJOR ALTITUDE
Battle Copter Pilot
(Includes: Helmet, Rifle)
Included with the G.I. Joe Battle Copter.

As a seven year old, Major Altitude announced that one day, he wanted to join the Joe team. After finding out the requirements for the elite fighting unit, he prepared his whole life for this daunting task. After years of hard work, he applied and was accepted to the team. His prototype code names were Air-Cav, Updraft, and Whirlwind.

MLC: **$10**

MERCER
Mercenary
(Includes: Machine Gun, Grenade Launcher, Backpack w/88mm Stanford Rocket Launcher, Missile, Battle Stand)

Once a member of Slaughter's Marauders (for a full bio, see Mercer [1987]), this former Cobra Viper (now wearing a beard) is still a member of the Joe team, but curiously wears the Cobra colors of blue, red, and silver.

NOTE: *His backpack and launcher might be slightly awkward to pose.*

MOC: **$15-20**, MLC: **$10**

RED STAR
Oktober Guard Officer
(Includes: Removable Hat, Knife, Backpack w/Antenna, Mini Gatling Gun w/Two Barrels, Ammo Belt, AK-47 Assault Rifle, Spring-Loaded Missile Launcher, Missile)

Red Star is the first G.I. Joe figure to hail from the Oktober Guard, the Russian version of the Joe team. With a bevy of fantastic weapons including the AK-47 assault rifle, an ammo belt, a Gatling gun, and a removable hat, Red Star was a popular figure from the 1991 releases.

NOTE: *Red Star was originally released on a "Cobra" file card, and then the file card came with a light blue "G.I. Joe" label applied over the top of the Cobra sigil. Eventually, Red Star would be released on the more common "G.I. Joe" card. The card with the sticker is quite rare, but can be found if collectors look frequently for it.*

Red Star on Cobra card with light blue Joe label.

MOC: *(Cobra file card, or light blue sticker on file card)* **$50-100**, *(Joe card)* **$15-20**, MLC: **$10**

SKYMATE
Glider Trooper
(Includes: Visor, Boomerang, Bow)
Included with Air Commandos glider.

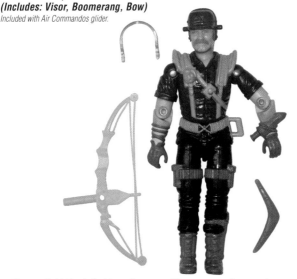

Skymate is highly desired by collectors, as his weapons and accessories are notoriously difficult to find. Between his neon pink boomerang that fits on his belt and light blue visor, he is a difficult figure to complete. His character hails from Queenstown, Australia, and is a member of the Australian S.A.S. [Special Air Service]. He is proficient with many exotic weapons. His prototype code names were Digger, Jackaroo, and Dingo.

MLC: **$15-20**

SCI-FI
Directed Energy Expert
(Includes: Helmet, Two Hoses, Backpack, Spring-Loaded Cannon, Laser Slug, Laser Rifle)

A fantastic update of an unusual figure from the 1986 line (for a full bio, see Sci-Fi, [1986]), this version of the former Laser Trooper turned "Directed Energy Expert" is clad in midnight black with some pretty cool accessories. He has now received his Master's in Electronic Engineering, and for his Master's Thesis, "was able to perfect an unparalleled defensive security system" (from the file card). It is hinted in his file card that he is a bit obsessed with his work.

MOC: **$15-20**, MLC: **$10**

SNAKE EYES
Commando
(Includes: Machine Gun, Grappling Hook w/String, Two Swords, Spring Loaded Backpack)

Neon colors do not a Ninja Commando make, and this version of Snake Eyes is widely regarded as the least favorite by many collectors. With two bright orange swords, a bright orange grappling hook, and a bright orange machine gun, this figure did not really capture the character's essence, moving from the esoteric to the borderline ridiculous. For a full bio, see Snake Eyes (1982).

MOC: **$20-30**, MLC: **$14**

TRACKER
Navy S.E.A.L.
(Includes: Machine Gun, Two Paddles, Inflatable Covert Insertion Raft, Battle Stand, Helmet/Visor)

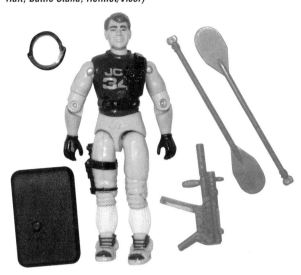

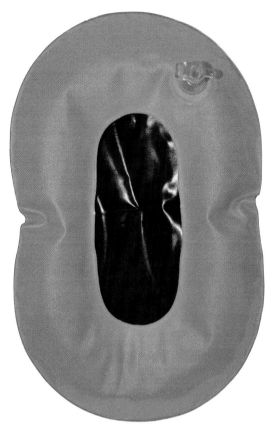

During a preliminary training exercise upon his acceptance onto the Joe team, Tracker captured both Snake Eyes and Spirit, his instructors when he repeated the "Escape and Evasion" exercise (from the file card). This figure is unusual, as it comes with an inflatable rubber raft, and a visor that does not fit over his eyes very well. His prototype code name was Bloodhound.

MOC: **$15-20**, MLC: **$10**

Tracker's raft.

ECO-WARRIORS

"The forces of nature are under attack from Cobra and only G.I. Joe can stop them! Using the most dangerous liquid toxins known to mankind, Cobra launches its most diabolical bid to contaminate the planet's fragile eco-system and bring civilization to its knees! Armed with a sophisticated Anti-Tox water solution that changes a figure's color on contact, and outfitted with special eco-suits that detect environmental contaminants, G.I. Joe moves out to "clean up" Cobra's act once and for all! Even now, the fate of the earth hangs in the balance."

NOTE: *The bottom of each character's file card included a brief attachment with "special tips" on how children can protect the environment.*

(ECO-WARRIORS) CESSPOOL
C.E.O. – Chief Environmental Operative
(Includes: Helmet, Chainsaw, Rifle, Hose, Backpack)

Before becoming the C.E.O. of Cobra Command, Cesspool was the "Chief Executive Officer of a huge multinational corporation" with a vested interest in businesses that poured toxic waste into the environment. An accident occurred while demonstrating a new product, and the disaster left him disfigured. He is as ruthless as he is despicable.

NOTE: *Cesspool is another character whose file card "real" name is that of an actual person. Vincent D'Alleva was the Hasbro executive in charge of the G.I. Joe Division.*

MOC: **$15-20**, MLC: **$10**

(ECO-WARRIORS) COBRA TOXO-VIPER
Hostile Environment Trooper
(Includes: Rifle, Backpack, Water Cannon, Figure Stand)

Updated and remolded for the Eco Warriors line, a full bio can be seen at Toxo-Viper (1988). Their suits have been updated and now they have state-of-the-art equipment, but their job is still abhorrent.

MOC: **$15-20**, MLC: **$10**

(ECO-WARRIORS) CLEAN-SWEEP

G.I. Joe Anti-Tox Trooper
(Includes: Helmet, Backpack, Pistol, Robot w/Lever)

With a large "robotic sludge sucker/ neutralizer gel dispenser" (from the file card), Clean-Sweep's job is fairly mundane, as he must "clean up Cobra's act," and un-blemish their pollution of the environment.

Clean Sweep's machine.

MOC: **$15-20**, MLC: **$10**

(ECO-WARRIORS) FLINT

Eco-Warriors Commander
(Includes: Helmet, Rifle, Water Rifle, Hose, Backpack)

As head of the new Eco-Warriors environmental force, Flint parachutes into a Cobra "toxic sludge operation... to stop evil polluters" (from the file card). For a full bio of this character, see Flint (1985).

MOC: **$15-20**, MLC: **$10**

(ECO-WARRIORS) OZONE

G.I. Joe Ozone Replenisher Trooper
(Includes: Helmet, Vacuum, Water Rifle, Hose, Backpack)

Ozone's the trooper who truly helps out the environment. He's the Joe with experience in "atmospheric dispersal toxins, and is equipped with a multi-purpose backpack, capable of neutralizing various forms of airborne sludge and other harmful chemicals while replenishing the ozone layer around the earth's atmposphere" (from the file card). His prototype code name was Fresh-Air.

MOC: **$15-20**, MLC: **$10**

[ECO-WARRIORS] SLUDGE VIPER

Cobra Hazardous Waste Viper
(Includes: Rifle, Backpack, Water Cannon, Missile, Figure Stand)

A pretty cool troop builder if his weapons weren't so bulky, the Sludge Viper has a sludge gun that "creates toxic sludge out of whatever is in hand, and propel it at lethal velocities." These were originally called Sludge Slingers.

MOC: **$15-20**, MLC: **$10**

SUPER SONIC FIGHTERS

"These specially trained front-line fighters blast into action, equipped with a devastating arsenal of battle-ready weapons! Take command of these front line commandos and put the sounds of battle at your fingertips! (Use your Sonic Backpack as a Hand-held Weapon!)"

In response to the Sonic Fighters line of figures, Larry Hama had this to say in a communiqué to Hasbro, "What is a 'Sonic Fighter'? Is it a special group of JOES who make NOISE? Is the noise itself a weapon? Are the weapons sonically activated or sonically driven or what? I really couldn't find an angle here that overcame my initial suspension of disbelief, so I have done the bios 'straight.'"

(SUPER SONIC FIGHTERS) LT. FLACON

Green Beret

(Includes: Machine Gun, Laser Rifle, Battle Stand, Copter Blades. Sonic Backpack capable of four sonic sounds: Laser Pistol, Machine Gun, Laser Rifle, Pistol)

For a full bio of this character, see Falcon (1987).

MOC: **$15-20**, MLC: **$10**

Falcon's sonic backpack.

(SUPER SONIC FIGHTERS) MAJOR BLUDD

Mercenary

(Includes: Sonic Disruptor Cannon, Laser Machine Gun, Battle Stand, Muzzle. Sonic Backpack capable of four sonic sounds: Laser Pistol, Sonic Disruptor Cannon, Rocket Launcher, Laser Machine Gun)

This version is interestingly different from the former incarnation of Major Bludd (1982), and it is curious to note the pronounced fangs on the mouth and grenades that he dangerously carries all over his body. For a full bio, see Major Bludd (1982).

MOC: **$15-20**, MLC: **$10**

Major Bludd's sonic backpack.

[SUPER SONIC FIGHTERS] PSYCHE-OUT

Deceptive Warfare

(Includes: Two Small E.C.M. Disks, Large E.C.M. Disk, E.C.M. Microphone, Antenna, Radar Dish, Radar Screen, Battle Stand, Hose. Sonic Backpack capable of four sonic sounds: Laser Pistol, Pistol, E.C.M. Laser, Laser Rifle)

The best re-sculpt of any Sonic Fighter or Super Sonic Fighter figure, Psyche-Out truly looks the part of a soldier whose MOS is Deceptive Warfare. For a full bio, see Psyche-Out (1987).

Larry Hama made an interesting handwritten margin note on this character's military specialty, "The use of t-shirts with anti Noriega slogans was an actual U.S. Army Psy-Ops operation along with the playing of heavy metal music outside the Vatican embassy."

MOC: **$15-20**, MLC: **$10**

Psyche-Out's sonic backpack.

[SUPER SONIC FIGHTERS] ROAD PIG

Dreadnok

(Includes: Machine Gun, Flamethrower, Battle Stand, Shoulder Pads. Sonic Backpack capable of four sonic sounds: Commando Rifle, Laser Pistol, Flamethrower, Machine Gun)

For a full bio of the character, see Road Pig (1988).

MOC: **$15-20**, MLC: **$10**

[SUPER SONIC FIGHTERS] ROCK 'N ROLL

Machine Gunner

(Includes: Machine Gun, Cannon, Battle Stand. Sonic Backpack capable of four sonic sounds: Laser Rifle, .50 Cal. Machine Gun, Mortar Launcher, M-50 Machine Gun)

For a full bio of the figure, see Rock 'N Roll (1982, 1989).

MOC: **$15-20**, MLC: **$10**

(SUPER SONIC FIGHTERS) ZAP

Ground Artillery Soldier

(Includes: Backpack Gun, Sonic Rocket Launcher, Helmet, Battle Stand, Double Barreled Rocket Launcher w/Muzzle. Sonic Backpack capable of four sonic sounds: Double Barreled Rocket Launcher, Grenade Launcher, Machine Gun, Pistol)

Zap's sonic backpack.

This version of Zap is a wonderful update of the original Zap (1982) and even captures his missed mustache. His MOS has changed from Bazooka Soldier to Ground Artillery Soldier. For a full bio of the character, see Zap (1982).

MOC: **$15-20**, MLC: **$10**

TALKING BATTLE COMMANDERS

These fearless leaders "command" attention! Equipped with state-of-the-art, voice/sound modification backpacks, these G.I. Joe and Cobra leaders are ready to shout out their orders loud and clear!

(TALKING BATTLE COMMANDERS) GENERAL HAWK

(#1) G.I. Joe Commander

(Says: "Eat Lead, Cobra!", "Yo Joe!", "Move Out!")
(Includes: Pistol, Rifle, Antenna, Figure Stand, Attached Backpack)

For a full bio of this character, see Hawk (1982, 1986). Many collectors consider this to be an excellent re-sculpt of Hawk, and for good reason.

MOC: **$15-20**,
MLC: **$10**

(TALKING BATTLE COMMANDERS) STALKER

(#2) Ranger

(Says: "Let's Party!", "Attack!", "Blitz 'Em!")
(Includes: Machine Gun, Laser Pistol, Figure Stand, Attached Backpack)

For a full bio of this character, see Stalker (1982).

MOC: **$15-20**, MLC: **$10**

(TALKING BATTLE COMMANDERS) COBRA COMMANDER

(#3) Cobra Leader

(Says: "I'll Get You!", "Cobra!", "Vipers Attack!")
(Includes: Missile Launcher, Two Missiles, Rifle, Figure Stand, Attached Backpack)

For a full bio of this character, see Enemy Leader: Cobra Commander (1982).

MOC: **$15-20**, MLC: **$10**

(Talking Battle Commanders) Overkill

(#4) B.A.T. Leader
(Says: "B.A.T.S. Attack!", "Wipe Out!", "Destroy!")
(Includes: Laser Rifle, Mechanical Claw, Red Right Hand, Figure Stand, Attached Backpack)

Pic of Overkill's hidden chest gun.

Begun as an "experimental prototype for the third generation of B.A.T.s [1986, 1991]... the cost projections were too high for profitable mass-production" (from the file card). Cobra Commander (1982) then decided to make use of the robot as a battlefield commander for the B.A.T.s. It should be noted that the figure's chest can open (careful, it is fragile) and two small .50-caliber machine guns pop out.

MOC: **$15-20**, MLC: **$10**

Cobra Commander

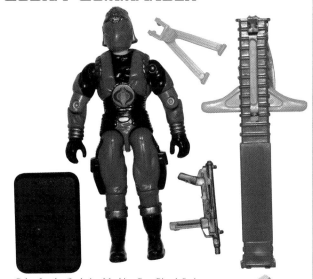

Cobra Commander's glider.

Cobra Leader (Includes: Machine Gun, Bipod, Spring-Loaded Flying Surveillance Weapon Launcher, Glider, Battle Stand)

Packaged with what can only be described as a "radio-controlled, buzz bomb, flying surveillance weapon" (from the file card), this bizarre version of Cobra Commander came in two variants: with or without eyebrows. The version with eyebrows is much more rare than the version without eyebrows. For a full bio, see Enemy Leader: Cobra Commander (1982).

MOC: *(eyebrows)* **$25-35**,
(no eyebrows) **$15-20**,
MLC: *(eyebrows)* **$15-20**,
(no eyebrows) **$10**

1991 Cobra Figures
Cobra B.A.T.

Battle Android Trooper
(Includes: Hand, Grenade Launcher, Battle Stand, Modular Missile Launcher, Missile)

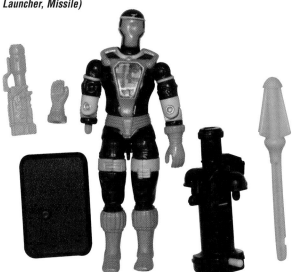

The second version of Cobra's Battle Android Troopers "can absorb enormous amounts of battle damage and still continue their missions" (from the file card). The usual method of deployment for B.A.T.s is to kick them out of low-flying aircraft without parachutes, letting the robots hit the ground and engage the enemy. "This delivery system is... quite demoralizing to opposing troops who happen to witness it." Although logically inferior to the original B.A.T.S. (1986), their weapons have been drastically upgraded.

MOC: **$15-20**, MLC: **$10**

Crimson Guard Immortal

Cobra Elite Trooper
(Includes: Ammo Belt, Backpack, Gun, Missile Launcher w/Propelled Missiles)

A very popular character with collectors, and fairly difficult to locate MOC, the Crimson Guard Immortals (what a fantastic name) are "fanatical super soldiers who swear a fearsome oath of absolute allegiance to Cobra Commander" (from he file card). Basically an update of the original "siegie" (see Crimson Guard, 1985), this figure includes some excellent weapons and a nice paint scheme.

When researching the figure, I found a full paragraph excised from the original prototype file card, "All Crimson Guard Immortals must have degrees in either law or accounting. They are equally proficient in advanced weapons systems marksmanship, classical martial arts and liability torts [civil act of wrongdoing]. Even if you dodge their bullets, and wriggle out of their 'Mystic-Death-Touch' strangle-holds, you can't avoid getting sued!"

MOC: **$25-35**, MLC: **$10**

DESERT SCORPION
Cobra Desert Trooper
(Includes: Pet Scorpion, Backpack w/Missile Rack and Hose, Missile, Two Digger Devices, Machine Pistol)

As punishment "to under motivated Vipers who refuse to follow orders," they are assigned to the Desert Scorpions. These soldiers "mimic the attack patterns of… the desert scorpions with which they live" (from the file card) in order to survive. If a punished trooper succeeds as a Desert Scorpion, they are reinstated to their former post, if they fail then it's the "leaky suit brigade" for them (see Toxo-Viper, 1988, 1991).

MOC: **$25-35**, MLC: **$10**

INCINERATORS
Cobra Flamethrowers
(Includes: Backpack, Hose, Flamethrower, Two Flame Canisters, Catapult Incendiary Grenade Launcher)

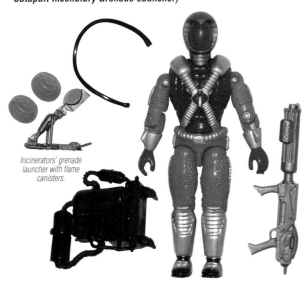

Incinerators' grenade launcher with flame canisters.

The Cobra Incinerators "are flame weapon and arson specialists of the Cobra Legions" (from the file card). They wield weapons that throw burning streams of gasoline, and are covered head-to-toe in fire-resistant, air-conditioned fighting suits." Their prototype code name was Salamander (until just before production).

MOC: **$15-20**, MLC: **$10**

INTERROGATOR
Cobra Battle Copter Pilot
(Includes: Rifle)
Included with Cobra Battle Copter.

With a strange original file card and prototype code names of Probe, Third Degree, and Inquisitor, the Interrogator figure was created over much debate. Mr. Hama tried to diffuse his "torture" aspect of the character as much as possible, and the figure that emerged is one who can siphon information out of the toughest of prisoners simply by talking to them.

MLC: **$8**

NIGHT VULTURE
Air Recon Trooper
(Includes: Crossbow)
Included with the Air Commandos glider.

The Night Vulture figure has a great face sculpt, and these troops act as "the airborne covert insertion and recon specialists of the Cobra Legions" (from the file card). In order to become a Night Vulture, you are "dropped with [your] gliders… over shark-infested waters at least five miles from land. Whoever makes it back is awarded the Night Vulture badge." Their prototype code names were the Owlhoots.

MLC: **$15**

SKY CREEPER
Air Recon Leader
(Includes: Rifle)
Included with the Air Commandos glider.

The man who became known as Sky Creeper constructed his first glider in order to break out of reform school. He then began a criminal career and was recruited into the ranks of Cobra at the behest of the Dreadnoks. He created and commands the Night Vulture corps, and his prototype code names were Sky Skull and Nightwing.

MLC: **$15**

SNOW SERPENT
Cobra Snow Trooper
(Includes: Jet Snow Board, Two Hoses, Gun, Pistol, Backpack, Spring-Loaded Missile Launcher w/Missile)

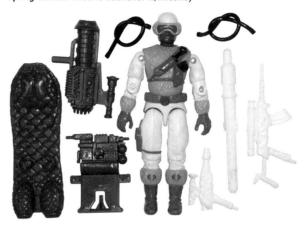

This updated version of the Snow Serpent comes replete with "down filled suits heated by the same backpack heating system that circulates hot air through the working parts of their weapons" (from the file card). For a full bio on the character, see Snow Serpent (1985).

MOC: **$15-20**, MLC: **$10**

1991 VEHICLES/PLAYSETS

G.I. JOE AIR COMMANDOS
(One-Man Aerial Craft Armed w/Pivoting Submachine Guns)
(Includes: Cloudburst figure)

Cloudburst's Air Commando Glider from 1991 is colored in blue and purple and gives the Joes some powerful air support. Each glider came with instructions to assemble and "fly" the glider.

MOMC: **$30**, MOC: **$18**, MLC: **$12**

G.I. Joe Air Commandos
(One-Man Aerial Craft Armed w/Pivoting Submachine Guns)
(Includes: Skymate figure)

Skymate's Air Commando Glider from 1991 is colored in orange and two shades of green camouflage and gives the Joes some powerful air support. Each glider came with instructions to assemble and "fly" the glider.

MOMC: **$40**, MOC: **$30**, MLC: **$15**

Cobra Air Commandos
(One-Man Aerial Craft Armed w/Pivoting Submachine Guns)
(Includes: Night Vulture figure)

Decked out in dark blue and black this Night Vulture's glider with mounted machine guns is a fantastic addition to Cobra's arsenal. Each glider came with instructions to assemble and "fly" the glider.

MOMC: **$30**, MOC: **$18**, MLC: **$12**

SERIES TEN

COBRA AIR COMMANDOS
(One-Man Aerial Craft Armed w/Pivoting Submachine Guns)
(Includes: Sky Creeper figure)

Colored in purple and orange, Sky Creeper's Air Commando Glider with mounted machine guns is a fantastic addition to Cobra's arsenal. Each glider came with instructions to assemble and "fly" the glider.

MOMC: **$30**, MOC: **$18**, MLC: **$12**

ATTACK CRUISER

The G.I. Joe Attack Cruiser signaled the end of the line to most Joe enthusiasts, as it was tricked-out in neon colors of blue, green, and hot pink.

Easily lost pieces include two mines, two missiles, and a launchable attack glider.

MISB: **$32**, MIB: **$20**, MLC: **$12**

The Attack Cruiser's easily lost pieces.

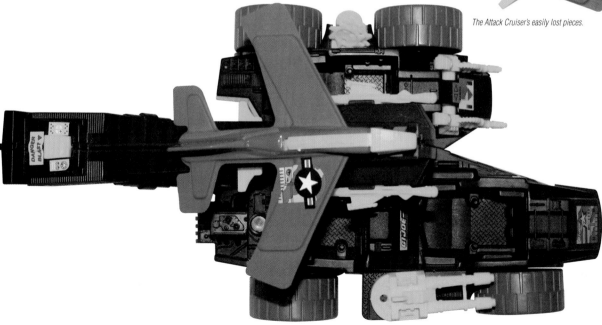

BADGER

The G.I. Joe Badger featured all-track radial tires, a 25,000 lb. tow hook with low drag stabilizer, and an auto-fire missile launcher adding mobility and firepower to the Joe's ground forces.

Easily lost pieces are its flag and three missiles.

MISB: **$20**, MIB: **$12**, MLC: **$6**

The Badger's easily lost pieces.

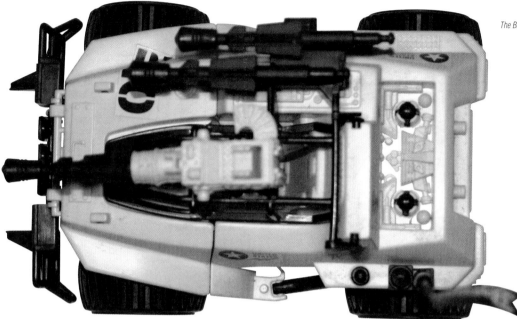

(MOTORIZED) BATTLE WAGON

The Battle Wagon in army green, light blue, and orange colors looked bulky and awkward but delivered an impressive payload. A detachable motorized rapid-fire cannon fired many of the twelve included missiles, and the vehicle was motorized itself.

Easily lost pieces are the twelve missiles.

MISB: **$40**, MIB: **$25**, MLC: **$15**

The Battle Wagon's easily lost pieces.

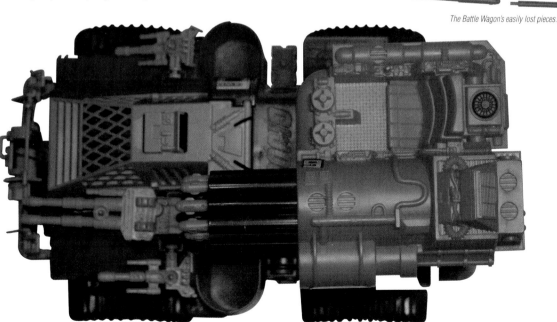

BRAWLER

The Brawler was an interesting addition to the Joe's ground forces, as it possessed weapons that really fired, a bevy of grenades that dotted its facade, missiles, and missile launchers.

Easily lost pieces include fifteen small orange grenades (some still attached to the body of the vehicle), two large missiles, and removable hatch cover.

MISB: **$40**, MIB: **$25**, MLC: **$15**

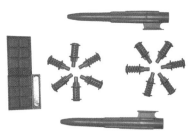

The Brawler's easily lost pieces.

COBRA BATTLE COPTER
(A Devastating High Altitude Flying Assault Craft)
(Includes: Interrogator figure)

This Cobra Battle Copter is done in red and silver and is another toy designed to actually fly. The zip-cord launcher is frequently missing.

MISB: **$20**,
MIB: **$12**,
MLC: **$6**

COBRA ICE SABRE

The Cobra Ice Sabre is one of the better vehicles from the 1991 line, as it showcases rear side-mounted cannons with anti-aircraft capabilities, a path-clearing injected cannon, a swinging missile launcher system with laser guidance adjusters, four long range terrain-hugging neuronic missiles (does this imply that the missiles were organic?), and a "cap firing" mechanism built into the missile launcher—when a missile fired, a cap would discharge.

Easily lost pieces include four missiles, and caps (usually not present in loose samples, so most collectors do not feel these are part of a complete vehicle).

MISB: **$25**, MIB: **$12**, MLC: **$8**

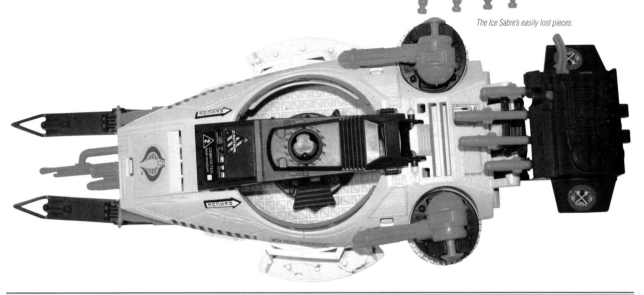

The Ice Sabre's easily lost pieces.

COBRA PARALYZER

The Cobra Paralyzer is a nice-looking tracked assault vehicle that sports a swiveling battle turret with 360-degree rotation, a double-barreled concussion cannon, and an inclined full-control cockpit with cranium-touch battle instructions.

Easily lost pieces are the three missiles.

MISB: **$25**, MIB: **$12**, MLC: **$8**

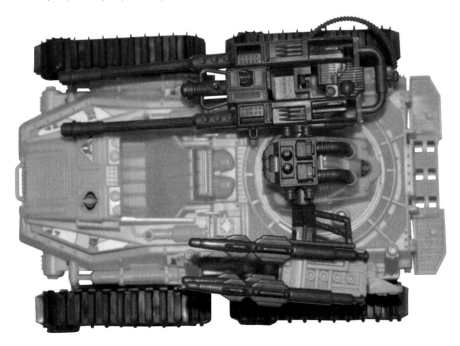

The Paralyzer's easily lost pieces.

SERIES TEN

COBRA SEPTIC TANK

The Cobra Septic Tank is the organization's latest addition to the Eco-Warriors (1991) line. The tank has two main features: a hydro powered sludge liquifier compressor/energized firing generator, and a hose that allows kids to feed water through this compressor, like a water pistol. The tank also featured color change battle damage, as did most Eco-Warriors products.

Easily lost pieces are the water cannon plunger and orange hose.

MISB: **$25**, MIB: **$12**, MLC: **$8**

The Septic Tank's easily lost pieces.

G.I. JOE BATTLE COPTER
A High Altitude, Quick-Strike Flying Aircraft
(Includes: Major Altitude figure)

This G.I. Joe Battle Copter is done in green and silver and another toy designed to actually fly. The zip-cord launcher is frequently missing.

MISB: **$20**, MIB: **$12**, MLC: **$6**

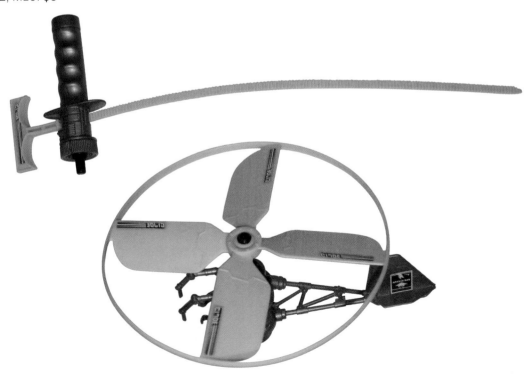

(SERIES XI, 1992)

This series marked a huge re-hashing of old Joe and Cobra characters, along with the introduction of a few new lines. The new D.E.F. (Drug Elimination Force) and Ninja Force lines were praised by kids and avoided by many Joe collector purists, as each Ninja Force figure sacrificed articulation for a power action spring-loaded ninja move. As brilliantly constructed as the vehicles of the 1982-1990 lines were, the vehicles and accessories from 1992-1994 were less articulated, more colorful, and the blueprints included with them avoided suspending the disbelief of children. This would signal the waning of kid and collector interest in the line, in spite of how hard Hasbro tried to promote the ethical ideas of crusading against drugs and repairing the environment.

"School Kit" Hasbro mailed this D.E.F. anti-drug kit to local schools.

1992 G.I. Joe mini-comics inserts.

1992 Collector's Case.

1992 catalog.

1992 G.I. JOE FIGURES

ACE
Battle Copter Pilot
(Includes: Helmet, Mask, Rifle)
Included with the G.I. Joe Battle Copter.

For a full bio, see Ace (1983).

MOC: **$12-15**, MLC: **$8**

BARRICADE
Bunker Buster (BC #9)
(Includes: Battering Ram Launcher, Battering Ram Missile, Battle Stand, Helmet, Submachine Gun, Backpack)

Barricade was the Joe team's "Bunker Buster" and functioned as the team's armored assault specialist. His suit is made of "flexible composite, laminate armor and a helmet with a built-in infrared heat source sensors" (from the file card).

NOTE: *This version of Barricade has a blue outfit, while the 1993 version of the figure has an orange outfit.*

MOC: **$12-15**, MLC: **$8**

BIG BEAR
Oktober Guard Anti-Armor Specialist (BC #4)
(Includes: Bazooka Launcher, Battle Stand, Rifle, Backpack, Two Missiles)

As the second G.I. Joe figure assigned from the Oktober Guard (see Red Star, 1991), Big Bear grew up in Archangel, Russia—a dank, cold, wet place. He believes that the Joe team is the U.S. counterpart to Russia's Oktober Guard team.

On his prototype file card, there was a hand-written note by Larry Hama, which stated, "NATO nomenclature for Soviet anti-tank weapons begin with 's', i.e.: SAGGER, SPIGOT, SPANDREL, SPIRAL, and SWATTER. My suggestion for a name would be SKULKER. Judging by the size and weight, the depicted ordnance launcher would be controlled by a SACLOS (Semi-Automatic Command Line-of-Sight) and guided by a self-deployed wire."

MOC: **$12-15**, MLC: **$8**

DUKE
Master Sergeant (BC #1)
(Includes: Cannon w/Seat, Battle Stand, Submachine Gun, Knife, Helmet, Tripod, Missile)

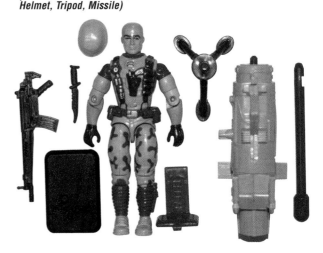

For a full bio, see Duke (1983). Duke is supposed to "sit" on the cannon he comes equipped with.

MOC: **$12-15**, MLC: **$8**

GENERAL FLAGG
G.I. Joe General (BC #7)
(Includes: Four-Piece Armored Catapult, Battle Stand, Rifle, Hat, Missile)

General Flagg is "the son of the original G.I. Joe Commanding General" (from the file card, and the Marvel comic). He graduated from Virginia Military Institute, and is "carrying on where his father left off."

NOTE: *This version of General Flagg has black gloves and a black undershirt, as opposed to the 1993 version of the figure that has a gray undershirt and gloves.*

MOC: **$12-15**, MLC: **$8**

General Flagg's catapult.

GUNG-HO
U.S. Marine (BC #8)
(Includes: Rocket Launcher, Missile, Battle Stand, Machine Gun, American Flag, Backpack)

For a full bio, see Gung-Ho (1983).

NOTE: *This version of Gung-Ho has a tattoo on his chest, not to be confused with Gung-Ho, 1993 who has a tattoo on his arm. Also, this 1992 version of Gung-Ho has a light green vest, where the 1993 version of the character has a maroon vest.*

MOC: **$12-15**, MLC: **$8**

ROADBLOCK
Heavy Machine Gunner (BC # 3)
(Includes: Machine Gun Launcher, Disk, Battle Stand, Knife, Machine Gun)

NOTE: *This Roadblock figure (pre- and post-recall, 1992) had black highlights, where the 1993 version of the figure had neon green highlights.*

MOC: *(launcher)* **$175-200**, *(no launcher)* **$12-15**,
MLC: *(launcher)* **$60-80**, *(no launcher)* **$8**

Roadblock's ultra-rare machine gun "disk" launcher.

This G.I. Joe action figure has possibly the most rare Joe accessory of all (next to Heavy Metal's microphone [1985])—Roadblock's "recalled" machine gun launcher. The machine gun/disk launcher broke too easily, prompting the recall, so finding one of these complete and unbroken is a true challenge, as is finding a mint condition carded sample of the figure and accessories. After the piece was recalled, the figure was re-released in 1993 without the machine gun launcher, but with other weapons (see Roadblock, 1993). For a full bio, see Roadblock (1984).

NOTE: *The large machine gun (apart from the machine gun launcher) that came with the pre-recalled Roadblock is also a fairly rare piece, as this was the only time it was made.*

SPIRIT
Air Commandos Leader
(Includes: Rifle)
Included with Air Commandos glider.

Spirit has now been promoted to leader of the G.I. Joe Air Commandos. For a full bio on this character, see Spirit (1984).

MOC: **$8**

WET-SUIT
S.E.A.L. (Sea, Air, and Land) (BC #2)
(Includes: Torpedo Sled, Battle Stand, Two Flippers, Helmet, Spear Gun, Three Missiles)

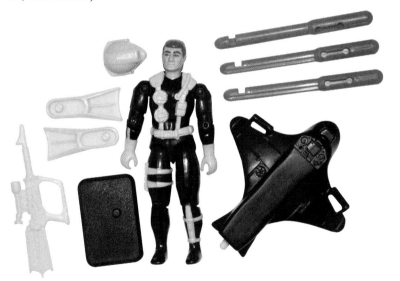

This version of Wet-Suit has yellow highlights, while his 1993 version has orange. For a full bio on this character, see Wet-Suit (1986).

MOC: **$12-15**, MLC: **$8**

WILD BILL
Air Cavalry Scout (BC #10 – black pants)
(Includes: Missile Launcher, Battle Stand, Pistol, Knife, Backpack, Hat, Missile)

Note that this version of Wild Bill has black pants, while his 1993 version sports white slacks. For a full bio on this character, see Wild Bill (1983).

MOC: **$12-15**, MLC: **$8**

1992 COBRA FIGURES
AIR DEVIL
Acrobatic Aerial Assault Trooper
(Includes: Face Shield, Pistol)
Included with Air Commandos glider.

The Cobra Air Devils "are the front line stealth assault and Air Commandos of the Cobra legions" (from the file card). They fight in a dirty and unorthodox manner, and "wreak havoc amid the support units and supply lines" of their enemies. Their alternate code names were Sky-Snakes and Vector-Vipers.

MLC: **$12**

COBRA EEL
Cobra Underwater Demolitions (BC #12 – blue outfit)
(Includes: Three-Piece Shark Missile Launcher, Battle Stand, Trident Gun, Two Flippers, Missile)

An update of the Cobra underwater specialists, these Eels have more training and are better equipped to take on the Joes. For a full bio, see Eels (1985).

NOTE: *This version of the figure has blue highlights and a mechanized shark accessory, while the 1993 version of the figure has purple highlights and no shark—he came with a yellow missile launcher instead.*

MOC: **$12-15**, MLC: **$8**

COBRA NINJA VIPER
(Includes: Two Ninja Swords)
Mail Away Exclusive

Quite a difficult catch in MIP condition, the Cobra Ninja Vipers were molded directly from Storm Shadow v.1 (1984), and were given blue and white highlights. Some versions of the bagged figure came with two black swords, while others did not. Obviously, the versions with the black swords are more desirable. Ninja Vipers are "no less than 10th level black belts in karate, jujitsu, and kung fu" (from the file card). They obey orders, function as covert ops specialists, and are recruited from the "highest ranks of Cobra's Viper Corps."

MISBaggie: *(w/swords)* **$35**, *(w/out swords)* **$25**

DESTRO
Enemy Weapons Supplier (BC #5)
(Includes: Disc Launcher, Battle Stand, Rifle, Two Discs)

This figure's file card hints again at the connection between Scotland and Destro, even stating that his home base is at "a grim castle in the Scottish highlands." For a full bio on this character, see Destro (1982, 1988).

MOC: **$12-15**, MLC: **$8**

FIREFLY
Cobra Saboteur (BC #11)
(Includes: Blade Launcher, Blade, Pull Tool, Rifle, Battle Stand)

Even though the first version of his figure is one of the most popular Joes, this version did not sell as well—perhaps because Firefly is supposed to be a stealthy saboteur, and this figure is molded almost entirely in neon green and comes with a rip-cord action blade launcher. This version of the figure has gray highlights, while the 1993 version of Firefly has black highlights. For a full bio on this character, see Firefly (1984).

On his prototype dossier, the file card was given a different quote, "Never stab when you can shoot! Never shoot when you can frag. Never frag when you can preset a directed shrapnel projector with a pressure sensitive piezo-electric fuse."

MOC: **$12-15**, MLC: **$8**

FLAK-VIPER
Cobra Anti-Aircraft Trooper (BC #6)
(Includes: Missile Launcher Backpack, Battle Stand, Rifle, Two Missiles)

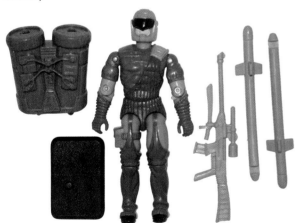

An interesting-looking troop-builder figure, the Flak-Viper fires his "tail biter" missiles at incoming Joe aircraft. "These are dedicated and motivated [anti-aircraft] troopers" (from the file card). This version of the Flak-Viper has light blue highlights, while the 1993 version of the figure has orange highlights.

MOC: **$12-15**, MLC: **$8**

HELI-VIPERS
Cobra Battle Copter Troopers
(Includes: Rifle)
Included with Air Commandos Glider.

The Heli-Vipers "are a fearless unit of Cobra agents trained for the most perilous aerial missions" (from the file card). Elite Cobra aviators, these troopers are "screened by Cobra Commander himself." Collectors weren't entirely sold on the figure's magenta and purple color scheme, however.

MLC: **$8**

NINJA FORCE

These swift and silent commandos are the true elite forces for G.I. Joe and Cobra! Each Ninja warrior is fully capable of neutralizing an adversary in milliseconds with his spring-action, martial art moves and lethal weapons! With this sub-set of figures, a lot of collectors bemoaned the death knell of the pure military feel of the Joe line, while others embraced the more martial arts aspects of the new additions to the Joe and Cobra forces.

DICE

Cobra Bo-Staff Ninja (NF #6)
(Includes: Spring Action "Flying Dragon," Axe, Bo, Figure Stand)

Dice was a Cobra Night Creeper (1990) who was removed from the group for being "too evil" (from the file card). His main weapon is a double-bladed bo-staff and his famous technique is the "Flying Dragon." The figure came with a special punching action. The character's current whereabouts are unknown.

MOC: **$12-15**,
MLC: **$8**

DOJO

Silent Weapons Ninja (NF #2)
(Includes: Spring Action "Lightning Strike," Two-Piece Sickle, Sword, Figure Stand)

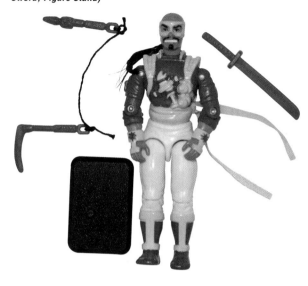

Dojo is the Silent Weapons Ninja for the G.I. Joe Team's Ninja Force. He was the "secret pupil of a Ninja master in hiding and was taught to utilize… [the] chain and sickle, three section staff, sai and throwing dirk" (from the file card). His special action is the "Lightning Strike" maneuver, and his figure's power action is a chopping right arm motion. Dojo has since retired from the Joe team, and currently runs a martial arts school.

MOC: **$12-15**, MLC: **$8**

NUNCHUK

Nunchaku Ninja (NF #3)
(Includes: Spring Action "Samurai Smash," Sword, Nunchaku, Figure Stand)

Nunchuk worked with silent weapons on Storm Shadow's (1984, 1988, 1992) new G.I. Joe Ninja Force team. On the team, Nunchuk specialized in nunchaku attack styles, and has learned the "Samurai Smash" method of attack. The figure possessed a spring action chopping motion in his right arm for swinging his nunchaku. Nunchuk has since retired from the Joe team, and currently runs a martial arts school.

MOC: **$12-15**, MLC: **$8**

SLICE

Cobra Ninja Swordsman (NF #5)
(Includes: Spring Action "Scorpion Slash," Knife, Sword, Figure Stand)

Slice, Cobra's evil Ninja Swordsman, "may be a renegade Ninja from Storm Shadow's (1984) very own [Arashikage] clan" (from the file card). He has perfected a move called the "Scorpion Slash," and his figure came with a special punching action. Slice's current whereabouts are unknown.

MOC: **$12-15**, MLC: **$8**

STORM SHADOW
Ninja Force Leader (NF #1)
(Includes: Spring Action "Screaming Whirlwind," Sickle, Sword, Figure Stand)

At this point in G.I. Joe continuity, Storm Shadow has defected to the G.I. Joe team, and heads their new Ninja Force. As their leader, he draws upon ancient martial arts techniques to help them win their battle against Cobra. This figure's noted move is the "Screaming Whirlwind," displayed by two spring action arms. For a full bio on this character, see Storm Shadow (1984, 1988).

MOC: **$12-15**, MLC: **$8**

T'JBANG
Ninja Swordsman (NF #4)
(Includes: Spring Action "Silent Backslash," Hooked Sword, Straight Sword, Figure Stand)

The skilled Ninja Swordsman of the G.I. Joe Ninja Force known as T-Jbang has taken an oath of silence, and therefore his special maneuver is the "Silent Backslash." He is a "former disciple of the master swordsman of Storm Shadow's [1984, 1988, 1992] [Arashikage] Ninja clan" (from the file card), and his spring action is a power punch.

MOC: **$12-15**, MLC: **$8**

D.E.F.
"Drug-fighting G.I. Joes battle Headman and his gang of drug-thugs for control of "Main Street U.S.A.!" Each drug enforcement agent and villain utilizes a Battle-Flash weapon to elevate this dangerous conflict to new heights of danger!"

NOTE: *In 1991 and 1992 particularly, Hasbro was trying to link its 3-3/4 Joe line with the nation's developing a social conscience by releasing figures with more responsible themes: Eco-Warriors, and the D.E.F.*

(D.E.F.) BULLET-PROOF
D.E.F. Leader (#1)
(Includes: Electronic Battle-Flash Missile Launcher, Helmet, Mouthpiece, Backpack, Rifle, Missile, Figure Stand)

As leader of the D.E.F., Bullet-Proof has served as a field officer for the D.E.A. (Drug Enforcement Agency) all over the world. His code name comes from his field experience: if he hasn't been hit yet, "He must be bullet proof!" (from the file card).

MOC: **$12-15**, MLC: **$8**

(D.E.F.) CUTTER
Sea Operations Specialist (#5)
(Includes: Electronic Battle-Flash Grappling Hook Launcher w/Base, Hook, Light, Submachine Gun, Figure Stand, String)

Making a change from vehicle driver to Sea Operations Specialist, Cutter is now working for the D.E.F., and intercepts "drug runners in coastal waters and the high seas" (from his file card). The file card suggests that prior to his experience piloting the Killer W.H.A.L.E. (1984) for the Joes, he was "the skipper of a high-speed drug interceptor craft." For a full bio, see Cutter (1984).

MOC: **$12-15**, MLC: **$8**

(D.E.F.) HEADHUNTERS
Headman's Narcotics Guard (#6)
(Includes: Electronic Battle-Flash Rocket Launcher, Missile, Shotgun, Backpack, Figure Stand)

The Headman (1992) recruits his Headhunters "from the greediest, most ruthless drug dealers and criminals in the world" (from the file card). They have a stake in Headman's operations, and are evil and ambitious.

MOC: **$12-15**, MLC: **$8**

(D.E.F.) HEADMAN
Drug Kingpin (#4)
(Includes: Electronic Battle-Flash Missile Launcher, Missile, Rifle, Figure Stand)

Headman's package art shows a pock-marked drooling evil-doer and his outward appearance matches his personality, "a hardened criminal... he created a drug empire based on paramilitary standards with strict discipline and a rigid chain of command" (from the file card). His figure, replete with ponytail and pinstriped suit, is one of the more ridiculous looking of all Cobra characters. His prototype code names were Big Man and High Roller.

MOC: **$12-15**, MLC: **$8**

(D.E.F.) MUTT & JUNKYARD
K-9 Officer & Attack Dog (#3)
(Includes: Dog [Junkyard], Electronic Battle-Flash Net Launcher, Pistol, Net, Figure Stand)

Mutt and his dog Junkyard are now assigned to the D.E.F.'s operations unit, where "Junkyard sniffs out contraband... [and] Mutt takes them down with his dual net launcher" (from the file card). Mutt's net launcher is one of the more interesting Joe weapons, as it is constructed with fabric cloth and plastic bolas to incapacitate captured Cobras. For a full bio of these characters, see Mutt (1984).

NOTE: *This 1992 version of Mutt has a blue vest, but his 1993 version sports a red vest.*

MOC: **$12-15**, MLC: **$8**

Mutt's net launcher.

(D.E.F.) SHOCKWAVE
S.W.A.T. Specialist (#2)
(Includes: Electronic Battle-Flash Battering Ram Tank, Battering Ram Missile, Helmet, Rifle, Figure Stand)

Shockwave was once the S.W.A.T. specialist of the Joe team who has now been assigned to the D.E.F., where "he had all the qualifications to be [their] point man" (from the file card). He includes a mobile robot-tank battering ram to aid in his "door-kicking" abilities. For a more complete bio, see Shockwave (1988).

MOC: **$12-15**, MLC: **$8**

ECO WARRIORS

[ECO WARRIORS] BARBECUE
Firefighter (#2)
(Includes: Rifle w/Hose, Backpack, Figure Stand)

   Once the Joe team's firefighter, now Barbecue is attached to the Eco-Warriors division of the Joe ranks, where his fireproof and solvent-resistant suit can stop catastrophes around the globe. For a full bio, see Barbecue (1985).

MOC: **$12-15**, MLC: **$8**

[ECO-WARRIORS] TOXO-ZOMBIE
Cobra Toxic Disaster Trooper (#3)
(Includes: Water Cannon, Figure Stand)

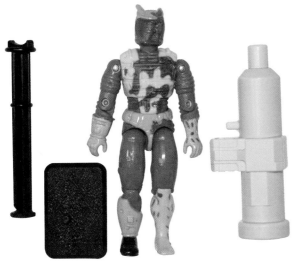

   A fascinating character, here we can see the tragic end result of a "Leaky Suit Brigade" trooper, as this figure shows a Toxo-Viper (1988, 1991) who has suffered from "prolonged exposure to… chemical wastes, radioactive by-products and toxic sludge" (from the file card). These mutated soldiers are highly dangerous, and "not quite among the living."

MOC: **$12-15**, MLC: **$8**

[ECO WARRIORS] DEEP-SIX
Deep Water Specialist (#1)
(Includes: Dolphin, Rifle, Two Flippers, Figure Stand)

   This, the latest incarnation of Deep-Six, comes with "Finback," his "highly trained dolphin sidekick" (from the file card). His diving suit has been upgraded to "withstand the pressures of deep water, [and is] specially coated to resist… corrosive action." He is the aquatic operations specialist of the Eco-Warriors. For a full bio, see Deep-Six (1984).

NOTE: *A handful of carded samples left the Hasbro warehouse (whether via salesmen or employees) with a killer whale packaged inside Deep-Six's bubble rather than a dolphin. These figures are impossible to track down, and can command prices exceeding $800 each (MOC).*

MOC: **$12-15**, MLC: **$8**

Deep Six's dolphin, "Finback."

1992 VEHICLES/PLAYSETS

AIR COMMANDOS

"Rule the skies with a fist of iron with Air Commandos. Highly trained, daredevil pilots who fear no one! Launch these aerodynamic, high-speed gliders into battle and watch them swoop and dive over hostile territory, leveling enemy forces with their pivoting submachine guns! Get ready for take-off!"

COBRA AIR COMMANDOS

(One-Man Aerial Attack Craft Armed w/Pivoting Submachine Guns)
(Includes: Air Devil figure)

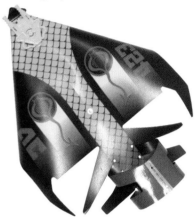

Decked out in red, black, and green, this Air Commando glider with mounted machine guns is a fantastic addition to Cobra's arsenal. Each glider came with instructions to assemble and "fly" the glider.

MOSC: **$30**, MOC: **$20**, MLC: **$18**

G.I. JOE AIR COMMANDOS

(One-Man Aerial Attack Craft Armed with Pivoting Submachine Guns)
(Includes: Spirit figure)

G.I. Joe's Air Commando Glider from 1992 is reminiscent of the American Flag and gives the Joes some powerful air support. Each glider came with instructions to assemble and "fly" the glider.

MOSC: **$30**, MOC: **$20**, MLC: **$18**

AH-74 DESERT APACHE

The AH-47 Desert Apache was the Sonic Fighter's (1990, 1991) air support. Strange that this vehicle was released in 1992, not in 1990 and 1991 when the Sonic Fighters and Super Sonic Fighters were released. The toy came with electronic sounds, spring-loaded missile launchers, a 30mm chin gun and a turboshaft thruster.

Easily lost pieces include eight small black missiles, two black missile racks, four larger green missiles, two missile launchers, and chin gun.

MISB: **$65**, MIB: **$40**, MLC: **$30**

The Desert Apache's easily lost pieces.

BARRACUDA

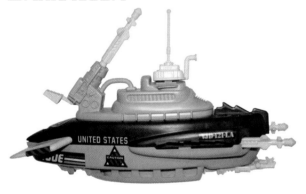

With real diving action (caused by the included baking soda tablets) and a torpedo launcher, the G.I. Joe Barracuda sports cutter fins on its hull, "Shredder" torpedoes, and movable stabilizer fins to aid the Joe team in naval combat. Collectors consider the vehicle complete without the baking soda tablets.

Easily lost pieces are the three torpedoes and the fuel pod cap.

MISB: **$20**, MIB: **$12**, MLC: **$8**

Area to place the baking soda tablets.

The Barracuda's easily lost pieces.

COBRA BATTLE COPTER
(Includes: Heli-Viper figure)

This Cobra Battle Copter is molded in black and gray (colors of the launcher mechanism). The zip-cord launcher is frequently missing.

MISB: **$20**, MIB: **$12**, MLC: **$8**

COBRA EARTHQUAKE

An awkwardly colored and constructed vehicle, Cobra's heavily armed earth-mover came with three mortar bombs ("drop 'n Shoot" missiles), a battle "scoop," a 50mm machine gun and four surface-to-surface missiles.

Easily lost pieces include three mortar bombs and four missiles.

MISB: **$45-50**, MIB: **$25-30**, MLC: **$15-20**

The Earthquake's easily lost pieces.

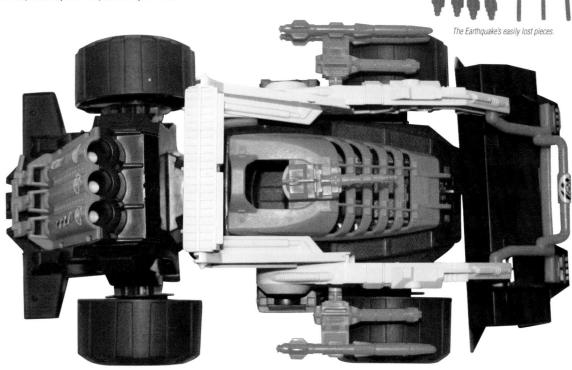

COBRA LIQUIDATOR A.T.F.
(Advanced Tactical Fighter)

Constructed as a one-piece water-shooting jet, this sleek black fighter jet is lightweight and acts as a type of water gun.

Easily lost pieces include four missiles and the rear landing gear.

MISB: **$25**, MIB: **$12**, MLC: **$8**

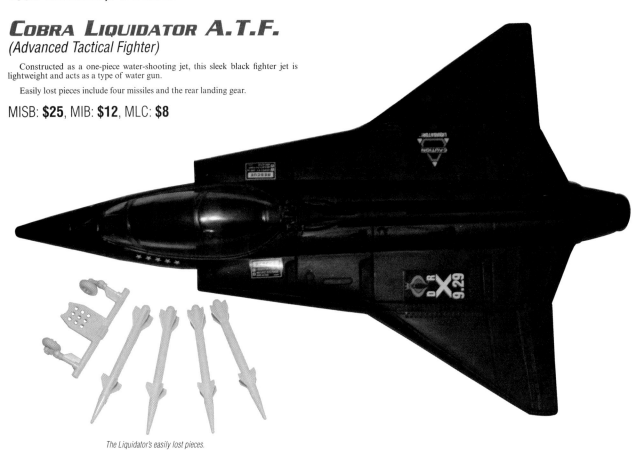

The Liquidator's easily lost pieces.

COBRA PARASITE

The Cobra Parasite is Cobra's new armored personnel character, and can carry up to 17 figures. It comes with a "bomb firing catapult," rotating laser chin gun, and three gyro-catapult bombs.

Easily lost pieces include three bombs, and one black rubber band (mine came with two by mistake).

MISB: **$25**, MIB: **$12**, MLC: **$8**

The Parasite's easily lost pieces.

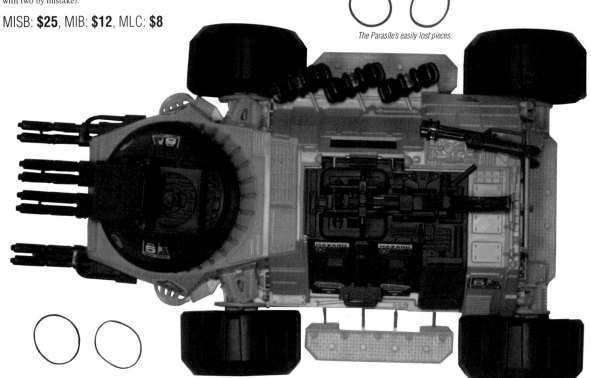

SERIES ELEVEN

COBRA RAT

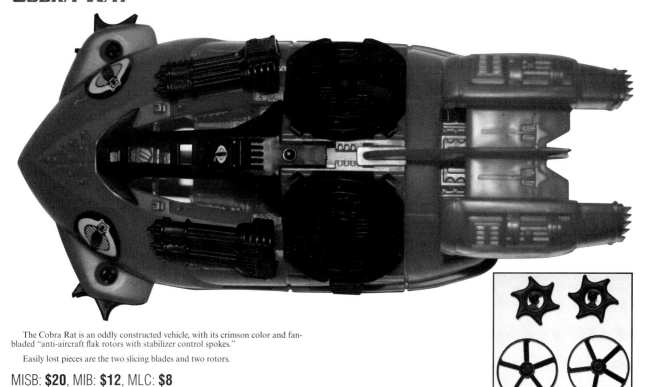

The Cobra Rat is an oddly constructed vehicle, with its crimson color and fan-bladed "anti-aircraft flak rotors with stabilizer control spokes."

Easily lost pieces are the two slicing blades and two rotors.

MISB: **$20**, MIB: **$12**, MLC: **$8**

The Rat's easily lost pieces.

COBRA TOXO-LAB PLAYSET

This version of the Cobra Toxo-Lab play set is the finalized version, and not the one actually portrayed in the 1992 catalog. It is a very hard-to-find piece with all of the components intact, and especially difficult to find MISB. Because of the nature of the playset, many loose samples have sticker wear for the use of water and other liquids involved with a child's play. This playset, with its toxo-gun, claw, access ladder, "Plasma-Tox" container with battle-damage, and "Toxo-Tank" (the blue thingy) was a staging Ground for Cobra's evil plots against the Eco-Warriors (see 1991, 1992).

Easily lost pieces include the ladder, toxo-gun, toxo-gun inner lever, orange hose, plasma-tox container, toxo-tank, and waste barrel.

NOTE: *The play set originally included baking soda tablets similar to the G.I. Joe Barracuda. Collectors do not consider the Toxo-Lab incomplete if they are missing.*

MISB: *(very hard to find)* **$65-90**, MIB: **$35-50**, MLC: **$20-25**

The Toxo-Lab's easily lost pieces.

ECO-STRIKER

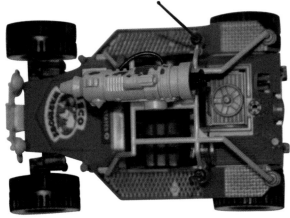

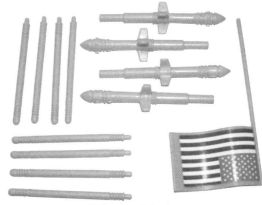

Fort America's easily lost pieces.

The Eco-Striker was a re-done A.W.E. Striker (1985) for G.I. Joe's Eco-Warriors (1991, 1992) forces. It has a water-firing gun, real front suspension, off-road tires, and a pollution-detection recording camera.

Easily lost pieces include the water gun, water gun inner lever, and two antennas.

MISB: **$30**, MIB: **$18-20**, MLC: **$12-15**

The Eco-Striker's easily lost pieces.

Transformed Fort America.

FORT AMERICA

The Fort America was the Sonic Fighter's (1990, 1991) mobile fortress. Unusual that this vehicle was released in 1992, not in 1990 and 1991 when the Sonic Fighters and Super Sonic Fighters were released. The toy came with electronic sounds, spring-loaded missile launchers, and changes from a "crushing combat tank to a battle fortress." With eight electronic combat sounds, this vehicle is still a pretty easy find MISB, and collectors should not pay too much for it.

Easily lost pieces include eight thin missiles, four thick missiles, and an American flag.

MISB: **$35-40**, MIB: **$25-28**,
MLC: **$12-20**

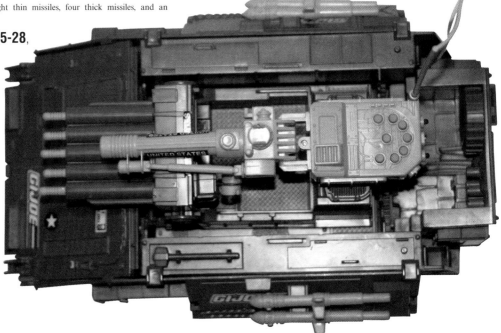

S
E
R
I
E
S

E
L
E
V
E
N

G.I. JOE BATTLE COPTER
(Includes: Ace figure)

This G.I. Joe Battle Copter is molded in blue and black. The zip-cord launcher is frequently missing.

MISB: **$20**, MIB: **$12**, MLC: **$8**

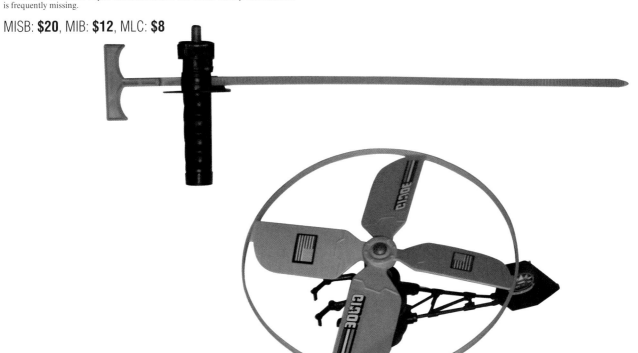

G.I. JOE STORM EAGLE A.T.F.
(Advanced Tactical Fighter)

Constructed as a one-piece water-shooting jet, this white-colored fighter jet is lightweight and acts as a type of water gun.

Easily lost pieces include four missiles, and the rear landing gear.

MISB: **$25**, MIB: **$12**, MLC: **$8**

The Storm Eagle's easily lost pieces.

HEADQUARTERS

This version of the G.I. Joe Headquarters is much different from the original, as it came with many push-button bells and whistles. From collapsible towers to break-out jail cells, this was a pretty interesting play set. It featured eight electronic battle sounds and a light up siren, spring loaded missile launchers, a removable bunker, a fuel hose for the Joes to fill up their vehicles, an armory to keep extra missiles, a movable elevator, and a feature that allowed the entire headquarters to fold up so a child could tote the heavy playset around. This was a fun toy.

This version of the Headquarters is becoming more difficult to find MISB. Rarely can you even find loose examples that are complete—unless its former owner was meticulously organized.

The Headquarters contains many easily lost pieces including three missile launchers, tripod, machine gun, flag barrel, tower support, battery cover, hose, gas pump, six thin missiles, and twelve larger missiles.

MISB: **$75**,
MIB: *(complete)* **$55**,
MLC: **$40**

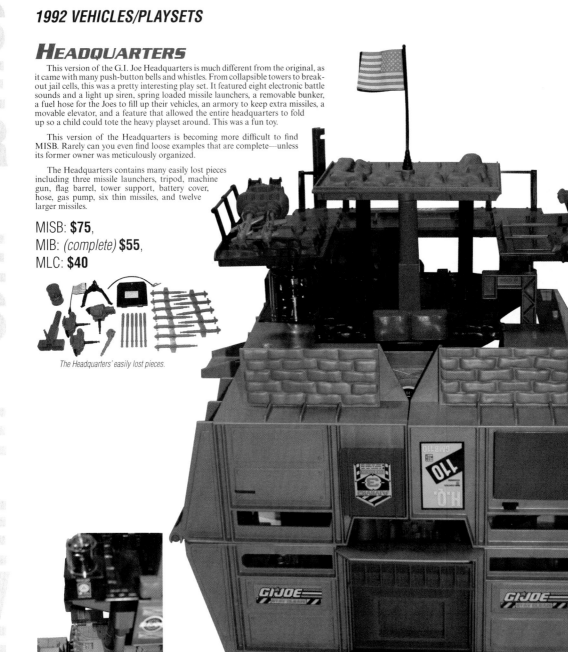

The Headquarters' easily lost pieces.

Armory and siren.

Headquarters, rear view."

Pop-out escape jail panel.

PATRIOT

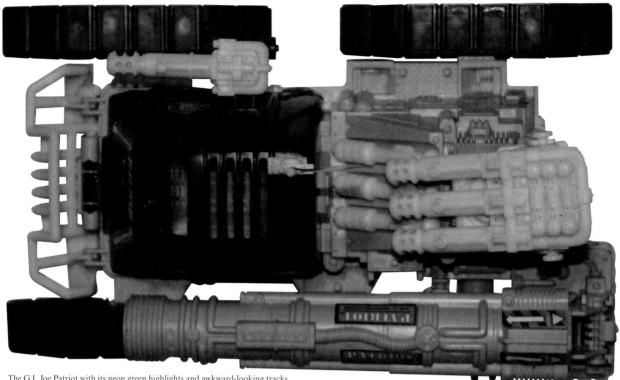

The G.I. Joe Patriot with its neon green highlights and awkward-looking tracks is less than popular with Joe collectors. It has a multi-terrain track system, a quick recoil side machine gun, and triple-barreled laser cannon to help support the Joes.

Easily lost pieces include three missiles, flag, and bumper.

MISB: **$25**, MIB: **$15**, MLC: **$8**

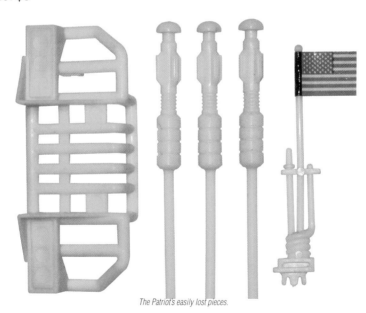

The Patriot's easily lost pieces.

(SERIES XII, 1993)

1993 is the most overwhelming of all of the various "vintage" 3-3/4 years. More than 100 figures were released from many different sub-sets including Street Fighter II, Ninja Force, Mega-Marines, Star Brigade, Armor-Tech Star Brigade, Battle Corps—and tons of different single- and mutli-packed mail-aways. It is an overwhelming year for collectors to handle, and most simply give up due to the enormous volume of releases. It is a long hard road to obtain all of the 1993 figures and vehicles, but there are a few stand outs from this morass of re-decorations and repaints of older figures from 1991 and 1992. Browse carefully!

1993 G.I. Joe catalog.

Promotional comics.

1993 Collector's Case.

1993 G.I. JOE FIGURES

BATTLE CORPS
(BATTLE CORPS) ACE
Fighter Pilot
(Includes: Helmet, Mask, Pistol)
Included with the Ghoststriker X-16.

Ace's MOS is once again "Fighter Pilot" as opposed to "Battle Copter Pilot" (see Ace, 1992). For a full bio, see Ace (1983).

MLC: **$10**

(BATTLE CORPS) BACKBLAST
Anti-Aircraft Soldier (BC #22)
(Includes: Mega-Blaster Missile Launcher, Two Missiles, Knife, Two Rifles, Figure Stand)

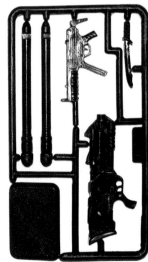

For a full bio on the character, see Backblast (1989).

MOC: **$12-18**, MLC: **$8**

(Battle Corps) Barricade
Bunker Buster (BC #17)
(Includes: Battering Ram Gun, Battering Ram Missile, Rifle, Helmet, Backpack, Figure Stand)

Note that this version of Barricade has an orange outfit, while the 1992 version of the figure has a blue outfit. For a bio of the figure, see Barricade (1992).

MOC: **$12-18**, MLC: **$8**

(Battle Corps) Bazooka
Missile Specialist (BC #1)
(Includes: Bazooka Missile Launcher, Two Missiles, Three Rifles, Figure Stand)

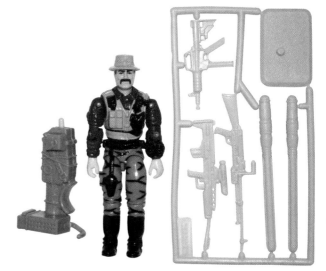

For a full bio on the character, see Bazooka (1985).

MOC: **$12-18**, MLC: **$8**

(Battle Corps) Beach Head
Ranger (BC #4)
(Includes: Missile Launcher, Two Missiles, Pistol, Two Rifles, Knife, Figure Stand)

Note that this figure has a black vest, while the 1994 version of the character wears a yellow vest. For a full bio on the character, see Beach Head (1986).

MOC: **$12-18**, MLC: **$8**

(Battle Corps) Bullet-Proof
Urban Commander (BC #34)
(Includes: Bullet Gun, Missile, Helmet, Backpack, Rifle, Figure Stand)

This version of Bullet-Proof has a much brighter yellow camouflage pattern than the one offered in 1992. For a full bio of this figure, see Bullet-Proof (1992).

MOC: **$12-18**, MLC: **$8**

(BATTLE CORPS) COLONEL COURAGE
Strategic Commander (BC #10)
(Includes: Armor Assault Gun, Missile, Knife, Machete, Pistol, Three Rifles, Figure Stand)

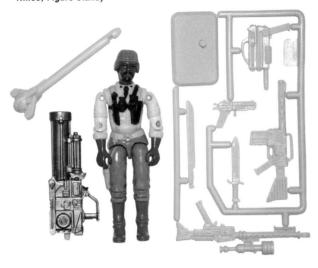

Colonel Courage stresses dress and discipline, and "works hard to impress these qualities upon his subordinates" (from the file card). He possesses a first-rate work ethic, and fantastic organizational skills.

MOC: **$12-18**, MLC: **$8**

(BATTLE CORPS) CROSS-COUNTRY
Transport Expert (BC #2)
(Includes: Cannon, Two Missiles, Pistol, Backpack, Two Rifles, Knife, Figure Stand)

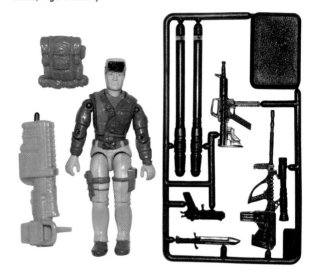

According to the file card, Cross-Country wears acid-washed jeans (sigh). For a full bio of this character, see Cross-Country (1986).

MOC: **$12-18**, MLC: **$8**

(BATTLE CORPS) CUTTER
Coast Guard Specialist
(Includes: Rifle)
Included with the SHARC 9000.

This version of Cutter is basically a repaint of the 1992 version of the figure. For a full bio, see Cutter (1984).

MLC: **$8**

DEEP SIX
Deep Sea Diver
(Includes: Helmet, Rifle, Battle Stand)
Mail Away Exclusive

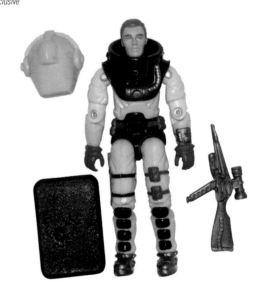

As a mail-away exclusive version of Deep-Six (1989), minus a few accessories, this was a pretty cool promotional, and is a fairly easy find. For a full bio, see Deep-Six (1984).

Mint in Mailer Baggie: **$15-25**, MLC: **$10-12**

(BATTLE CORPS) DUKE
Battle Commander (BC #19)
(Includes: Missile Cannon, Two Missiles, Machete, Three Rifles, Figure Stand)

For a full bio of this character, see Duke (1983).

MOC: **$12-18**, MLC: **$8**

(BATTLE CORPS) FROSTBITE
Arctic Commander (BC #20)
(Includes: Thermal Cannon, Two Missiles, Mask, Three Rifles, Machete, Figure Stand)

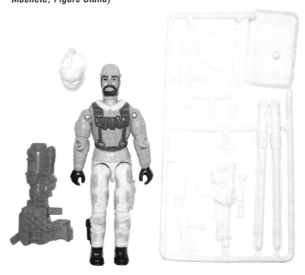

A nicely updated version of Frostbite, this figure comes with a removable mask that looks strangely haunting. For a full bio, see Frostbite (1985).

MOC: **$12-18**, MLC: **$8**

(BATTLE CORPS) GENERAL FLAGG
G.I. Joe General (BC #26)
(Includes: Four-Piece Missile Launcher, Missile, Hat, Rifle, Figure Stand)

General Flagg's missile launcher.

This figure is a simple repaint of the 1992 version of General Flagg, but with a gray undershirt and gloves. The 1992 version had a black undershirt and gloves. For a full bio, see General Flagg (1992).

MOC: **$12-18**, MLC: **$8**

GENERAL HAWK
G.I. Joe Commander
(Includes: Helmet, Face Shield, Rifle, Sonic Backpack, Figure Stand)
Mail Away Exclusive

General Hawk backpack.

This mail-away version of General Hawk (1982, 1986, 1991) is a simple repaint of the 1991 version with a Super Sonic Fighter Backpack included (a variant of the Super Sonic Fighter Major Bludd backpack, 1991). These General Hawk exclusives are plentiful, even MISB, and collectors should not pay much for them.

MISP: **$12**, MLC: **$6-8**

(Battle Corps) Gung-Ho
U.S. Marine (BC #16)
(Includes: Missile Launcher, Missile, Backpack, Machine Gun, American Flag, Figure Stand)

This version of Gung-Ho is similar to the 1992 version, except the '93 Gung-Ho has a tattoo on his arm, not on his chest. Also, the 1993 figure has a maroon vest, where the 1992 version has a light green vest. For a full bio, see Gung-Ho (1983).

MOC: **$12-18**, MLC: **$8**

(Battle Corps) Iceberg
Arctic Assault Trooper (BC #3)
(Includes: Launcher, Two Missiles, Snowboard, Knife, Machete, Pistol, Rifle, Figure Stand)

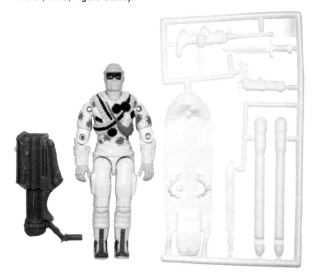

This version of Iceberg is regarded by collectors as one of the nicer of the vast lot of figures produced in 1993. With all-white equipment and a muted dark-green missile launcher accompanied by a snowboard, this figure is sometimes considered an upgrade of the original. Take note that Iceberg's snowboard has two variations, one has a more detailed Joe logo on the bottom of the board, while the other is less pronounced. Neither is more expensive or difficult to find. For a full bio, see Iceberg (1986).

MOC: **$12-18**, MLC: **$8**

(Battle Corps) Keel-Haul
Admiral (BC #21)
(Includes: Anti-Aircraft Launcher, Two Missiles, Two Rifles, Knife, Figure Stand)

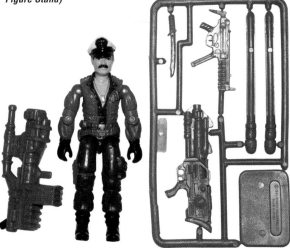

A strange character for Hasbro to update, as he was originally included as the Admiral of the U.S.S. FLAGG aircraft carrier (1985), Keel-Haul is a nice looking figure. Basically a re-paint of the original, collectors should note that this version has two variations of the patch located on the figure's back. One patch is small, while the other takes up the entirety of the figure's back. The smaller-logo Keel Haul(s) are a bit more rare, and should command a few dollars more. For a full bio, see Keel-Haul (1985).

MOC: **$12-18**, MLC: **$8**

Keel-Haul with large logo variant.

(Battle Corps) Law
MP (BC #28)
(Includes: Enforcer Gun, Two Missiles, Shield, Two Rifles, Knife, Figure Stand)

Another unusual update, this version of Law does not come with his German Shepard, Order, instead he comes with a fascinating costume texture—a texture not often used by Hasbro to mold figures. For a full bio, see Law (1986).

MOC: **$12-18**, MLC: **$8**

(BATTLE CORPS) LEATHERNECK
Infantry/Training Specialist (BC #11)
(Includes: Ripple Rocket, Missile, Three Rifles, Pistol, Knife, Figure Stand)

For a full bio of this character, see Leatherneck (1986).

MOC: **$12-18**, MLC: **$8**

(BATTLE CORPS) LONG ARM
First Strike Specialist (BC #31)
(Includes: Mega-Blaster, Two Missiles, Shield, Helmet, Two Rifles, Knife, Figure Stand)

As the Joe's new First Strike Specialist, this was a well-molded figure for 1993, as Long Arm came with a new helmet and visor, and a "Mega-Blaster." Like Barricade (1992) and Shockwave (1988), he was usually the "first in and last out" for many G.I. Joe assault operations.

MOC: **$12-18**, MLC: **$8**

(BATTLE CORPS) MACE
Undercover Operative (BC #29)
(Includes: Stealth Gun, Two Missiles, Three Rifles, Knife, Helmet, Figure Stand)

One of the newly minted figures for the 1993 series, Mace acts as an undercover specialist for the Joe's Battle Corps line. As a character, Mace indeed takes risks, but to him, "no risk is too great to continue the war on crime" (from the file card).

MOC: **$12-18**, MLC: **$8**

(BATTLE CORPS) MUSKRAT
Heavy-Fire Specialist (BC #30)
(Includes: Helmet Gun, Two Missiles, Three Rifles, Helmet, Knife, Figure Stand)

This updated version of Muskrat is not very popular with most collectors. His Battle Corps mission is new as his character hunts "criminals like the Headhunters in the swamps along the Florida coast" (from the file card). For a full bio, see Muskrat (1988).

MOC: **$12-18**, MLC: **$8**

S E R I E S

T W E L V E

(BATTLE CORPS) MUTT & JUNKYARD

K-9 Officer & Attack Dog (BC #36)

(Includes: Launcher, Missile, Rifle, Pistol, Dog [Junkyard], Figure Stand)

Basically a re-paint of the 1992 D.E.F. Mutt & Junkyard, this version has a red vest, while the 1992 D.E.F. version dons a blue vest. For a full bio, see Mutt & Junkyard (1984, 1992).

MOC: **$12-18**, MLC: **$8**

(BATTLE CORPS) SNOW STORM

High-Tech Snow Trooper (BC #12)

(Includes: Glacier Gun, Two Missiles, Two Rifles, Pistol, Knife, Figure Stand)

Snow Storm w/revised color. Eco-Warrior Snow Storm.

Yet another Arctic trooper for the Joe team, I have always been quite fond of the design of Snow Storm's figure, as his helmet and legs seem well proportioned for the character's body. As a character, he accomplishes his missions with great success, and does so while wearing a technologically advanced high-tech thermal suit. Snow Storm's figure was originally slated to be a member of the G.I. Joe sub-line of Eco-Warrior troopers (see Eco-Warriors, 1991, 1992), and this figure, like Outback (1993), was actually released in a limited quantity in Eco-Warriors colors early in 1993. The Eco-Warriors version of Snow Storm is somewhat more rare than the regular release, but is really a collectable for most completionists [those collectors who need one version of every figure for their collection]. The file cards of these two differently colored versions of Snow Storm did not indicate any change.

MOC: *(Eco-colors or not)* **$12-18**, MLC: **$8**

(BATTLE CORPS) OUTBACK

Survival Specialist (BC #13)

(Includes: Pummel Gun, Two Missiles, Three Rifles, Figure Stand)

Outback w/revised colors. Eco-Warrior Outback.

Outback's new file card hints at his specialization for the Joe's Eco-Warriors sub-line (see Eco-Warriors, 1991, 1992), and the figure, like Snow Storm (1993), was actually released in a limited quantity with Eco-Warriors colors early in 1993. The Eco-Warriors version of this character is somewhat more rare than the regular release, but is really a collectible for most completionists [those collectors who need one version of every figure for their collection]. The file cards of these two differently colored versions of Outback did not indicate any change. For a full bio, see Outback (1987).

MOC: *(Eco-colors or not)* **$12-18**, MLC: **$8**

(BATTLE CORPS) ROADBLOCK

Heavy Machine Gunner (BC #7)

(Includes: Launcher, Two Missiles, Two Rifles, Pistol, Knife, Figure Stand)

This Roadblock was released without his infamous machine gun launcher (see Roadblock, 1992), and his figure has neon-green highlights, while his 1992 figure had black highlights. The changes in his weapon, from the machine gun launcher to a "tree" of accessories, were also reflected on the painting on his card front and file card. As in 1993, the machine gun launcher was deleted from both. For a full bio, see Roadblock (1984).

MOC: **$12-18**, MLC: **$8**

(BATTLE CORPS) WET-SUIT
Navy S.E.A.L. (BC #8)
(Includes: Sea Sled, Three Missiles, Two Flippers, Helmet, Rifle, Figure Stand)

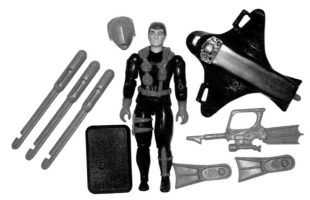

This version of Wet-Suit had orange highlights, as opposed to his 1992 figure that sported yellow highlights. For a full bio, see Wet-Suit (1986).

MOC: **$12-18**, MLC: **$8**

(BATTLE CORPS) WILD BILL
Aero-Scout (BC #25)
(Includes: Hyper Launcher, Missile, Knife, Pistol, Calvary Hat, Backpack, Figure Stand)

This version of Wild Bill wore white pants, while the 1992 version wore black slacks. For a full bio, see Wild Bill (1983).

MOC: **$12-18**, MLC: **$8**

DINO HUNTERS
[DINO HUNTERS] AMBUSH
Dinosaur Camouflage Specialist
(Includes: Two Rifles, Two Pistols, Helmet, Knife, Machete, Figure Stand)
Included with the Toys 'R Us Exclusive Dino-Hunter Mission Play set (along with Low-Light).

As a Dinosaur Camouflage Specialist, Ambush has studied ancient history, and possesses "prehistoric knowledge and stealth-like qualities [that] made him a perfect choice to capture and save dinosaurs from Cobra Island" (from the filecard). For a full bio, see Ambush (1990).

MLC: **$25**

[DINO-HUNTERS] LOW-LIGHT
Dinosaur Night Spotter
(Includes: Three Rifles, Pistol, Helmet, Visor, Knife, Figure Stand)
Included with the Toys 'R Us Exclusive Dino-Hunter Mission Play set (along with Ambush).

This version of Low-Light was modeled after his 1991 incarnation, but his file card changed to reflect his new MOS—Dinosaur Night Spotter. His facial hair has been corrected and turned back to its original yellow, but the history of the character was altered to match his new MOS. Apparently, his night spotting skills will come in handy during night missions when trying to capture dinosaurs on Cobra Island. For a full bio, see Low-Light (1986, 1989).

MLC: **$25**

1993 COBRA FIGURES

(BATTLE CORPS) COBRA ALLEY VIPER

Urban Assault Trooper (BC #6)

(Includes: Assault Gun, Two Missiles, Cobra Shield, Crossbow Backpack, Two Rifles, Helmet, Figure Stand)

This is one of my favorite sculpts of all of the 1993 figures, as it really nails the essence of the Alley Viper character. With a "Cobra laser-proof shield" and "computerized missile launcher with urban assault gun" (from the file card), this "elite contingent of ruthless marauders... [are] true masters of brutality!" This 1993 version of the figure is cast in yellow and black colors, while the 1994 version of the figure is done over in the more traditional blue and orange. For a full bio, see Alley Viper (1989).

MOC: **$15-22**, MLC: **$12**

(BATTLE CORPS) COBRA COMMANDER

Cobra Supreme Leader (BC #24)

(Includes: "Cobra Cannon," Two Missiles, Four Rifles, Figure Stand)

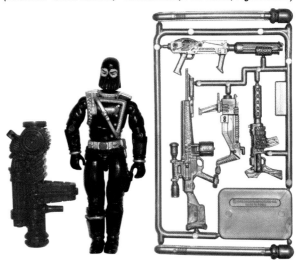

Recast in a darker blue color from the Talking Battle Commander mold of Cobra Commander (1991), this version of Cobra Commander is fairly popular with collectors. Fro a full bio, see Enemy Leader: Cobra Commander (1982).

MOC: **$14-20**, MLC: **$10**

(BATTLE CORPS) COBRA EEL

Underwater Demolitions Specialist (BC #27)

(Includes: Torpedo Launcher, Two Missiles, Two Flippers, Four Guns, Figure Stand)

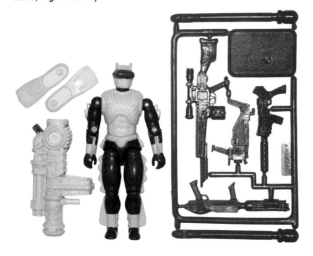

This version of the figure has purple highlights and does not come with the mechanized shark accessory from the 1992 version of the figure. The 1993 Eels has purple highlights and no shark, he came with a yellow missile launcher instead. For a full bio, see Cobra Eel (1992), and Eels (1985).

MOC: **$12-18**, MLC: **$8**

(BATTLE CORPS) COBRA FIREFLY

Saboteur (BC #18)

(Includes: Two-Piece Blade Launcher, Blade, Rifle, Figure Stand)

Firefly's blade launcher.

This version of the figure has black highlights, while the 1992 version of Firefly has gray highlights. For a full bio on this character, see Firefly (1984).

MOC: **$12-18**, MLC: **$8**

(BATTLE CORPS) COBRA FLAK-VIPER

Anti-Aircraft Trooper (BC #9)
(Includes: Backpack Launcher, Two Missiles, Rifle, Figure Stand)

This version of the Flak-Viper has neon orange highlights, while the 1992 version of the figure has light blue highlights. Note that the code name for this figure has changed from Flak-Viper (1992) to Cobra Flak-Viper (1993).

MOC: **$12-18**, MLC: **$8**

(BATTLE CORPS) H.E.A.T. VIPER

(High-Explosive Anti-Tank) Trooper (BC #5)
(Includes: Tank Gun, Two Missiles, Three Guns, Figure Stand)

This, the second incarnation of Cobra's anti-tank trooper, are "equipped with the latest in hyper-kinetic, high-speed, armor-piercing technology" (from the file card). With a 360 degree helmet tracking system and a "Fang" II anti-tank high-impact weapon, the Cobra H.E.A.T. Vipers provide a lot of firepower for Cobra ground forces.

MOC: **$12-18**, MLC: **$8**

(BATTLE CORPS) COBRA NIGHT CREEPER LEADER

Ninja Supreme Master (BC #14)
(Includes: Shock Gun, Missile, Two Crossbows, Two Swords, Shield, Knife, Figure Stand)

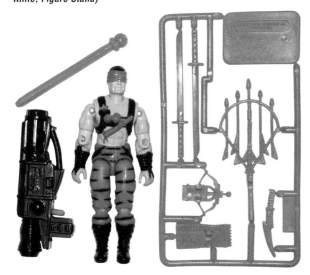

The Cobra Night Creeper Leader is the leader of the Night-Creepers (1990), and as such "is believed to conduct all field intelligence and covert operations of Cobra" (from the file card). Unscrupulous, manipulative, and armed with sophisticated weaponry, the Night Creeper Leader is a deadly adversary for the Joe team. This version of Night Creeper Leader has orange highlights, while the 1994 version sports purple highlights.

MOC: **$12-18**, MLC: **$8**

CREATE-A-COBRA ACTION FIGURE

(Includes: Rifle, Sticker Sheet, Battle Stand)
Mail Away Exclusive

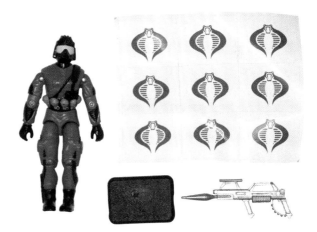

With a custom-made file card indicating Code Name, Primary Military Specialty, Secondary Military Specialty, Weapons Specialty, Martial Arts Expert(ise), and School Training (as well as Traits, Abilities, and Personality blurbs), the Create-A-Cobra mail-away was the lesser produced of the Hasbro's two Create-A-Figure programs (see Steel Brigade, 1987). When you sent in your form, money, and Flag Points (proof-of-purchase seals for Joe packages), Hasbro sent this figure along with the aforementioned custom file card, rifle, and a set of Cobra labels. This is a fairly rare mail-away exclusive to find, especially complete with the file card and sticker sheet (both are very difficult to obtain).

Mint in Mailer Baggie: **$35-40**, MLC: **$20-25**

(BATTLE CORPS) CRIMSON GUARD COMMANDER
Cobra Elite Officer (BC #23)
(Includes: Laser Launcher, Two Missiles, Four Guns, Figure Stand)

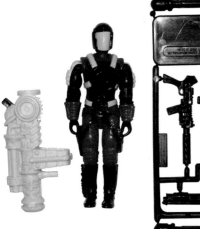

The Crimson Guard Commander character is a bit confusing, as the last "Crimson Guard Commanders" were Tomax and Xamot (1985), and this character seems to be one in an army of many. Their file card suggests that 1993's Crimson Guard Commanders are "Cobra Elite *Officers*," and not "Cobra Elite *Troopers*" (elite troopers like the Crimson Guard [1985] or Crimson Guard Immortals [1991]). Regardless, they are described as formidable officers that carry "modified AK-47 laser assault rifles" (from the file card).

MOC: **$12-18**, MLC: **$8**

(BATTLE CORPS) DR. MINDBENDER
Master of Mind Control (BC #15)
(Includes: Driller Gun, Missile, Knife, Five Guns, Figure Stand)

This version of Dr. Mindbender is a very common 1993 figure to find carded, and collectors should not pay much for him. His character, after being rooked by Cobra Commander and buried in a tanker "deep beneath a volcano on Cobra Island" (from the file card), the good (or bad) doctor was repaired and bionically enhanced "with various machine parts," and eventually escaped the freighter. He is currently an active member of Cobra Command. For a full bio, see Dr. Mindbender (1986).

MOC: **$12-18**, MLC: **$8**

(BATTLE CORPS) GRISTLE
Urban Crime Commander (BC #32)
(Includes: Tracker Gun, Two Missiles, Knife, Two Rifles, Figure Stand)

Gristle, as despicable looking on his card art as the disgusting Headman (1992), acts as Cobra's Urban Crime Commander—a vile and deadly corrupt crime boss. He has worked his way up from the ranks of the Headhunters (1992, 1993) to attain his position of power, and is easily recognizable by his "blood-shot eyes, or by the sunglasses he uses to shield them from the daylight" (from the file card).

MOC: **$12-18**, MLC: **$8**

(BATTLE CORPS) HEADHUNTERS
Cobra Street Troopers (BC #35)
(Includes: Rocket Launcher, Missile, Backpack, Shotgun, Figure Stand)

This, the second version of the Cobra Headhunters is different has neon green highlights, as opposed to the 1992 versions more muted brown tones. For a short bio, see Headhunters (1992).

MOC: **$12-18**, MLC: **$8**

(BATTLE CORPS) HEADHUNTER STORMTROOPERS

Elite Urban Crime Guard (BC #33)
(Includes: Stun Gun, Two Missiles, Two Guns, Knife, Figure Stand)

A fascinatingly constructed figure, the Headhunter Stormtroopers are quite popular as troop builders with Joe collectors. The figure is dotted with spikes all over their uniform, and their painted eye visor is quite pronounced as it is done in blood-red. These Stormtroopers act as "rapid-assault, specially trained urban terrorists who oversee large criminal operations" (from the file card). Their suits are made of steel-spiked leather, and combine this accoutrement with their deadly tempers and you've got foes who are not easily restrained.

MOC: **$14-22**, MLC: **$12**

(BATTLE CORPS) NITRO-VIPER

(Includes: Pistol)
Included with the Cobra Detonator.

The Nitro-Viper figure has the notoriety of being the only Joe figure not to come with a file card. In 1994, 3-3/4" G.I. Joe collector, Michael Livanos, created a Nitro-Viper file card that was officially sanctioned by Hasbro. It states that Nitro-Vipers are highly motivated Cobra Track-Viper Troopers who combat each other to get the chance to drive the Cobra Detonator—a super high-tech Cobra land vehicle. Some of the requirements of Nitro-Viper training includes, "blowing up video game arcades and amusement parks" (from the file card). The super-rare file card itself might sell for $20.

MLC: **$8**

MEGA-MARINES

"This specialized team was formed for one specific mission: to repel and destroy Cobra's Mega-Monsters! These bio-tech fighters also battle new Cobra Vipers, and feature moldable Bio-Armor, a breakthrough in bio-mechanical armament! The "bug-hunt" is on!" The "moldable bio-armor" included with each figure is akin to children's modeling dough.

"From the evil labs of Dr. Mindbender come the hideous, genetically enhanced Cobra Mega-Monsters! These soldiers are the toughest troops Cobra's ever come up with. Watch out Joes! There's a monster of a fight brewing!"

(MEGA-MARINES) BIO-VIPERS

(MM #7)
(Includes: Missile Launcher, Missile)

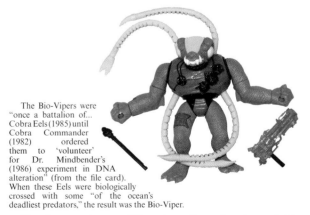

The Bio-Vipers were "once a battalion of... Cobra Eels (1985) until Cobra Commander (1982) ordered them to 'volunteer' for Dr. Mindbender's (1986) experiment in DNA alteration" (from the file card). When these Eels were biologically crossed with some "of the ocean's deadliest predators," the result was the Bio-Viper.

These figures are large, unwieldy, and are either embraced or reviled by collectors. The figure's plastic was sprayed with a perfumed "Monster Smell," and it sports four tentacles that, with a depression of a button, would "grab" a Joe character—but not really.

MOC: **$12-18**, MLC: **$8**

(MEGA-MARINES) BLAST-OFF

Flame Thrower (MM #5)
(Includes: Missile Launcher, Two Missiles, Helmet, Two Rifles, Knife, Body Armor, Can of Moldable Bio-Armor, Figure Stand)

Blast-Off was the Joe team's new Flame Thrower for the 1993 line. A former firefighter, his "courageous effort of persistence and skill earned him a spot on the G.I. Joe team" (from the file card). As Cobra's Mega-Monsters are vulnerable to flames, Blast-Off may succeed where others fail. He wears a number "2" on his chest.

MOC: **$12-18**, MLC: **$8**

(MEGA-MARINES) CLUTCH
Monster Blaster A.P.C. Driver (MM #2)
(Includes: Concussion Cannon, Can of Moldable Bio-Armor, Two Missiles, Shotgun, Two Rifles, Machete, Armor, Figure Stand)

The second re-sculpt of Clutch (1982), the Joe team's original transportation expert, was not included with the vehicle he is designated to drive, the Monster-Blaster A.P.C. (Armored Personnel Carrier). His new file card states that as a mechanic, Clutch "helped win the Indy 500," and then he was recruited to the Joe team. Clutch wears a number "3" on his chest. For a full bio, see Clutch (1982).

MOC: **$12-18**, MLC: **$8**

(MEGA-MARINES) CYBER-VIPERS
Cybernetic Officers (MM #6)
(Includes: Missile Launcher, Two Missiles, Four Guns, Armor, Can of Moldable Bio-Armor, Figure Stand)

A fairly difficult find MOC, the Cyber-Vipers are "half-man and half-robot" (from the file card) with evil brains enhanced "by Dr. Mindbender (1986) himself." These troopers control higher-level operations of the Mega-Monsters "and are responsible for initiating their destructive attacks... [as] guardians of the monsters."

MOC: **$14-20**, MLC: **$9**

(MEGA-MARINES) GUNG-HO
Mega-Marine Commander (MM #1)
(Includes: Xeno-Blaster, Two Missiles, Can of Moldable Bio-Armor, Armor, Helmet, Machete, Shotgun, Two Rifles, Figure Stand)

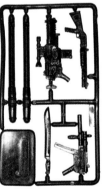

Gung-Ho has now been promoted to the Mega-Marines Commander, as his acquaintance with "hostile environments and experience in the U.S. Marine Corps made him a natural choice to command" (from the file card). He wears the number "1" on his uniform. For a full bio, see Gung-Ho (1983).

MOC: **$12-18**, MLC: **$8**

(MEGA-MARINES) MEGA-VIPERS
Mega-Monster Trainers (MM #3)
(Includes: Missile Launcher, Two Missiles, Can of Moldable Bio-Armor, Armor, Four Guns, Figure Stand)

Like the Cyber-Vipers, the Mega-Viper figures are a little difficult to find MOC, yet are similarly in fairly low demand. These troops act as trainers for the Bio-Vipers (1993) and Monstro-Vipers (1993) and the soldiers are skilled warriors and possess a "fight to the finish" attitude (from the file card).

MOC: **$14-20**, MLC: **$9**

(MEGA-MARINES) MIRAGE
Bio-Artillery Expert (MM #4)
(Includes: Bio-Bazooka, Two Missiles, Can of Moldable Bio-Armor, Armor, Two Guns, Knife, Figure Stand)

Mirage is one of the most impressive sculpts of the entire 1993 line of figures. His character serves as a heavy weapons specialist, with experience in firing "bazookas, AK-47 assault rifles, MAC-10 submachine guns and 'ripple fire' rocket launchers" (from the file card). He was taught his skills by Roadblock (1984), and is the Joe's first choice to handle heavy firepower weapons.

MOC: **$12-18**, MLC: **$8**

(MEGA-MARINES) MONSTRO-VIPERS
(MM #8)
(Includes: Rifle, Ball and Chain, Can of Moldable Bio-Armor)

Like their brother-projects, the Bio-Vipers, Monstro-Vipers were once a team of wilderness troopers (Range-Vipers [1990]) "until Cobra Commander (1982) ordered them to 'volunteer' for Dr. Mindbender's (1986) experiment in DNA alteration" (from the file card). These Range Vipers were crossed with rabid werewolves, "bigfoot" creatures, and grizzly bears—the result was the Monstro-Viper. The figure came with moldable bio-armor that could be formed into the shape of a stomach-regurgitating "gut bomb" and "flung" from the figure's spring-loaded hand.

MOC: **$12-18**, MLC: **$8**

NINJA FORCE

"These swift and silent commandos are the true elite forces for G.I. Joe and Cobra! Each ninja warrior is fully capable of neutralizing and adversary in milliseconds with his [or her] spring-action, martial-arts moves and lethal weapons!" There are some card variations (with and without small parts warning stickers) and some misrepresentations of the Ninja Force figures' spring action moves. These variations have little to no effect on the value of carded samples.

(NINJA FORCE) BANZAI
Rising Sun Ninja (NJF #5)
(Includes: Spring-Action Suzushi Slam, Axe, Sickle, Knife, Two Swords, Two Dueling Knives, Figure Stand)

With his "Samurai Slam," Banzai is one of the world's premiere nunchaku masters. He is the blood brother of Budo (1988), and is a disciplined martial artist and always ready for combat (from the file card), and after perfecting his skills joined G.I. Joe's Ninja Force. His figure comes with a spring-action punching motion.

MOC: **$12-18**, MLC: **$8**

(NINJA FORCE) BUSHIDO
Snow Ninja (NJF #6)
(Includes: Spring-Action Teicho Chop, Axe, Sickle, Knife, Two Swords, Two Dueling Knives, Figure Stand)

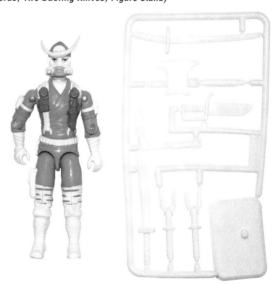

With his MOS as Snow Ninja, Bushido practiced his martial arts skills in "freezing temperatures to heighten his sense of awareness and discipline" (from the file card). After studying many ninja techniques, he moved to Iceland to hone his skills and then returned to the U.S. to join G.I. Joe's Ninja Force.

MOC: **$12-18**, MLC: **$8**

(NINJA FORCE) NIGHT CREEPER
Cobra Ninja (NJF #3)
(Includes: Spring-Action Banzai Bash, Two Knives, Sickle, Two Swords, Bow, Figure Stand)

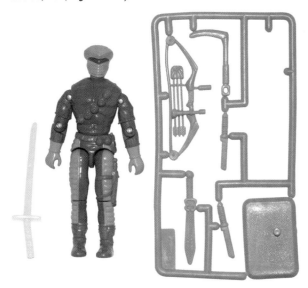

This latest incarnation of the Night Creeper figure states in the file card that it comes with a cape, yet it does not. It is a passable ninja figure, and very easy to come by. His spring action is in his arms that can be raised up to snap back down. For a full bio, see Night Creeper (1990).

MOC: **$12-18**, MLC: **$8**

(NINJA FORCE) RED NINJAS
Battle Ax Operators
(Includes: Axe)
Included with the Ninja Raider Battle Ax.

The Red Ninjas were the single most disappointing Joe figure I ever purchased. Thinking them to be akin to the Red Ninjas as portrayed in the Marvel comic (see Marvel Comics, *G.I. Joe #21*), I was shocked to find them draped in neon magenta and deep blue, and not looking one bit like the characters in the comic. However (and surprisingly), their file card is first-rate, citing that Red Ninja mercenaries "are the most feared ninja warriors since the No Kan-Doo ninja dynasty terrorized China in the 15th century". The figure's spring action was a "roundhouse" punching motion.

MLC: **$7-8**

(NINJA FORCE) SCARLETT
Counter Intelligence Specialist (NJF #4)
(Includes: Spring-Action Kato Kick, Nunchuks, Two Claws, Three Swords, Knife, Figure Stand)

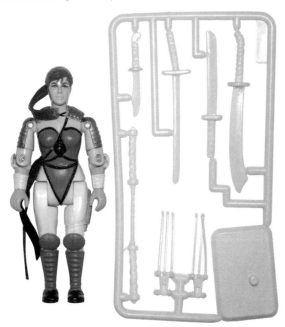

The first Scarlett figure with rooted hair becomes the Counter Intelligence Expert of the G.I. Joe Ninja Force team. Her spring action is a kicking ability. The figure itself came with two different types of ball jointed heads, and neither is worth more than the other. For a full bio, see Scarlett (1982).

MOC: **$14-20**, MLC: **$10**

(NINJA FORCE) SLICE
Cobra Ninja Swordsman (NJF#7)
(Includes: Spring-Action Scorpion Slash, Sword, Axe, Two Double-Bladed Knives, Spear, Knife, Figure Stand)

The 1993 edition was a repainted orange version of Slice (1992). See that reference for a full bio. His figure's spring-action move was a "punching" right arm.

MOC: **$12-18**, MLC: **$8**

(NINJA FORCE) SNAKE EYES
Covert Mission Specialist (NJF #1)
(Includes: Spring-Action Basami Slice, Knife, Two Claws, Three Swords, Nunchuks, Figure Stand)

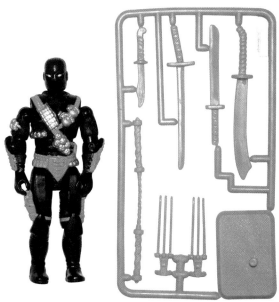

    A new member of the Ninja Force, Snake Eyes became a Covert Mission Specialist and launched all-out Ninja-mania in the Joe universe. His spring action was chopping arms activated with a squeeze of his legs. For a full bio, see Snake Eyes (1982).

MOC: **$15-22**, MLC: **$10**

(NINJA FORCE) ZARTAN
Master of Disguise (NJF #2)
(Includes: Spring-Action Moroto Chop, Two Knives, Sickle, Two Swords, Bow, Figure Stand)

    The second Zartan figure produced by Hasbro showcased an orange mohawk and finally included his true weapon of choice in the Marvel comic universe—a "high-tension ninja Yumi bow" (from the file card). His spring action was in the form of a punching motion. For a full bio, see Zartan (1984).

MOC: **$12-18**, MLC: **$8**

(NINJA FORCE) T'GIN-ZU
Pile Driver Operator
(Includes: Sword)
Included with the Ninja Raider Pile Driver.

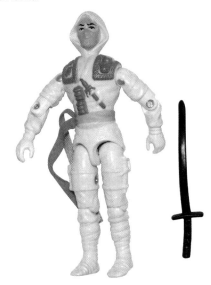

    Clad in the prefect Ninja colors of orange and white, T'Gin-Zu (a pun on the brand of steak knives) was one of Storm Shadow's prized students who studied, "...martial arts for over 20 years until he earned the right to be called a ninja master" (from the file card). He volunteered to drive the Ninja Raider, and his spring action is a two-handed "punching" motion.

MLC: **$8**

ARMOR TECH STAR BRIGADE
    "Battle-armored warriors rocket into space! With futuristically styled, built-in Robo-Armor and spring fired missile launchers, these high-tech fighters take the battle action into distant galaxies… and beyond!" These figures are unpopular with collectors, and many carded samples can be found cheap in good condition.

(ARMOR TECH STAR BRIGADE) COBRA B.A.A.T.
Battle Armored Android Trooper (AT SB #6)
(Includes: Cyber-Tech Launcher, Two Missiles, Four Guns, Knife, Figure Stand)

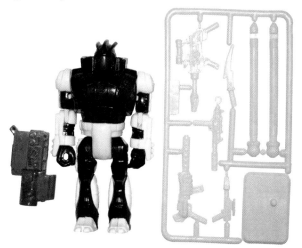

    This is the "outer-space" version of Cobra's B.A.T.s (1986). Like the B.A.T. v.2 (1991), the 1993 B.A.A.T.'s weapons systems have been upgraded, while their logic has been downplayed, yet again. These robots are as brainless as they are trigger-happy.

MOC: **$12-18**, MLC: **$8**

(ARMOR TECH STAR BRIGADE) DESTRO

Cobra Tech Commander (AT SB #5)

(Includes: Cobra-Tech Arm Launcher, Two Missiles, Knife, Four Guns, Helmet, Figure Stand)

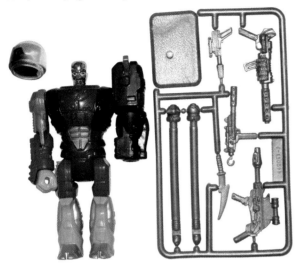

His file card states that Destro has a "new armor-plated space fortress guarded by Cobra B.A.A.T.s [1993]," and this is where Destro "peddles his galactic destruction" (from the file card). For a full bio, see Destro (1983).

MOC: **$12-18**, MLC: **$8**

(ARMOR TECH STAR BRIGADE) DUKE

Star Brigade Commander (AT SB #2)

(Includes: Robo-Arm, Two Missiles, Rifle, Knife, Helmet, Laser Gun, Figure Stand)

As commander of the Star Brigade Force, Duke uses his robotic battle armor to ferret out Cobra troopers. The armor reportedly gives Duke the strength of ten men, and is bullet and laser-proof. For a full bio, see Duke (1983).

MOC: **$12-18**, MLC: **$8**

(ARMOR TECH STAR BRIGADE) GENERAL HAWK

G.I. Joe Armor-Tech Commander

(Includes: Helmet, Rifle)

Included with the Armor-Bot.

General Hawk dons his robotic battle armor when his pilots the Armor-Bot. This incarnation of Hawk has a file card that makes mention of him being an old space campaigner, who "has seen plenty of interstellar combat, and was even present during the brutal battle to liberate the moon from Cobra." For a full bio, see Hawk (1982).

NOTE: *Hawk came with either a pink or black rifle. Neither variant is harder to find.*

MLC: **$8**

(ARMOR TECH STAR BRIGADE) HEAVY DUTY

Heavy Ordnance Specialist (AT SB #4)

(Includes: Macro-Missile Gun, Two Missiles, Rifle, Knife, Laser Gun, Helmet, Figure Stand)

The second version of Heavy Duty sends the character into space, where he utilizes his robotic battle armor to enhance his already prominent strength and durability. For a full bio, see Heavy Duty (1991).

MOC: **$12-18**, MLC: **$8**

(ARMOR TECH STAR BRIGADE) ROBO-JOE

Jet-Tech Operations Expert (AT SB #1)
(Includes: Synchro-Tech Launcher, Two Missiles, Three Guns, Machete, Helmet, Figure Stand)

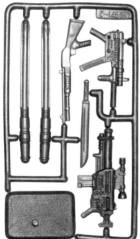

Greg Scott was a genius who drafted the plans for the Armor-Tech robotic battle armor. Destro attacked the lab by one night, stole the plans and badly wounded Scott. Joe scientists rebuilt the young researcher, and now he is hunting down Destro (1982, 1988, 1993) for "justice" and "revenge" (from the file card).

MOC: **$12-18**, MLC: **$8**

(ARMOR TECH STAR BRIGADE) ROCK 'N ROLL

Robo-Gunner (AT SB #3)
(Includes: Robotizer Cannon, Two Missiles, Three Guns, Machete, Helmet, Figure Stand)

Rock 'N Roll now functions as the Robo-Gunner of the Star Brigade Force, where he "braves laser fire, jumps on live grenades, and even chases Cobra B.A.A.T.s right into the sun" (from the file card). For a full bio, see Rock 'N Roll (1982).

MOC: **$12-18**, MLC: **$8**

STAR BRIGADE

"High-tech astronauts take the battle action into the darkened depths of space to protect the universe from Cobra invaders. With specialized deep-space battle suits and shooting weapons, this cosmic clash is hotter than the sun!" These Star Brigade figures sold at a cost like most carded Joe figures at retail and at lower price points than the Armor-Tech Star Brigade.

(STAR BRIGADE) ASTRO-VIPER

Cobranaut (SB #11)
(Includes: Astro-Smasher, Two Missiles, Two Guns, Knife, Helmet, Figure Stand)

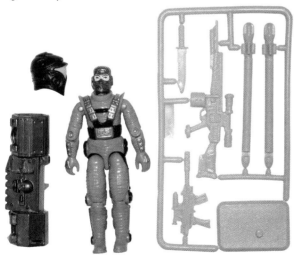

For a full bio, see Astro-Viper (1988).

MOC: **$12-18**, MLC: **$8**

(STAR BRIGADE) COUNTDOWN

Combat Astronaut (SB #8)
(Includes: Fazer Gun, Two Missiles, Two Guns, Knife, Helmet, Figure Stand)

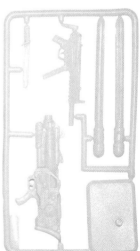

For a full bio, see Countdown (1989).

MOC: **$12-18**, MLC: **$8**

(STAR BRIGADE) OZONE

Astro-Infantry Trooper (SB #10 a & b)
(Includes: Solar Shooter, Two Missiles, Three Guns, Machete, Helmet, Figure Stand)

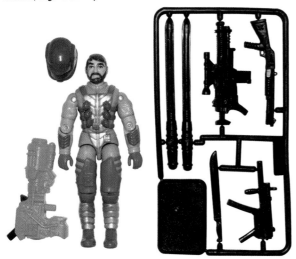

Ozone has now switched from the Eco-Warriors to the Star Brigade, where his experience as an ozone replenisher trooper is called into play. This version of Ozone is tan with red and blue highlights. Ozone also came in gray with red and blue highlights this year. Neither is color scheme is more rare. For a full bio, see Ozone (1991).

MOC: **$12-18**, MLC: **$8**

(STAR BRIGADE) PAYLOAD

Astro-Pilot (SB #7)
(Includes: Quasar Gun, Two Missiles, Three Guns, Knife, Figure Stand)

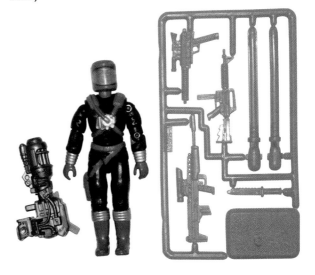

This version of Payload is black with green highlights and another version was released in black with blue highlights. Neither color scheme is more rare. For a full bio, see Payload (1987).

MOC: **$12-18**, MLC: **$8**

(STAR BRIGADE) ROADBLOCK

Space Gunner (SB #9)
(Includes: Star Blaster, Two Missiles, Three Guns, Machete, Helmet)

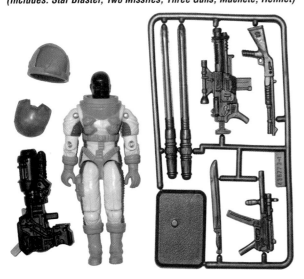

Acting as a "space-gunner" for the Star Brigade, he was the Heavy Machine Gunner for the Joe team. For a full bio, see Roadblock (1984).

MOC: **$12-18**, MLC: **$8**

(STAR BRIGADE) SCI-FI

Starfighter Pilot
(Includes: Helmet, Rifle)
Included with the Starfighter.

From Directed Energy Expert (see Sci-Fi, 1991) to Starfighter Pilot, Sci-Fi has a "fascination with electronics and high-tech laser optics" (from the file card). His Master's Thesis security program was adopted by NASA, and eventually this led to his appointment with the Joe team's Star Brigade.

MLC: **$8**

(STAR BRIGADE)
T.A.R.G.A.T.

Trans Atmospheric Rapid Global Assault Trooper (SB #12)

(Includes: Lunar Launcher, Two Missiles, Three Guns, Face Shield, Figure Stand)

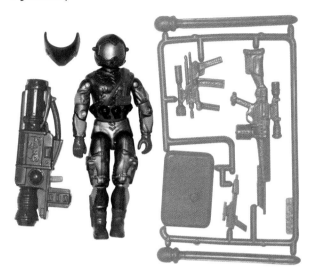

Now the T.A.R.G.A.T. soldiers are truly trans-atmospheric troopers, as they man Cobra Invaders (1993) while orbiting the moon (from the file card). For a full bio, see T.A.R.G.A.T. (1989).

MOC: **$12-18**, MLC: **$8**

MAIL AWAY
EXCLUSIVES
ARCTIC COMMANDOS

Cobra has created a "giant thermal conversion laser cannon" on the top of Mt. Everest to strike at strategic targets (from the file card). Can G.I. Joe's Arctic Attack Force stop Cobra? This set sells for $25-40 Mint in Mailer Baggie.

[ARCTIC COMMANDO]
DEE-JAY

(Includes: Rifle, Microphone)
Mail Away Exclusive

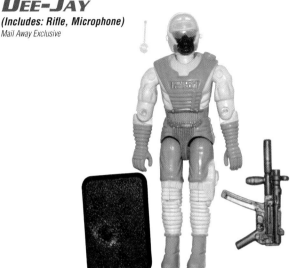

For a full bio, see Dee-Jay (1989).

MLC: **$6-8**

[ARCTIC COMMANDO]
SNOW SERPENT

(Includes: Rifle, Battle Stand)
Mail Away Exclusive

For a full bio, see Snow Serpent (1985, 1991).

MLC: **$6-8**

[ARCTIC COMMANDO]
STALKER

(Includes: Knife, Battle Stand)
Mail Away Exclusive

For a full bio, see Stalker (1982, 1989).

MLC: **$6-8**

[ARCTIC COMMANDO] SUB-ZERO

(Includes: Rifle, Battle Stand, Antenna)

Mail Away Exclusive

For a full bio, see Sub-Zero (1990).

MLC: **$6-8**

BATTLE COPTER PILOTS

The B.C.P.'s fight against one another over the skies of Eastern Europe, while Cobra's Interrogator tries to disrupt the flow of air traffic. "Can Major Altitude and his contingent of G.I. Joe Battle Copters stop him?" (from the file card). This set sells for $15-20 Mint in Mailer Baggie.

[B.C.P.] INTERROGATOR

(Includes: Knife, Battle Stand)

Mail Away Exclusive

For a full bio, see Interrogator (1991).

MLC: **$6-8**

[B.C.P.] MAJOR ALTITUDE

(Includes: Rifle, Helmet, Battle Stand)

Mail Away Exclusive

For a full bio, see Major Altitude (1991).

MLC: **$6-8**

INTERNATIONAL ACTION FORCE

"The I.A.F. is a group of four international G.I. Joe combat specialists who have been called on to hit Cobra hard! From Russia, England, Japan, and Native America, these four Joes are impelled to fight the Cobra threat!" (from the file card). This set sells for $30-45 Mint in Mailer Baggie.

[I.A.F.] BIG BEAR

(Includes: Rifle, Battle Stand)

Mail Away Exclusive

For a full bio, see Big Bear (1992).

MLC: **$6-8**

[I.A.F.] Big Ben
(Includes: Rifle, Battle Stand)
Mail Away Exclusive

For a full bio, see Big Ben (1991).

MLC: **$6-8**

[I.A.F.] Budo
(Includes: Helmet, Sword, Battle Stand)
Mail Away Exclusive

For a full bio, see Budo (1988).

MLC: **$6-8**

[I.A.F.] Spirit
(Includes: Knife, Battle Stand)
Mail Away Exclusive

For a full bio, see Spirit (1983, 1992).

MLC: **$6-8**

Rapid Deployment Force

"The R.D.F. commandos are issued a communiqué to stop Cobra's latest nuclear threat, and only this team of three soldiers can stop them!" (from the file card). The R.D.F. figures were offered together as a three-pack, along with three guns, figure stands, and a re-cast black Pocket Patrol Pack (1983) with Rapid Deployment Force decals. This set sells for $25-40 Mint in Mailer Baggie.

[R.D.F.] Fast Draw
Mail Away Exclusive

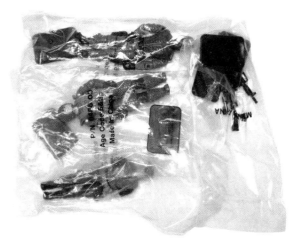

For a full bio, see Fast Draw (1987).

MLC: **$6-8**

S
E
R
I
E
S

T
W
E
L
V
E

[R.D.F.] REPEATER
Mail Away Exclusive

[R.D.F.] SHOCKWAVE
Mail Away Exclusive

For a full bio and photo of this "Night Force" version of Repeater, see Repeater (1988).

MLC: **$8**

For a full bio and photo of this "Night Force" version of Shockwave, see Shockwave (1988).

MLC: **$6-8**

CAPCOM STREET FIGHTER II

"The Capcom Street Fighter II World Warrior's tournament is underway! The best of the best and meanest of the mean battle in the greatest martial arts conflict ever! The title of World's Toughest Fighter is at stake—collect them all and let the battle begin!" These figures are official versions of the video game characters.

(STREET FIGHTER II) BALROG
Heavyweight Boxer (STF #11)
(Includes: Knockout Launcher, Two Missiles, Two Boxing Gloves, Two Rifles, Knife, Grappling Hook, String, Figure Stand)

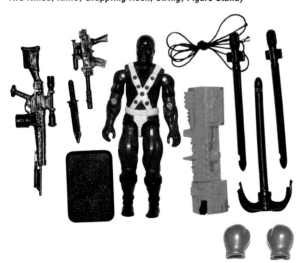

Balrog was a former heavyweight champion who ignored the rules (from the file card). He's currently a street brawler and "occasionally" works for M. Bison (1993).

MOC: **$12-18**, MLC: **$6-10**

(STREET FIGHTER II) BLANKA
Jungle Fighter (STF #5)
(Includes: Beast Blaster, Two Missiles, Grappling Hook, Two Guns, Knife, String, Figure Stand)

Blanka hails from Brazil and is a half-man half-beast creature who roams the rain forests (from the file card). He is "normally passive and docile, [but] when enraged [he] attacks like an uncaged animal." This version of Blanka has green skin, while the Blanka included with the Beast Blaster has blue skin (1993).

MOC: **$12-18**, MLC: **$6-10**

(STREET FIGHTER II) BLANKA
(Championship Edition)
Included with the Beast Blaster (along with Championship Edition Chun Li).

For a short bio, see Blanka (1993). This version of Blanka has blue skin, while the carded version of Blanka has green skin (1993).

MLC: **$6-8**

(STREET FIGHTER II) CHUN LI
Kung Fu Fighter (STF #4)
(Includes: Spring Action Whirlwind Kick, Nunchuks, Three Swords, Two Claws, Knife, Figure Stand)

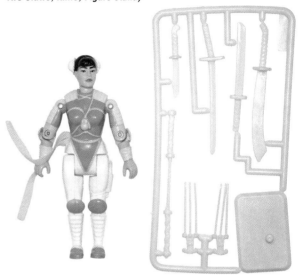

Chun Li has entered the Street Fighter tournament to secretly track the movements of the "international smuggling operation known as Shadoloo" (from the file card). She is motivated by justice. Her action figure has a spring action kick. This version of her figure wears a blue outfit, as opposed to the red outfit worn by Chun Li included with the Beast Blaster (1993).

MOC: **$12-18**, MLC: **$6-10**

(STREET FIGHTER II) CHUN LI
(Championship Edition)
Included with the Beast Blaster (along with Championship Edition Blanka).

For a short bio, see Chun Li (1993). Her figure has a spring action kick. This version of her figure wears a red outfit, as opposed to the blue outfit worn by the carded version of Chun Li (1993).

MLC: **$6-8**

(STREET FIGHTER II) DHALSIM
Yoga Fighter (STF #8)
(Includes: Spring Action Fire Fist, Two Knives, Sickle, Two Swords, Bow, Figure Stand)

As a Yoga Fighter, Dhalsim is patient and a master of control over his body, and is a merciful warrior. His figure has a spring action chopping punch motion.

MOC: **$12-18**, MLC: **$6-10**

(STREET FIGHTER II) EDMOND HONDA
Sumo Wrestler (STF #7)
(Includes: Spring Action Hundred Hand Slap, Sickle, Axe, Two Swords, Two Dueling Knives, Broad Knife, Figure Stand)

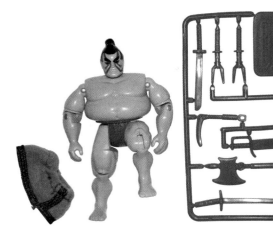

E. Honda has trained all his life to be a sumo wrestler, and has achieved the rank of grand champion (from the file card). His figure was originally supposed to have a chopping hand motion, but instead was replaced with an awkward kicking motion spring action leg.

MOC: **$12-18**, MLC: **$6-10**

(STREET FIGHTER II) GUILE
Special Forces Fighter (STF #3)
(Includes: Sonic Boom Bazooka, Two Missiles, Grappling Hook, String, Shield, Two Guns, Knife, Figure Stand)

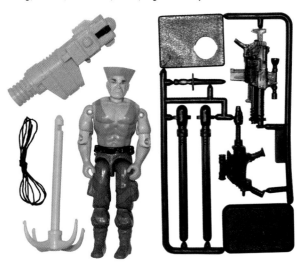

This version of Guile sports a green shirt, as oppose to the other Guile included with the Sonic Boom Tank who wears a brown shirt. Guile was "an ex-member of an elite Special Forces team" (from the file card). He is driven by an inner rage, and combines his Special Forces skills with street fighting knowledge.

MOC: **$12-18**, MLC: **$6-10**

(STREET FIGHTER II) GUILE
(Championship Edition)
Included with the Sonic Boom Tank.

This is the "brown-shirted" version of Guile, as opposed to the green shirt as worn by his carded version (1993). For a short bio, see Guile (1993).

MLC: **$6-8**

(STREET FIGHTER II) KEN MASTERS
Shotokan Karate Fighter (STF #2)
(Includes: Spring Action Double Fireball Fists, Two Knives, Two Swords, Bow, Sickle, Figure Stand)

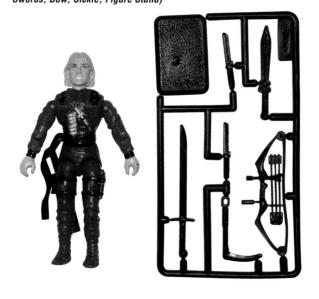

Ken Masters is a "disciple of the Shotokan school of karate" (from the file card), but he has an enormous ego; he "loves to show off during a fight." This version of Ken Masters sports a red outfit, while the version of Ken included with the Dragon Fortress wears a purple outfit (1993). His spring action mimicked his "double fireball fists."

MOC: **$12-18**, MLC: **$6-10**

S E R I E S   T W E L V E

(STREET FIGHTER II) KEN MASTERS

(Championship Edition)

Included with the Dragon Fortress (along with Championship Edition Ryu).

This version of Ken Masters is purple/blue in color, while the carded version of Ken wears a red outfit. His spring action mimicked his "double fireball fists." For a brief bio, see Ken Masters (1993).

MLC: **$6-8**

(STREET FIGHTER II) M. BISON

Grand Master (STF #6)

(Includes: Flaming Torpedo Launcher, Shoulder Pads [see note], Two Missiles, Grappling Hook, String, Three Guns, Figure Stand)

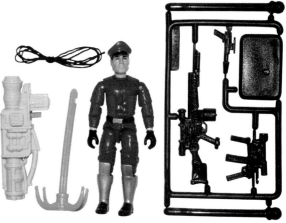

M. Bison has a secretive past, and currently runs the criminal Shadoloo organization, wielding immense power (from the file card). Some versions of M. Bison's figure came with a set of silver shoulder pads, and some did not. Further, this version of M. Bison wears a red outfit, while the version included with the Crimson Cruiser is dressed in aqua-blue colors.

MOC: **$12-18**, MLC: **$6-10**

(STREET FIGHTER II) M. BISON

(Championship Edition)
(Includes: Shoulder Pads)

Included with the Crimson Cruiser.

This version of M. Bison is dressed in aqua-blue, while the carded figure wears red fatigues. For a brief bio, see M. Bison (1993).

MLC: **$6-8**

(STREET FIGHTER II) RYU

Stotokan Karate Fighter (STF #1)

(Includes: Spring Action Dragon Punch, Two Swords, Sickle, Axe, Knife, Two Dueling Knives, Figure Stand)

Ryu is a student of Shotokan karate, and "has devoted all his life to the perfection of his fighting skills" (from the file card). He is so dedicated to his craft, that he has made himself a loner. This version of the figure has a spring-loaded right arm, and wears a white outfit, as opposed to the Ryu figure included with the Dragon Fortress who sports a gray outfit.

MOC: **$12-18**, MLC: **$6-10**

(STREET FIGHTER II) RYU
(Championship Edition)
Included with the Dragon Fortress (along with Championship Edition Ken Masters).

This version of Ryu has a spring-loaded right arm, and wears a gray outfit, as opposed to the carded Ryu figure that sports a white outfit. For a quick bio, see Ryu (1993).

MLC: **$6-8**

(STREET FIGHTER II) VEGA
Spanish Ninja (STF #10)
(Includes: Spring Action Matador Mash, Two Swords, Sickle, Axe, Knife, Two Dueling Knives, Figure Stand)

Vega is one of the more difficult Street Fighter II figures to find, as he has an attractive and interesting figure sculpt. His character was "of noble blood" and has practiced Ninjitsu (from the file card). His nickname is the "Spanish Ninja" because of the combination of his Spanish matador techniques with ninja skills.

MOC: **$12-18**, MLC: **$6-10**

(STREET FIGHTER II) SAGAT
Thai Fighter (STF #12)
(Includes: Spring Action Thai Chop, Three Swords, Knife, Nunchuks, Two Claws, Figure Stand)

He was once nicknamed the "King of the Street Fighters" (from the file card), and was narrowly defeated at the hands of Ryu (1993). He is rumored to have the most powerful fighting style in the world.

MOC: **$12-18**, MLC: **$6-10**

(STREET FIGHTER II) ZANGIEF
Russian Bear Wrestler (STF #9)
(Includes: Spring Action Pile Driver, Two Missiles, Grappling Hook, String, Three Guns, Figure Stand)

As a man who "wrestles bears for fun" (from the file card), Zangief adores the art of fighting. He is fearless and has a devastating finishing move.

MOC: **$12-18**, MLC: **$6-10**

1993 VEHICLES/PLAYSETS

ARMOR-BOT
(Includes: Hawk figure)

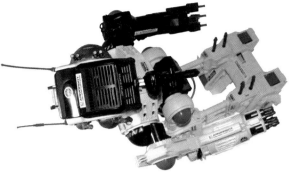

The Star Brigade Armor-Bot, with five electronic voice commands has a pivoting laser rifle, rocket guns, armor plated wheel treads, body shielding, and a battle-grip cyber claw to aid the Joe team on deep space landings. It also comes with a firing missile launcher.

Easily lost pieces include twelve missiles and two antennas.

MISB: **$35-50**, MIB **$25**, MLC: **$12-18**

Armor-Bot's easily lost pieces.

BEAST BLASTER
(Includes: Championship Edition Blanka and Chun Li figures)

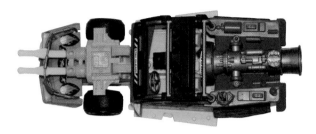

The Street Fighter II Beast Blaster has an armor-plated combat windshield, jet powered engine (from an F-16), 4-wheel drive all-terrain tires, and a firing rocket launcher that shoots four SF-2 surface-to-surface missiles that helps Blanka and Chun-Li defeat the evil Shadoloo forces. The designs of the Beast Blaster were based on the Dreadnok Thunder Machine (1986), and it comes with similar accessories.

Easily lost pieces include four missiles, antenna, two doors, and the roof.

MISB: **$25**, MIB: **$15-20**, MLC: **$10-12**

The Beast Blaster's easily lost pieces.

COBRA DETONATOR
(Includes Nitro-Viper figure)

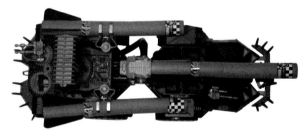

With the Detonator in their arsenal, the forces of Cobra utilize this wrecking force with six monster-tires, three long-range ICBM rockets, and a targeting seat with AAK gun to plow through the Joe's defenses.

The easily lost pieces are its three foam ICBM missiles.

MISB: **$35-40**, MIB: **$20-25**, MLC: **$15**

COBRA ICE SNAKE

Cobra's Ice Snake is a fast-attack snow vehicle with a spring-action 360-degree rotating Arctic-assault missile launcher, a roll-cage canopy, and heavy duty treads. The main missile fired from its launcher is attached by a string, so switching missiles is a bit awkward unless you use the same one over and over.

Easily lost pieces include three missiles, (one with) string, missile launcher, black rubber band (not pictured, as it was attached to the interior of the vehicle).

MISB: **$20**, MIB: **$12**, MLC: **$8**

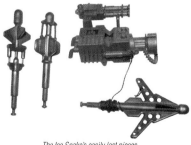

The Ice Snake's easily lost pieces.

CRIMSON CRUISER
(Includes: Championship Edition M. Bison figure)

M. Bison's Crimson Cruiser is from the Street Fighter II line of Joes, and sports a "Bison Blaster" missile launcher with three concussion missiles, all terrain tires, and a "cement crusher" spiked bumper—all to do M. Bison's nefarious bidding.

Easily lost pieces include three missiles, antenna, and missile launcher.

MISB: **$20**, MIB: **$12**, MLC: **$8**

The Crimson Cruiser's easily lost pieces.

DINO-HUNTER MISSION PLAYSET
(Dino-Hunter Jeep and Dinosaur)
(Includes: Low-Light and Ambush figures)
Toys 'R Us Exclusive

The Dino-Hunters mission play set was launched in response to capitalize on the dinosaur craze that captured kids' imaginations in the early 1990s. It is a strange set, as it comes with two re-decorated figures, a re-colored jeep (see the Desert Fox 6WD vehicle, 1988), and a funky medium-sized plastic dinosaur. The playset is fairly rare, and collectors should expect to pay a pretty penny for boxed examples.

Easily lost pieces include the Dinosaur (pictured next to jeep), two grappling hooks, two sonic missiles, antenna, launcher stand, missile launcher (pictured on jeep—note, this looks exactly like the Flak-Viper backpack [1992, 1993], but the launcher has two holes one either side of it that snap into the launcher stand).

MISB: **$80-100**, MIB: **$50-60**, MLC: **$35-45**

The Dino Hunter Playset's easily lost pieces.

DRAGON FORTRESS
(Includes: Championship Edition Ken Masters and Ryu figures)

Based on the design of the 1992 Cobra Toxo-Lab, the Dragon Fortress was used as a training facility for the members of G.I. Joe's Street Fighter II contingent. With a bungee jump, trampoline launcher, and double barreled cannon, this fortress is the perfect training ground for the Street Fighters. This is an uncommon piece to find MISB, but should not command too high of a price, as the Street Fighter II line is not very popular with most collectors.

Easily lost pieces include four missiles, missile launcher, bungee jump (3 pieces: leg attachment, black rubber band, roof attachment), and a missile rack.

MISB: **$35-40**, MIB: **$30**, MLC: **$20**

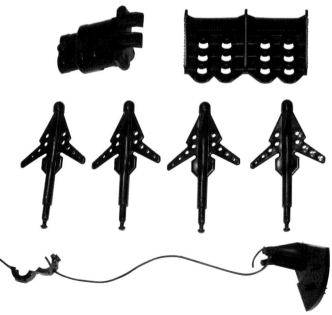

The Dragon Fortress' easily lost pieces.

GHOSTSTRIKER X-16
(Includes: Ace figure)

The latest in the Joe team's flight technology, the Ghoststriker is armed with two sidewinder missiles, four phoenix missiles, retractable landing gear—and for kids, an image projection unit built inside the toy. Now, kids could project the illuminated image of an enemy jet on their bedroom wall, "fire a missile" at the bad guy, and electronically neutralize him. This was pretty high-tech stuff for 1993.

Easily lost pieces include six missiles, top wing, and, if loose, the jet's "projection disc" located right behind the nosecone underneath the jet (not pictured as it can sometimes break while being removed).

MISB: **$50**,
MIB: **$35**, MLC: **$20**

The Ghoststriker's easily lost pieces.

COBRA INVADER

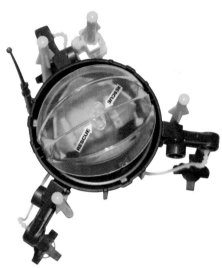

The Cobra Invader is the spaceborne version of the Pogo: Ballistic Battle Ball (1987), and without its newer modifications is nearly the same vehicle. Note the three green cords in the vehicle's main picture, one cord is attached to each leg, not unlike the gray cords on the legs of the Pogo.

Easily lost pieces include four missiles, missile launcher, gold antenna, coolant hose, and three hoses.

MISB: **$15**, MIB: **$10**,
MLC: **$6-8**

The Invader's easily lost pieces.

MONSTER BLASTER A.P.C.
(Armored Personnel Carrier)

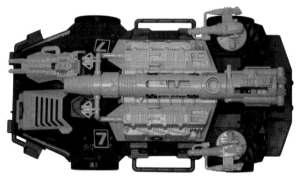

The Mega-Marine's Monster Blaster is driven by Clutch (1982, 1993), and is a heavily armored troop transporter designed to encounter and defeat the Bio-Vipers (1993) and Monstro-Vipers (1993). The toy featured a fascinating bolt-action "Lock 'N Load" missile launcher (very cool), four heat-seeking missiles, and puncture proof "monster crushing" tires. Even though Clutch (1993) was designated as the driver of this vehicle, he was not included with it but sold separately MOC.

Easily lost pieces are the four missiles.

MISB: **$35**, MIB: **$20**, MLC: **$12-15**

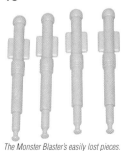
The Monster Blaster's easily lost pieces.

MUDBUSTER

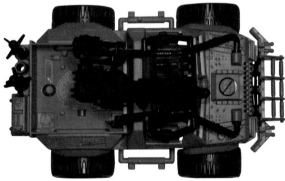

The Mudbuster is G.I. Joe's all terrain 4x4 battle truck with a "smash 'n bash" bumper, 360-degree rotating missile launcher, and puncture proof tires. Its color does not detract from the durability of the toy, yet at this point in the Joe line, vehicles were a tough sell (usually) because of their colors.

Easily lost pieces include the missile launcher (with attached string), three missiles, roll bar, and black rubber band (not pictured, as it would not come off the interior of the vehicle).

MISB: **$20**, MIB: **$12**, MLC: **$8**

The Mudbuster's easily lost pieces.

NINJA LIGHTNING

With its easily repeatable rip-cord pull action and firing surface-to-surface stealth missiles, the G.I. Joe Ninja Force's Ninja Lightning motorcycle was the preferred mode of transportation for Snake Eyes, Storm Shadow, and the team. With its neon colors, some collectors disliked its design, and it's not popular with collectors.

Easily lost pieces are the two missiles.

MISB: **$15-18**, MIB: **$10**, MLC: **$6**

The Ninja Lightning's easily lost pieces.

NINJA RAIDER BATTLE AX
(Includes: Red Ninja figure)

The Ninja Raider Battle Ax had a spring-loaded "Cyclone Slash" blade mechanism and top mounted rapid-fire double machine guns for Cobra's Red Ninja to run amok with. It was a very simple toy.

The easily lost piece is the missile gun.

MISB: **$20**, MIB: **$12**, MLC: **$8**

The easily lost pieces.

NINJA RAIDER PILE DRIVER
(Includes: T'Gin-Zu figure)

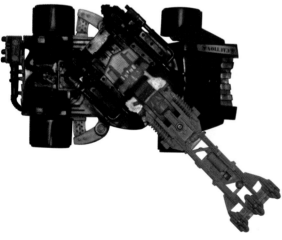

G.I. Joe's Pile Driver, with its spinning "Ninja Knockout" hammer mechanism and rapid fire missile grenade guns protects the driver from line fighters of Ninja Force. Like its brother vehicle, Cobra's Ninja Raider Battle Ax, this is a very simple vehicle.

The missile grenade gun is the only easily lost piece.

MISB: **$20**, MIB: **$12**, MLC: **$8**

The Ninja Raider Pile Driver's missile grenade gun.

RAPID DEPLOYMENT FORCE POCKET PATROL PACK

MLC: **$2-3**

SHARK 9000
(Includes: Cutter figure)

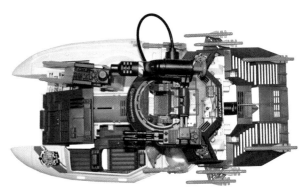

The SHARK 9000 was originally slated to be part of the G.I. Joe D.E.F. (1992) sub-line of figures and vehicles, but instead was given a nod to the "Battle Corps" line. It is a complicated vehicle to construct, with many pieces and parts, from its Aqua-Attack missile launcher to its H20 X-1 machine guns.

Easily lost pieces include the water cannon, missile launcher, two torpedoes, four mines, thick hose, and eight missiles.

MISB: **$35-45**,
MIB: **$20-25**,
MLC: **$12-15**

The SHARK 9000's easily lost pieces.

SONIC BOOM TANK
(Includes: Championship Edition Guile)

The designs of the Street Fighter II Sonic Boom Tank were based on the Cobra Paralyzer (1991), and it comes with similar accessories. With three high-impact sonic boom missiles, an armor-plated canopy, and a double-barreled recoiling "Boom Boom" gun, Guile can attack the opposition with great force.

Easily lost pieces include the three missiles.

MISB: **$20**, MIB: **$12**, MLC: **$8**

The Sonic Boom Tank's easily lost pieces.

STARFIGHTER
(Includes: Sci-Fi figure)

Based on the designs of Cobra's Stellar Stiletto (1988), the G.I. Joe Starfighter is a light-speed rocket that adds to Star Brigade's outer space arsenal.

Easily lost pieces include two coolant hoses, four laser rockets, and the rocket launcher.

MISB: **$20**, MIB: **$12**, MLC: **$8**

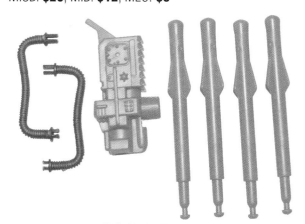
The Starfighter's easily lost pieces.

TRIPLE "T"
(Tag Team Terminator)
Mail Away Exclusive

In 1993, Sgt. Slaughter's Triple "T" was offered as a mail-away vehicle. This version of the Triple "T" included neon magenta colored guns and missiles. Note that mint-in-baggie specimens came with a note from Hasbro explaining the color change and re-decoration of the tank.

Mint in Mailer Baggie: **$25**, MLC: **$8**

(SERIES XIII, 1994)

The 1994 series, the swan song of the "vintage" 3-3/4" Joe line, is a bit complicated to reveal to collectors, because of packaging changes made during the year. Most carded Battle Corps figures released early in the year came with regular-sized file cards, while those released later in the assortment (#'s 8-13) came with two versions of packaging and alternative, baseball card-sized file cards.

Some figures were released with two different packaging versions. The first features cards with a horizontal G.I. Joe logo, with borders, and regular file card, and the second features cards with a vertical G.I. Joe logo, non-bordered, and baseball-card size file cards. The figures released in both of these types of packaging were Ice Cream Soldier, Lifeline, Major Bludd, Night Creeper Leader, Snow Storm, and Stalker. These six figures are more difficult to find with the earlier colored borders and regular-sized file cards, therefore these MOC characters command two to three dollars more on those colored-bordered cards.

As an added treat in 1994, the original G.I. Joe, Joseph Colton, a throwback from the true vintage line (1964), was released in 3-3/4" form as a mail away exclusive from Hasbro Direct. Salivating collectors were treated to a second original G.I. Joe promotional—a 12" Joseph Colton version with accessories and a battle stand that smacked of the vintage 12" Joes. [I must note that I ordered the figure, and waited for what seemed an eternity just to get a letter from Hasbro stating they had run out of the 12" Joe Colton promotionals. They refunded my money and flag points (these refund forms are quite rare now), and I was left disappointed. A few months later, I was surprised to receive a package from Hasbro, and inside was a 12" G.I. Joe! But he was re-done in Arctic camouflage! (Hasbro really pulled through, as per usual.)

The 1994 series was the end of the line, and Hasbro re-used and re-cast many figures and sculpts to create new characters and vehicles in order to save on production costs. Unfortunately, nothing Hasbro could do would save G.I. Joe, and all the projects still in planning (the Ninja Commandos, and more military-looking Battle Corps figures) were scrapped.

The 1994 catalog.

The "original" G.I. Joe mail-away.

12" Joseph Colton mail-away form.

1994 G.I. JOE FIGURES

(BATTLE CORPS) BEACH-HEAD
Ranger (BC #6)
(Includes: Missile Launcher, Two Missiles, Three Guns, Knife, Figure Stand)

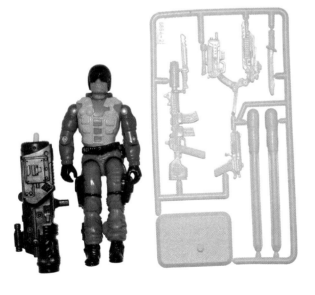

The 1994 Beach-Head figure has a yellow vest, while the 1993 version wears a black vest. For a full bio, see Beach-Head (1986).

MOC: **$12-18**, MLC: **$8**

(BATTLE CORPS) FLINT
Desert Paratrooper (BC #1)
(Includes: Sand-Blaster, Two Missiles, Three Guns, Helmet, Figure Stand)

This version of Flint throws Dashiell Faireborne into the desert, as his new MOS is "Desert Paratrooper." For a full bio, see Flint (1985, 1991).

MOC: **$12-18**, MLC: **$8**

(BATTLE CORPS) DIAL-TONE
Communications Expert (BC #2)
(Includes: Sonic Launcher, Two Missiles, Three Guns, Knife, Helmet, Figure Stand)

Still acting as the Joes' RTO (Radio Telephone Operator), Dial-Tone is always in constant radio contact with his team. For a full bio, see Dial-Tone (1986).

MOC: **$12-18**, MLC: **$8**

G.I. JOE
(Includes: Machine Gun)
Mail Away Exclusive

This mail-away exclusive was a very important and popular one, as it was for the "original" G.I. Joe—Joseph B. Colton. He was the first soldier to earn the official code name of G.I. Joe, and created the original "ultimate freedom fighting force" (from the file card).

Mint in Mailer Baggie: **$20**, MLC: **$12**

(BATTLE CORPS) ICE CREAM SOLDIER
Flamethrower Commando (BC #10)
(Includes: Missile Launcher, Two Missiles, Pistol, Two Rifles, Small Sword, Figure Stand)

Yet another flame specialist is added to the Joe's ranks with the Ice Cream Soldier. It is rumored that Cobra troopers do not take this soldier seriously given such a ridiculous code name, but they do after he "fires up his super-charged flamethrower" (from the file card).

MOC: **$12-18**, MLC: **$8**

(BATTLE CORPS) LIFELINE
Rescue Trooper (BC #8)
(Includes: Missile Launcher, Grappling Hook, Knife, Flashlight, Gun, Attached Mouthpiece, Briefcase, Rope, Figure Stand)

With this version of Lifeline, his true face is revealed. For a full bio, see Lifeline (1986).

MOC: **$12-18**, MLC: **$8**

1994 G.I. JOE FIGURES

(BATTLE CORPS) SHIPWRECK
Navy S.E.A.L. (Sea, Air and Land) (BC #3)
(Includes: Hydro-Blaster, Two Missiles, Two Flippers, Two Rifles, Pistol, Knife, Air Mask, Figure Stand)

With this incarnation of the salty sailor, Shipwreck has completed Naval Gunnery School Training (from the file card) and become a member of the Navy SEALS (like Torpedo, 1983; and Wet-Suit, 1983). His accessories are well assigned for this figure, and for a full bio, see Shipwreck (1985).

MOC: **$12-18**, MLC: **$8**

(BATTLE CORPS) SNOW STORM
High-Tech Snow Trooper (BC #12)
(Includes: Glacier Gun, Two Missiles, Two Rifles, Pistol, Knife, Figure Stand)

Now decked out in a black and white outfit (as opposed to his differently colored outfits in 1993), Snow Storm is still the Joe's resident Arctic trooper. For a full bio, see Snow Storm (1993).

MOC: **$12-18**, MLC: **$8**

(BATTLE CORPS) STALKER
Ranger (BC #9)
(Includes: Missile Launcher, Two Missiles, Three Guns, Machete, Figure Stand)

Stalker's figure, like many of the 1994 Joes, has different highlight variations that don't seem to effect the value of the figure, but are a "must" for completionists out there. Along with Stalker's paint variations, Flint, Dial-Tone, Shipwreck, and Lifeline from 1994 have minor variations that do not effect their values. Stalker's character is again a Ranger, and there is a mention of his being on the same LRRP (Long Range Reconnaissance Patrol) as Storm Shadow and Snake Eyes. He has known these two characters for a long time, witnessing Storm Shadow saving Snake Eye's life, and the bitter feud that erupted between the two. For a full bio, see Stalker (1982).

Stalker color variations.

MOC: **$12-18**, MLC: **$8**

(BATTLE CORPS) WINDCHILL
Blockbuster Driver (BC #62)
(Includes: Rifle)
Included with the Blockbuster.

This version is the weaker-looking version of the two Windchill figures, with quick paint applications that seem slapped-on. His file card is quite difficult to find, as it was attached to the Blockbuster's box, and there were a tremendous amount of mail-order bagged Windchill figures available. For a full bio, see Windchill (1989).

MLC: **$8**

1994 COBRA FIGURES

(Battle Corps) Alley Viper

(BC # 7)

(Includes: Assault Gun, Two Missiles, Two Rifles, Shield, Helmet, Face Mask, Figure Stand)

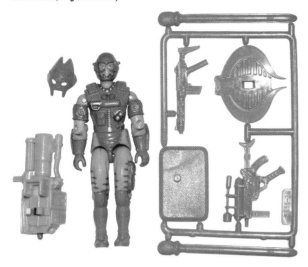

This 1994 version of the figure is cast in its traditional 1989 colors of blue and orange, while the 1993 version of the figure is yellow and black. For a full bio, see Alley Viper (1989).

MOC: **$15-22**, MLC: **$8**

(Battle Corps) Major Bludd

Mercenary *(BC #11)*

(Includes: "Bludd" Launcher, Two Missiles, Two Rifles, Knife, Figure Stand)

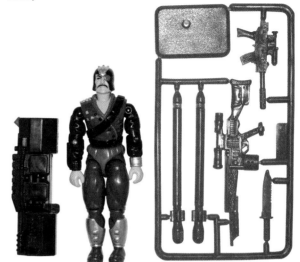

For a full bio, see Major Bludd (1983).

MOC: **$12-18**, MLC: **$8**

(Battle Corps) Metal-Head

Anti-Tank Specialist (BC #4)

(Includes: Tank-Blaster, Two Missiles, Three Guns, Figure Stand)

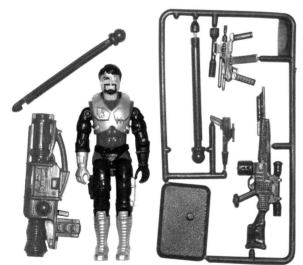

This version of Metal-Head is well sculpted and reminiscent of his original incarnation, and he is still a "walking anti-tank weapon" (from the file card). For a full bio, see Metal-Head (1990).

MOC: **$12-18**, MLC: **$8**

(Battle Corps) Night Creeper Leader

Cobra Ninja Supreme Master (BC #13)

(Includes: Shock Gun, Two Missiles, Two Swords, Two Crossbows, Knife, Shield, Figure Stand)

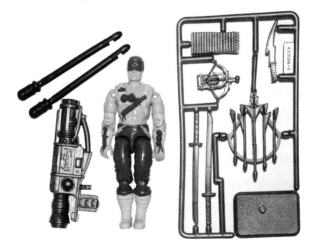

Note that this version of Night Creeper Leader has purple highlights, while the 1993 version sports orange highlights. For a brief bio, see Night Creeper Leader (1993).

MOC: **$12-18**, MLC: **$8**

[BATTLE CORPS] VIPER

Cobra Infantry Trooper (BC #5)
(Includes: Master-Blaster, Two Missiles, Trident Rifle, Two Pistols, Knife, Figure Stand)

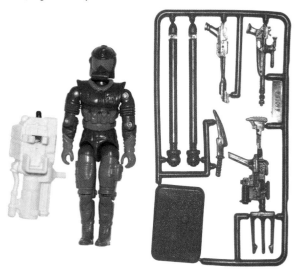

This figure is an updated version of the standard Cobra Viper from 1986, and for a full bio, see Viper (1986).

MOC: **$14-20**, MLC: **$8**

ACTION PILOT

Air Force Fighter Pilot

This version of the Action Pilot: Air Force Fighter Pilot is based loosely on the design of Hasbro's original 12″ Action Pilot from 1964. He comes with appropriate weapons for the figure, and this particular version is powder blue in color and is included with the 30th Edition Commemorative Collection: Original Action Team boxed set. The yellow version of the Action Pilot was individually packaged.

Individually boxed MIB: **$15**; MLC: **$8**; with the boxed set MLC: **$8**

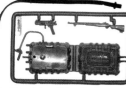

Action Pilot: Air Force Fighter Pilot accessories.

COMMEMORATIVE COLLECTION/EDITION [30TH ANNIVERSARY BOXED SET]

Boxed Set: **$35-45**

ACTION MARINE

Marine Corps Commando

This version of the Action Marine: Marine Corps Commando is based loosely on the design of Hasbro's original 12″ Action Marine from 1964. He comes with appropriate weapons for the figure, and besides being released in individual packaging, he is included with the 30th Edition Commemorative Collection: Original Action Team boxed set. This figure is the same individually boxed as in the boxed set.

Individually boxed MIB: **$15**; MLC: **$8**; with the boxed set, MLC: **$8**

Action Marine: Marine Corps Commando accessories.

Action Marine and Action Soldier—boxed variations.

ACTION PILOT
Astronaut

This version of the Action Pilot: Astronaut is based loosely on the design of Hasbro's original 12″ Action Pilot from 1964. He is included with the 30th edition Commemorative Collection: Original Action Team boxed set, and some collectors pair him with the space capsule included with that set.

MLC: **$8**, **$15** with the capsule.

ACTION SAILOR
Navy Frogman

This version of the Action Sailor: Navy Frogman is based loosely on the design of Hasbro's original 12″ Action Sailor from 1964. He comes with appropriate weapons for the figure, and this particular version of the figure is orange in color. He is included with the 30th Edition Commemorative Collection: Original Action Team boxed set w/black accessories. The black version of the Action Pilot was individually packaged w/blue accessories.

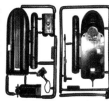

Action Sailor accessories.

Individually boxed MIB: **$15**; MLC: **$8**; with the boxed set, MLC: **$8**

ACTION SOLDIER
U.S. Army Infantry

This version of the Action Soldier: U.S. Army Infantry is based loosely on the design of Hasbro's original 12″ Action Soldier from 1964. He comes with appropriate weapons for the figure, and this particular version has weapon sets that are black in color.

He is included with the 30th Edition Commemorative Collection: Original Action Team boxed set. The individually boxed Action Soldier came with brown accessories.

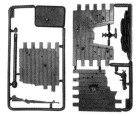

Action Soldier variant accessories from the individually boxed figure.

Individually boxed MIB: **$15**; MLC: **$8**; with the boxed set, MLC: **$8**

SHADOW NINJAS

"G.I. Joe's elite martial arts commandos now battle Cobra's fiercest fighters with Inviso-Power, turning both forces into the most secretive stealth ninjas the world has ever NOT seen! Also featuring spring-action moves, ninja weapons and specialized accessories!" The "Inviso-Power" for these figures actually seems to work, turning the figures a white color when submerged in water.

(SHADOW NINJAS) BUSHIDO
Snow Ninja (#39)
(Includes: Spring-Action Teisho Punch, Two Swords, Two Dueling Knives, Sickle, Knife, Axe, Figure Stand)

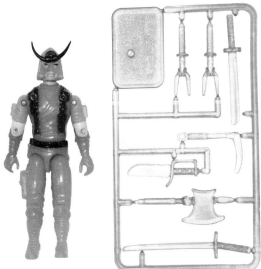

This figure is molded exactly like the earlier version of Ninja Force Bushido, except for its color-change properties. For a full bio, see Bushido (1993).

MOC: **$12-18**, MLC: **$8**

(SHADOW NINJAS) NIGHT CREEPER

Cobra Ninja (#42)

(Includes: Spring-Action Creeper Chop, Two Knives, Two Swords, Sickle, Bow, Figure Stand)

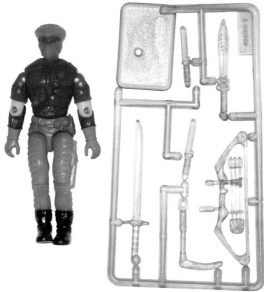

This figure is molded exactly like the earlier version of Ninja Force Night Creeper, except for its color-change properties. For a full bio, see Night Creeper (1990, 1993).

MOC: **$12-18**, MLC: **$8**

(SHADOW NINJAS) NUNCHUK

Nunchaku Ninja (#41)

(Includes: Spring-Action Samurai Slash, Two Swords, Two Knives, Sickle, Bow, Figure Stand)

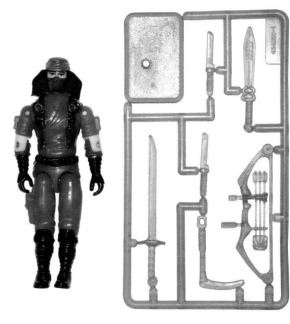

This figure is molded exactly like the earlier version of Ninja Force Nunchuk, except for its color-change properties. For a full bio, see Nunchuk (1992).

MOC: **$12-18**, MLC: **$8**

(SHADOW NINJAS) SLICE

Cobra Ninja Swordsman (#40)

(Includes: Spring-Action Scorpion Slash, Spear, Sword, Axe, Knife, Two Double-Ended Knives, Figure Stand)

 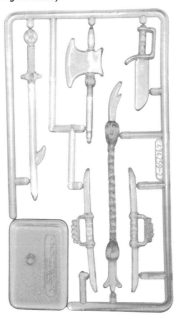

This figure is molded exactly like the earlier version of Ninja Force Slice, except for its color-change properties. For a full bio, see Slice (1992).

MOC: **$12-18**, MLC: **$8**

(SHADOW NINJAS) SNAKE EYES

Covert Mission Specialist (#37)

(Includes: Spring-Action Basami Bash, Three Swords, Two Claws, Nunchuks, Knife, Figure Stand)

This figure is molded exactly like the earlier version of Ninja Force Snake Eyes, except for its color-change properties. For a full bio, see Snake Eyes (1982, 1993).

MOC: **$12-18**, MLC: **$8**

(SHADOW NINJAS) STORM SHADOW

Shadow Ninja Leader (#38)
(Includes: Spring-Action Scissor Slice, Three Swords, Two Claws, Nunchuks, Knife, Figure Stand)

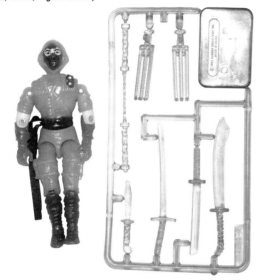

This figure is molded exactly like the earlier version of Ninja Force Storm Shadow, except for its color-change properties. For a full bio, see Storm Shadow (1984, 1993).

MOC: **$12-18**, MLC: **$8**

STAR BRIGADE

"High-tech astronauts race-to-space to protect the universe from Cobra. With specialized space suits, battle action backpacks and shooting weapons, this cosmic clash is hotter than the sun!

"Star Brigade Lunartix characters are alien bounty hunters that join the galactic battles as they stalk the stars in search of alien or humanoid prey!"

(STAR BRIGADE) CARCASS

Alien Destroyer (#52)
(Includes: Bendable Monster Arms, Four Guns, Knife, Figure Stand)

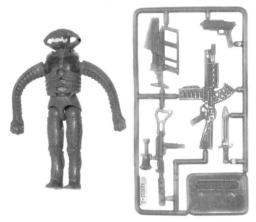

One of the most controversial Joe figures, Carcass "leaves nothing but broken bones and smashed dwellings" in his evil wake (from the file card). Carcass has wire-rooted arms that are poseable, and it should be noted that his outer chest pieces are not movable and if you try to move them, they may break.

NOTE: *If you find a Lunartix Alien (Carcass, Predacon, or Lobotomaxx) that is of a different color than pictured here, you have a Mexican variant.*

MOC: **$12-18**, MLC: **$8**

(STAR BRIGADE) COUNTDOWN

Combat Astronaut (#53)
(Includes: Fazer Gun, Two Missiles, Two Guns, Knife, Helmet, Figure Stand)

For a full bio, see Countdown (1989).

MOC: **$12-18**, MLC: **$8**

(STAR BRIGADE) EFFECTS

Explosives Expert (#49)
(Includes: Missile Launcher, Three-Piece Catapult, Two Disks, Helmet, Rifle, Figure Stand)

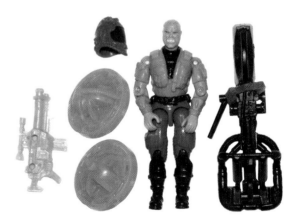

With a grimace on his face, Effects is the Explosives Expert of the Star Brigade team. He is a wizard with special effects, dazzling lights, sounds, and explosions that keep Cobra space troopers off their guard (from the file card).

MOC: **$12-18**, MLC: **$8**

(STAR BRIGADE) GEARS

Invention Technician (#60)

(Includes: Helmet)

Included with the G.I. Joe Power Fighter.

One of the more difficult to obtain Joes, Gears "is a technological genius... [who] helped to bring Robo-Joe (1993) to life" (from his file card). This process led to his development of "Robotic Battle Armor... [and] the Power Fighter Units that operate as an extension of the pilot's own body." He is a masterful inventor.

MLC: **$10-15**

(STAR BRIGADE) LOBOTOMAXX

Stellar Explorer (#50)

(Includes: Bendable Neck and Tail, Five Guns, Knife, Figure Stand)

The Lunartix alien known as Lobotomaxx hates everything human and alien, and is proud of his nefarious reputation (from the file card). He sports a tail and four legs and his figure stands quite awkwardly, easily standing out among all of the troops in your Joe collection.

NOTE: *If you find a Lunartix Alien (Carcass, Predacon, or Lobotomaxx) that is of a different color than pictured here, you have a Mexican variant.*

MOC: **$12-18**, MLC: **$8**

(STAR BRIGADE) OZONE

Astro-Infantry Trooper (#54)

(Includes: Solar Shooter, Two Missiles, Three Guns, Machete, Helmet, Figure Stand)

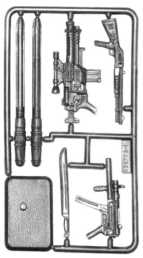

Yet another version, and he still maintains the ozone layer of Earth's atmosphere for the Joe team. This version of Ozone is colored maroon. For a full bio, see Ozone (1991, 1992).

MOC: **$12-18**, MLC: **$8**

(STAR BRIGADE) PREDACON

Alien Bounty Hunter (#51)

(Includes: Four Guns, Two Knives, Figure Stand)

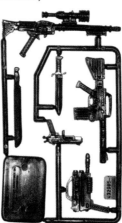

The last of three Lunartix aliens, Predacon comes with four arms and a hunched position that attributes to the figure never seeming to stand "right." As a bounty hunter, his character makes a living by "capturing criminals and selling them to back to the Galactic Authorities" (from the file card).

NOTE: *If you find a Lunartix Alien (Carcass, Predacon, or Lobotomaxx) that is of a different color than pictured here, you have a Mexican variant.*

MOC: **$12-18**, MLC: **$8**

(STAR BRIGADE) TECHNO-VIPER

Cobra Battlefield Technician (#61)

Included with the Cobra Power Fighter.

This version of the Techno-Viper acts as a Power Fighter pilot, and as battlefield technicians, they helped to design Cobra's Power Fighter vehicles. For a full bio, see Techno-Viper (1987).

MLC: **$10-15**

(STAR BRIGADE) COBRA COMMANDER

Cobra Supreme Leader (#24)

(Includes: Three-Piece Cobra Space Crawler, Helmet, Pistol)

The strangest version of Cobra Commander to date, the Cobra Supreme Leader comes with an unusual "crawler" vehicle with suction cups on the ends of it in order to attach it to a wall. His helmet is huge, his pistol is neon green, and he wears a space suit "to set up battle stations on the moon" and motivate his troops (from the file card). For a full bio, see Enemy Leader: Cobra Commander (1982).

MOC: **$14-18**, MLC: **$8**

(STAR BRIGADE) COBRA BLACKSTAR

Elite Space Pilot (#25)

(Includes: Blackstar Blaster, Two Missiles, Backpack, Gun, Figure Stand)

These pilots have "formed an alliance with the Blackstar forces, a secretive legion of space pilots whose origins remain unknown" (from the file card). Yet, this figure is not a troop builder, but the best of all the Cobra Blackstars—a character who behaves as if space is his natural habitat.

MOC: **$12-18**, MLC: **$8**

(STAR BRIGADE) DUKE

Star Brigade Commander (#21)

(Includes: Back Blaster, Missile, Backpack, Helmet, Gun)

With interesting accessories appropriate to a space trooper, Duke has the "high-pressure responsibility to command in the dangerous depths of outer space" (from the file card). For a full bio, see Duke (1983).

MOC: **$12-18**, MLC: **$8**

(STAR BRIGADE) PAYLOAD

Astro-Pilot (#26 a & b)
(Includes: Quasar Gun, Two Missiles, Three Guns, Knife, Figure Stand)

This version of the 1994 Payload is black with blue highlights. For a full bio, see Payload (1987).

MOC: **$12-18**, MLC: **$8**

(STAR BRIGADE) ROADBLOCK

Space Gunner (#27)
(Includes: Star Blaster, Two Missiles, Three Guns, Machete, Helmet, Figure Stand)

Now with orange and black highlights (as opposed to his 1993 version with light-blue and red highlights), Roadblock still acts as the Space Gunner for Star Brigade. For a full bio, see Roadblock (1984).

MOC: **$12-18**, MLC: **$8**

(STAR BRIGADE) SCI-FI

Star Brigade Pilot (#22)
(Includes: Sonic Backpack/Missile Launcher, Two Missiles, String, Two Weights, Helmet, Pistol)

With a fascinating new outfit, Sci-Fi retains the title of Star Brigade Pilot, but does not come included with a vehicle. For a full bio, see Sci-Fi (1986, 1991, 1993).

MLC: **$8**

(STAR BRIGADE) SPACE SHOT

Combat Freighter Pilot (#23)
(Includes: Cosmic Climbing Backpack, Pistol, Helmet)

Space Shot is the all-new Combat Freighter Pilot on the Joe's Star Brigade team. He is "known throughout the galaxy as a fly-by-night freighter pilot with a rebellious reputation" (from the file card). He was recruited by Duke for the Joe team, and after joining, became "less of a rebel, and more of a hero."

MOC: **$12-18**, MLC: **$8**

1994 VEHICLES/PLAYSETS

SPACE CAPSULE FROM COMMEMORATIVE COLLECTION
(Belongs to Action Pilot: Action Astronaut)

BLOCKBUSTER
(Includes: Windchill figure)

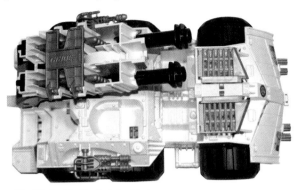

The G.I. Joe Blockbuster is the latest heavily-armed vehicle in the Joe's massive arsenal, with a double-barreled pom-pom cannon, anti-aircraft gun, and front mounted Gatling gun, it can give the Joes some added firepower. The toy itself has a ten shot auto-feeding rocket chamber that kids must have adored.

Easily lost pieces include ten missiles, two cannons, two hatch covers, and the missile launcher cover.

MISB: **$40**, MIB: **$25**, MLC: **$15**

The Blockbuster's easily lost pieces.

MANTA RAY

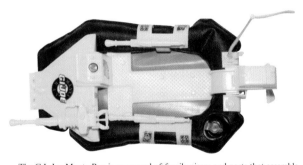

The G.I. Joe Manta Ray is composed of fragile pieces and parts that assemble to form an inflatable attack raft. It consists of MANY different pieces that fit together like a puzzle. With three lock-on torpedoes, a front mounted super-charged torpedo launcher, and a turbo-blast engine with removable cover, the Joes add to their formidable naval forces.

Easily lost pieces include three torpedoes, torpedo launcher (with one torpedo inside), hull top and bottom, engine and engine cover, rubber band, flag, propeller and propeller shaft (assembled), and two side-mounts for torpedoes.

MISB: **$20**,
MIB: **$15**,
MLC: **$8**

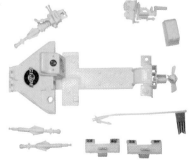

The Manta Ray's easily lost pieces.

RAZOR-BLADE

The G.I. Joe Razor-Blade helicopter is a strange vehicle with an intricate design. By holding one of the two handles and pulling the strings tight, the helicopter glides along the string (via the attached trolley guide way). The vehicle also comes with a figure rescue backpack to "scoop" troops out of harm's way.

Easily lost pieces include two handles with string, trolley to attach to helicopter, three missiles, rescue backpack, and rotor blade pivot shaft.

MISB: **$28**,
MIB: **$15**,
MLC: **$12**

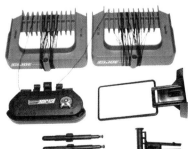

The Razor-Blade's easily lost pieces.

COBRA SCORPION

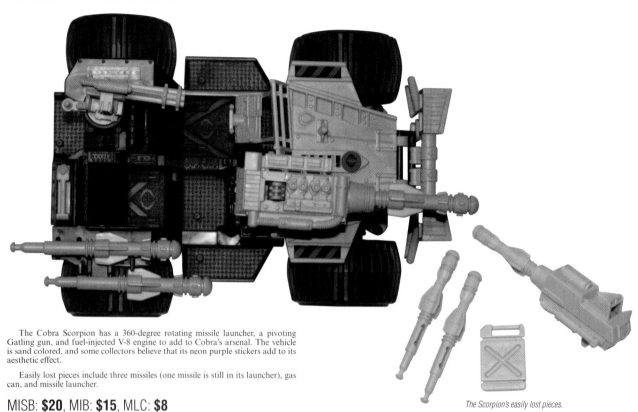

The Cobra Scorpion has a 360-degree rotating missile launcher, a pivoting Gatling gun, and fuel-injected V-8 engine to add to Cobra's arsenal. The vehicle is sand colored, and some collectors believe that its neon purple stickers add to its aesthetic effect.

Easily lost pieces include three missiles (one missile is still in its launcher), gas can, and missile launcher.

MISB: **$20**, MIB: **$15**, MLC: **$8**

The Scorpion's easily lost pieces.

STAR BRIGADE POWER FIGHTERS

"The heavily armed Power Fighter units can be classified as one-man Armor-Bots. They greatly enhance a soldier's battle capability when engaging Cobra or alien enemies on any type of terrain. Whether battling among the giant craters of the moon, or scouting treacherous Martian canyons, Power Fighters lead Joe to victory… and beyond!"

G.I JOE POWER FIGHTER
(Includes: Gears figure)

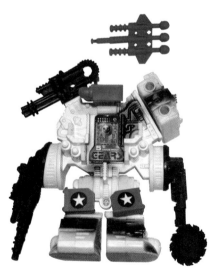

The Power Fighter battle suit worn by Gears has a positionable rocket launcher, a spinning slasher saw, and two pivoting laser guns to aid the Joe team in their battles for outer space.

The removable rocket cluster missile is the only easily lost piece.

MISB: **$40**, MIB: **$25**, MLC: **$15**

COBRA POWER FIGHTER
(Includes: Techno-Viper figure)

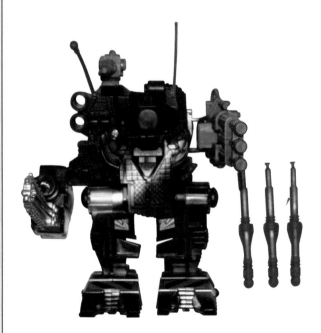

The Cobra Power Fighter is a formidable opponent in space with its positionable missile launcher, giant chainsaw mechanism, all-terrain planetary treads, and two laser guns.

Easily lost pieces are the three removable missiles.

MISB: **$40**, MIB: **$25**, MLC: **$15**

INDEX